Bureaucracy and Revolution in Eastern Europe

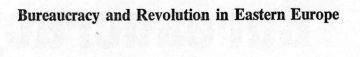

Bureaucracy

Chris Harman

and Revolution

in Eastern Europe

Pluto Press

First published 1974 by
Pluto Press Limited
Unit 10, Spencer Court, 7 Chalcot Road, London NW1 8LH

Copyright © Pluto Press 1974

ISBN paperback 0 902818 49 3
ISBN hardback   0 902818 50 3

Designed by Richard Hollis, GrR

Printed in Great Britain by
Bristol Typesetting Company Limited
Barton Manor, St Philips, Bristol

Contents

Introduction ☆ 9

Part One: Repression

1. **Eastern Europe after World War II** ☆ 23
   The Pre-War Regimes ☆ The Communist Parties at the Close
   of the War ☆ The Revolutionary Wave and the 'People's
   Governments' ☆ The Warsaw Uprising ☆ Revolution from
   Above ☆ The Fate of Peasant and Socialist Parties ☆ The
   Growth of the Communist Parties ☆ Slav against Teuton ☆
   Nationalization ☆ The Prague Coup – Workers' Uprising?

2. **The Russian Interest** ☆ 49
   Reparations ☆ Mixed Companies ☆ Trade ☆ Conclusion

3. **From Control to Subjection** ☆ 56
   The Purges ☆ Economic Changes ☆ The Pattern of Economic
   Development ☆ 1952 or 1984?

Part Two: Revolt and Revolution

4. **1953: The German Workers' Revolt** ☆ 69
   The Uprising ☆ The Real Causes ☆ The Bureaucracy Split

5. **1953-56 Prelude to Revolution** ☆ 86
   The Hungarian 'New Course' ☆ The Twentieth Congress

6: **1956: Poland – Aborted Revolution** ☆ 94
   Intellectuals in Revolt ☆ Insurrection Below ☆ Reforms ☆
   Gomulka versus the Left ☆ The October Left ☆ The Fight for
   Control ☆ Workers' Councils ☆ Strike and Repression

7. 1956: The Hungarian Revolution ☆ 124
The Revolution Breaks ☆ The New Government ☆ The
Emergence of Workers' Councils ☆ Revolution or Counter-
Revolution? ☆ Class Forces in the Hungarian Revolution ☆
Mass Insurgency ☆ Dual Power ☆ Concessions . . . ☆
Betrayal ☆ The Counter-Revolution ☆ The Second Period of
Dual Power ☆ The Destruction of the Workers' Councils ☆
Conclusion

8. 1968: Czechoslovakia – Arrested Reform ☆ 188
Origins of the Crisis ☆ Novotny's Fall ☆ The New Leadership
☆ The Reformers and the Invasion ☆ 'Normalization' ☆
Slovakia ☆ The Intellectuals ☆ Ideological Confusion ☆ The
Workers ☆ Democratization within the Unions ☆ Resistance
to 'Normalization' ☆ The Workers' Councils ☆ Conclusion

9. 1970: Poland ☆ 242
The Economy ☆ Gdansk

Conclusion: Reform or Revolution ☆ 254
Economic Malaise ☆ Waste and Competition ☆ A Vicious
Circle ☆ The Crisis ☆ The Failure of Reform ☆ Revolution

Notes ☆ 273

Index ☆ 290

A Note on Terminology

For the sake of convenience, I refer to the regimes of Eastern Europe, Russia, China and so on as 'communist', because that is how they are generally known in Britain. That is not meant in any way to link them with the communist traditions as propounded by Marx, Engels, Lenin, Luxemburg and Trotsky, nor to see their ruling parties as identical with the Communist Parties of the West.

I also refer to the ruling group in these countries at various points as 'the bureaucracy'. By this I do not mean that every clerk who works in a government office is somehow a member of a class opposed to the mass of the population. By 'the bureaucracy' I mean a much smaller group, those who occupy the key positions of power in industry and the governmental apparatus, those who gain massive material privileges from enforcing accumulation in competition with other ruling classes and in opposition to the interests of the working class.

Introduction

For half a century an idea has dominated the thinking of the left throughout the world – the idea that socialist countries already exist. Loyalty to the governments of the socialist third of the world has been the first claim on the solidarity of those struggling against capitalism, both in the west and in the third world.

Yet, in recent years, enthusiasm has been replaced by confusion. In 1956 Khrushchev stunned Communists everywhere by his revelation that Stalin, 'the greatest leader, sublime strategist of all times and nations', had been responsible for rigged trials leading to the deaths of 'many thousands of honest and innocent Communists', that Stalin had carried through 'mass arrests and deportations of many thousands of people, execution without trial and without normal investigation' and had used 'mass repression' causing 'misery and suffering to whole nations'.

Since Khrushchev's speech, events themselves have rained crushing blows on the heads of those who hold the 'Communist' societies to be intrinsically superior to those of Western capitalism. In Hungary in 1956 and Poland in 1970 the established regimes were shaken by movements whose working-class character could not be denied: general strikes, factory occupations, election of workers' committees, the storming of police stations and prisons. In 1968 Russian troops invaded Czechoslovakia, despite the vehement protest of the Communist government of that country. So blatant was the contradiction between myth and reality that even the official Communist Parties of the West felt compelled to protest.

The characteristic drive of capitalism to militaristic adventures and to war no longer seems absent from the relationships between the different 'Communist' states. More troops are now stationed along Russia's border with China than along its European border with the West. The rival 'red' armies have clashed and their soldiers have died, over the possession of a few barren acres on the Ussuri or a few sheep in Sinkiang.

To left-wing militants in the rest of the world such developments have brought severe disillusionment and demoralization. They have tried to defend the indefensible, to hide from themselves what they could not hide from others, to cover up their own uncertainty with empty rhetorical phrases. But to no avail: time and again real historical developments have caught them unawares and left them without arguments, as successive leaders have pointed to the 'crimes' and 'mistakes' of their predecessors, as the rulers of one 'Communist' power have heaped abuse upon the rulers of another.

The traditions of the past, wrote Marx, weigh like a nightmare on the brain of the living. His aphorism is cruelly true of the revolutionary left today. Those whose loyalties are with the 'Communist' countries are threatened by every new development, every new revelation, which bring them only further disillusionment and further loss of will in their fight against their own oppressive ruling classes in the west.

The power of the marxist world view has always rested on its sharp vision of socialism as a real historic possibility, offering humanity for the first time the opportunity to overcome alienation and exploitation, inhumanity and misery, violence and war.

An essential step forward along this path is the establishment of socialist workers' states. Yet, if a third of the world is both socialist and at the same time dominated by these ills, then the very value of the marxist approach is put into question.

Marxism's survival as a theory capable of giving realistic hope to the oppressed everywhere depends upon its coming to terms with the reality of Russia and Eastern Europe. If marxism cannot do so, it can offer no alternative to a humanity that is in need of social revolution as never before. The hunger of the third world, the stockpiling of monstrous means of destruction by the great powers, the daily grind of life for workers in the advanced West, must all appear immutable insofar as they are paralleled in the East, if the East is 'socialist'.

According to a Russian joke, 'capitalism is the exploitation of man by man, and socialism is the exact reverse'. If marxism cannot solve that conundrum, it is truly a nightmare on the brain of the living.

This book's contention is that we can understand the 'Communist' world coherently in marxist terms, but only if we first recognize that what exists in Russia and Eastern Europe (and for that matter China and North Korea) is bureaucratic state capitalism, not socialism, and consequently that progress is only possible for the majority of the people of those countries through anti-bureaucratic working-class revolution.

The Russian Revolution of 1917 was undeniably a working-class revolution. But the working class was a small minority in the population, an island in a vast sea of peasants, able to seize power because of its concentration in the cities, at the key centres for communications and governmental administration, but not able to rule indefinitely on such a basis.

The Bolsheviks were keenly aware of the problems this posed. They argued that the long term balance of forces could only be altered in favour of the working class by bringing to bear the much greater weight of the working classes in the advanced western countries. As Lenin put it in March 1918, 'the absolute truth is that without the revolution in Germany, we shall perish'.

The German revolutionary, Rosa Luxemburg, underlined the connection between the isolation of the Bolshevik revolution and the difficulties facing it early in 1918 in her book *The Russian Revolution*.

> Everything that happens in Russia is comprehensible and represents an inevitable chain of causes and effects, the starting point and end term of which are: the failure of the German proletariat and the occupation of Russia by German imperialism. It would be demanding something superhuman from Lenin and his comrades if we should expect from them that under such circumstances they should conjure forth the finest democracy, the most exemplary dictatorship of the proletariat, and a flourishing socialist economy. By their determined revolutionary stand, their exemplary strength in action and their unbreakable loyalty to international socialism, they have contributed whatever could possibly be contributed under such devilishly hard conditions.

Subsequent history was to show that the price paid for isolating the revolution was to be immense. Instead of the Western working classes giving muscle to the Russian workers, the Western ruling classes sent their armies into Russia.

Three years of foreign intervention and civil war devastated the economy of Russia. Lack of raw materials and supplies produced wholesale factory closures. The cities were denuded of workers: by 1920 the number of industrial workers was half what it had been in 1917. Large numbers of socialist militants had hastened to the front, where many died in defence of the revolution. Many of those who survived were no longer part of a collectivity which laboured together to produce wealth; instead they found themselves with positions of authority imposing discipline on a largely peasant army. Those workers who remained in the towns produced very little; half-starved, their meagre rations often had to be obtained by the state at gun point from the peasants.

Marxists speak of the withering away of the state. In Russia, however, a by-product of the fight to defend the revolution was a withering away of the working class. And without a real, active working class, the institutions of working-class power thrown up in 1917 – in particular, genuine workers' councils – could hardly survive.

The Bolshevik leaders continued to rule Russia – but in the name of a class that hardly existed. In the vacuum that was left they had somehow to erect a structure that could hold together a vast, sprawling country, to keep the allegiance of tens of millions of peasants, to lay the basis for a resumption of economic life in the towns, and to direct the movements of millions of soldiers.

The human material available for manning this structure was far from perfect. The decimation of the already small working class meant that often the only literate personnel who were trained to routine work were the remnants of the old Czarist bureaucracy.

As Lenin told the Fourth Congress of the Comintern in 1922:

> We took over the old machinery of state and that was our misfortune. . . . We have a vast army of government employees, but lack the educated forces to exercise real control over them. . . . At the top we have, I don't know how many, but at all events no more than a few thousand . . . Down below there are hundreds of thousands of old officials we got from the Czar and from bourgeois society . . .[1]

It was by no means clear, even in Lenin's time, that the Bolshevik leaders ran the bureaucracy. Often it was the other way round. Again Lenin enunciated the problem (at the Party Congress in 1922):

> Let us look at Moscow. . . . Who is leading whom? The 4,700 responsible Communists the mass of bureaucrats, or the other way round? I do not believe that you can say that the Communists are leading this mass. To put it honestly, they are not the leaders, but the led . . . It must be recognized that the Party's proletarian policy is determined at present not by the rank and file, but by the immense and undivided authority of the tiny section of what might be called the Party's 'old guard'.

Had there been a strong working class, able to impose its will on the administrative apparatus, all this might not have mattered. But in the conditions of economic devastation and famine at the end of the civil war in the early 1920s, it was all-important. The administrative machine did not just have to implement plans worked out by the working class as it attempted to improve conditions and living standards: it had somehow to reconcile the competing needs of tens of millions of hungry peasants with the demands of hundreds of thousands of virtually non-productive workers, as well as maintain a large army and the growing administrative structure itself.

To the functionary on the ground it often seemed more realistic to decide which claims to concede and which to refuse according to the relative power of the different claimants, if necessary using repression to contain the demands of the less powerful. Pragmatic adjustments to the local balance of class forces became more important than any instruction from the party leadership about fulfilment of socialist principles. And when it came to putting pressure on the functionaries, the decimated, declassed working class was often much less significant than the well-to-do peasant or the medium size trader. Meanwhile, arbitrating between the demands of the different social groups, the bureaucracy began to accumulate power which raised it above all of them.

The 'tiny sections' of the 'old guard' in the party could not remain immune to these pressures indefinitely themselves. Men change history, but in the process they themselves are transformed. The Bolsheviks were inevitably corrupted by the attempt to play different social forces off against one another. Just as 'realism' for the low level functionary came to mean making concessions to non-working-class elements, 'realism' to some of the party leaders came to mean placating the low-level functionaries. Formally, orders were passed from the top downwards; but powerful, informal pressures began to develop in the opposite direction.

Lenin's illness and subsequent death provided the occasion for the differing forces to express themselves openly, in the form of divisions within the party leadership. 'Realism' for Stalin and Zinoviev (later Stalin and Bukharin, with Zinoviev moving into opposition) meant organizing lower level functionaries in a campaign against Trotsky – and that, in turn, meant pandering to the prejudices of the bureaucrats. The party leadership argued for increased concessions to the well-to-do peasants, for separating the fate of Russia from the fate of world revolution (with the doctrine of 'socialism in one country') and against the traditions of internal party democracy which once were taken for granted by every Bolshevik.

The principles of October were abandoned one by one. Those who continued to speak in the tones of 1917 were driven first from leadership, then from the party, and finally into exile or prison. They were replaced by people who had hardly figured in the revolution. And all the time there was a growth in the power of the bureaucracy – until in 1928 it felt compelled to attack the living standards of both workers and peasants, simultaneously suppressing once and for all the last elements of free discussion either in the party or in society. Those Bolsheviks such as Bukharin and Tomsky who had aligned themselves with Stalin during the faction fights of the 1920s were now deprived of power and independence. And in the mid 1930s they were to find themselves in torture cells and execution chambers, along with most of Stalin's own protégés, as well as with the left oppositionists of the 1920s – for, under the sort of regime Stalin was now running, every remnant of the Bolshevik tradition had to be eradicated.

By 1938 more than 90 per cent of the surviving Bolsheviks of 1917 had left or been driven out of the party.

What took place was a counter-revolution. It was not violent in the classic sense, insofar as the working class, decimated in the civil war and despondent in the harsh economic conditions that followed, had few forces with which to resist the growing power of the bureaucracy. But it was certainly bloody: a one-sided civil war waged on both the workers, deprived of their right to strike, their real wages slashed, and the peasants, driven from the land into state farms and 'collectives'. Those who resisted saw their homes burned, their neighbours killed, their families carted off to labour camps.

However, to say that a new bureaucratic ruling group took power in Russia is not in itself a sufficient explanation of the horrors of the Stalin period. What has to be explained is why the new ruling group was driven to attack the living standards of the mass of the population and to create a totalitarian political structure. After all, even Stalin did not consciously set out with the intention of putting millions of people in slave camps and murdering the leaders of 1917.

The explanation lies in the immensity of the task which confronted the new ruling group. To maintain their control over the country, they had somehow to defend it against military threats from more industrially advanced countries. Initial attempts to evade this problem (in the mid 1920s) only made it all the more serious later on (after 1927).

The revolutionaries of 1917 had seen the only hope for survival of the Soviet Union in the spreading of the revolution. The new rulers rejected that classic perspective, in favour of 'socialism in one country'. The bureaucrats on whom they depended did not understand revolution and even feared it – apart from anything else, it might lead the Russian working class to question their own privileges. Given their adopted perspective of 'socialist' isolation, they had no alternative, if they were to defend Russia against the massive military machines of the west, but to build up a similar military machine of their own. But that demanded a massive expansion of industry, and particularly heavy industry, to provide the basis for an output of modern armaments. As Stalin put it:

> to slacken the pace (of industrialization) would mean to lag behind; and those who lag behind are beaten. We do not want to be beaten. No, we don't want to . . . We are fifty or a hundred years behind the advanced countries. We must make good this lag in ten years. Either we do so or they crush us.[2]
> The environment in which we are placed . . . at home and abroad . . . compels us to adopt a rapid rate of industrialization.[3]

But accumulation on the scale necessary inevitably meant attacks on the living standards of peasants and workers. When peasants resisted, the army was used to seize their crops and to drive them from their holdings into collectives. When workers resisted, threats and physical force were used to keep them working.

The drive to accumulate also explains the particular social, political and cultural features of the Stalin era. In order to hammer down the living standards of workers and peasants, the bureaucracy itself had to be a solid, impregnable, monolithic structure. Each bureaucrat had to identify his own personal future with the bureaucracy's goal, of raising still further the level of accumulation. Those whose backgrounds or sentiments held them back from employing the necessary means to this end had to be purged mercilessly.

> In 1932 strikes broke out among the textile workers in the Ivanovo district. Provoked by famine and lower pay, they were put down with more than usual ferocity by Kaganovich. Fairly high local officials were punished as well as the strikers . . . Outraged by the conditions, some party officials . . . insisted on sharing these conditions themselves. They and their wives boycotted the special shops, wore workers' clothes and stood in the food queues. It was for this they were punished. As Kaganovich explained, the use of special shops by the privileged was party policy – to boycott them was therefore aggression against the government. It was a sign of aping workers and following their moods.[4]

In the purges of the thirties, the last elements of Bolshevik revolutionary tradition were eliminated from the party. But that meant giving the police apparatus dominance over the rest of the bureaucracy and then carrying through still bloodier purges in order to keep the police apparatus itself in line.

In *The Communist Manifesto* Marx distinguished between the dynamic of capitalism and the dynamic of socialism: 'In bourgeois society, living labour is but a means to increase accumulated labour. In Communist society, accumulated labour is but a means to widen, to enrich and to promote the existence of the labourer.'

In *Capital* he described the internal dynamic of capitalist society in greater detail:

> The development of capitalist production makes it constantly necessary to keep increasing the amount of capital laid out in a given industrial undertaking, and competition

makes the immanent laws of capitalist production to be felt by each individual capitalist, as external coercive laws. It compels him to keep constantly extending his capital, in order to preserve it, but extend it he cannot, except by means of progressive accumulation.[5]

Fanatically bent on making value expand itself, he (the capitalist) ruthlessly forces the whole human race to produce for production's sake . . .

Therefore, save, save. i.e. reconvert the greatest possible portion of surplus value or surplus product into capital! Accumulation for accumulation's sake, production for production's sake.[6]

Marx's account of the motive power of the nineteenth century capitalist is an apt description of the ruling group in Russia under Stalin, Khrushchev and Brezhnev.

Within western capitalism, competition between different firms to sell their products provides the main drive to accumulate. In the case of Russia the most important pressure is international arms competition. The mechanism is slightly different, but the outcome is the same: workers are continually told that their living standards must be held back because of the need to invest so as to remain competitive. In short, the rulers of Russia behave as if the whole country were a single capitalist firm.

Even in western capitalism, military competition provides a stimulus of growing importance. In the United States in the early 1960s arms spending was equal to 60 per cent of gross domestic fixed capital formation. As Bukharin noted at the Fourth Congress of the Comintern:

Competition between various industrialists whose methods consisted in lowering the price of commodities . . . is almost the only form of competition mentioned by Marx. But in the epoch of imperialist competition we find many other forms of competition wherein the method of reducing prices is of no significance . . . The main groups of the bourgeoisie are now of the nature of trustified groups within the framework of the state. They are nothing else but combined enterprises . . . It is quite conceivable that such a form of enterprise . . . should resort chiefly to violent forms of competition . . . Thus arise the new forms of competition which lead to military attack by the state.[7]

Military competition, like competition for markets, knows no end. Every time one country succeeds in driving up the level of exploitation and accumulation, it forces other countries to do the same. Each ruling group is trapped in an endless upward spiral, from which there is no escape. Each working class is kept under relentless pressure to work harder in order to keep its rulers abreast of their rivals.

Forty years after Stalin first put Russia on the path of competition with the west, Brezhnev was still dwelling on

> the question of the economic competition between two world systems. This competition takes different forms. In many cases we are coping successfully. But the fundamental question is not only how much you produce, but also at what cost, with what outlays of labour. It is in this field that the centre of gravity lies in our time.[8]

The rulers of Russia do not merely suffer the effects of the international pressures to accumulate. They themselves contribute to these pressures. In their search for resources to build up industry, they have expanded beyond the boundaries of the Soviet Union itself. Their armies rolled across Eastern Europe and remained to dominate, and they attempted, in the 1950s and early 1960s, to impose their will on China. But this demanded further military expenditures and further efforts at accumulation. Today their armed forces do not simply point towards the western powers, but are equally concerned with preserving Eastern Europe against internal rebellion and with threatening the Chinese. Indeed, the only occasions they have been in operation over the last twenty years have been against internal insurgents or other Communist governments (in Hungary, in Czechoslovakia and on the Chinese border). Accumulation is fostered by imperialist expansion. But expansion in turn demands a higher level of accumulation.

Accumulation is not just an external constraint upon the bureaucracy. The very functioning of the bureaucracy itself has come to depend on it. Individual bureaucrats see that the road to personal advancement runs through the expansion of the particular area of industry under their control. That expansion rests upon accumulation, which has become as much second nature to them as it is to the corporate capitalists of the West.

A social class, for Marx, was not just a group of people who enjoyed a particular pattern of consumption or who shared a certain life style. It was, fundamentally, a group of people whose relations to the means of production forced them to act continually in opposition to other social groups. In this sense, the bureaucrats of Russia are a class. They control the means of production, which they attempt to expand at a faster speed than their rivals internationally. This they can only do by holding back workers' living standards, by acting as a bitter opposition to working-class interests, both domestically and internationally.

From 1924 to 1953 many revolutionaries went along with and defended Stalinism because it seemed 'realistic' to do so. But theirs was the 'realism' of the lady who went riding on a tiger. They were carried remorselessly towards covering up, denying or defending exploitation, gross social inequality, anti-semitism, national oppression, slave camps and rigged trials.

But there was always an alternative to Stalinism. It meant, in the late 1920s, returning to genuine workers' democracy and consciously linking the fate of Russia to the fate of world revolution. That did not imply ignoring the need to protect Russia in the meantime: a limited development of heavy industry was possible in the mid-1920s (while Stalin himself was rejecting the need for such a development) without vicious attacks on the workers and peasants. Living standards and industry could have developed in harmony together, up to a certain point – but only providing it was not assumed that the revolution would remain indefinitely isolated. And there was a real possibility of spreading the revolution – if policies other than Stalin's had been followed: the actual policies pursued in Germany, France and Spain were the other side of the coin of the policy of industrialization in one country.

Such a society could have been genuinely transitional in type, moving consciously from a state of affairs in which workers were dominated by accumulation to one in which the accumulation was 'but a means to widen, to enrich, to promote the existence of the labourer'.

The historical merit of the Left Opposition in the Russian Communist Party was that it framed a policy along these lines. It did link the question of the expansion of industry with that of working-class democracy and internationalism.* It quickly grasped that

*It should be added, though, that some sections of the Left Opposition were by no means clear as to the necessity of the link. The capitulation to

the whole concept of 'socialism in one country' was 'a reactionary utopia', even though its most important member, Trotsky, continued to his death to harbour the illusion that somehow, despite the lack of workers' democracy, Russia was a 'workers' state'.

The last twenty years have shown that the societies of Eastern Europe provide ground at least as fertile for social revolution as those of the West and the third world. To understand why, it is necessary to look concretely at the effects of the drive to accumulate. It is then possible to see how Stalinism has not only reproduced all the problems that plague the capitalist West, but has also given rise to its own gravedigger – a modern, industrial working class. That, briefly, is the aim of this book.

The theoretical framework is not new. It was first worked out in detail by Tony Cliff more than twenty-five years ago, and a similar position has been elaborated more recently by the Polish marxists, Jacek Kuron and Karol Modzelewski.[10] I attempt to use the theory to explain the major crises arising in the societies of Eastern Europe (with the exception of Yugoslavia) and to indicate the consequences of these crises for the future prospects of the Russian regime itself.

Stalin of men like Preobrazhensky and Radek seems to indicate that they came to regard industrialization *per se* as important, regardless of the other questions. By contrast, Trotsky insisted that workers' living standards 'must become the main criterion for measuring the success of socialist evolution'.[9]

1.

Repression

1.

Eastern Europe after World War II

The fate of Eastern Europe was decided with the defeat of the German armies in 1944 and 1945. The leaders of the various allied powers came together in a series of conferences and meetings, hoping to reach some amicable agreement about the division of the spoils of war and the allocation of influence in the post-war world.

The last thing any of those involved in the negotiations considered was the desires of the people of Europe. In later years, western politicians were to spin a fine web of rhetoric on the suffering of the populations of the East European countries. At the time, however, the most cynical *Realpolitik* was the order of the day. Talks between Churchill and Stalin in 1944 were typical.

> The moment was apt for business, so I said 'Let us settle about our affairs in the Balkans. Your armies are in Roumania and Bulgaria. We have interests, missions and agents there. Don't let us get at cross-purposes in small ways. So far as Britain and Russia are concerned, how would it do for you to have 90 per cent predominance in Roumania, for us to have 90 per cent of the say in Greece, and go 50-50 about Yugoslavia?' While this was being translated, I wrote on a half sheet of paper:
> Roumania: Russia 90% – The others 10%
> Greece: Great Britain 90% – Russia 10%
> Yugoslavia: 50-50%
> Hungary: 50-50%
> Bulgaria: Russia 75% – The others 25%
> I pushed this across to Stalin, who had by then heard the translation. There was a slight pause. Then he took his pencil and made a large tick upon it, and passed it back to us. It was all settled in no more time than it takes to set down . . .
> After this there was a long silence. The pencilled paper lay

on the centre of the table. At length I said, 'Might it not be thought rather cynical if it seemed we had disposed of these issues, so fateful to millions of people, in such an off-hand manner? Let us burn the paper.' 'No, you keep it,' said Stalin.[1]

Out of such meetings emerged an agreement on the fundamental aspects of a division of Europe, although at first there were significant differences between the various powers as to what form this division should take. The Americans, in particular, tried to avoid a formal demarcation of spheres of influence, assuming that without this they would be able to dominate the whole of Europe with their superior economic strength. However, the Russians, and to a lesser extent the British, were able to force the US into effective acceptance of such a division.[2]

The powers drew a line between them that both the West and the Russians took for granted through all the trials and tribulations of the cold war. Although there were nasty jostlings at certain key points along this border – Berlin and Korea, for instance – neither side made any serious attempt to alter the bases of the division.

In Greece in 1944-45, for example, although the majority of the Greek people clearly supported the war-time resistance force, EAM-ELAS, the Communist leaders of that movement were under clear orders from Moscow not to prevent British dominance of the country:

> Of all the groups in EAM the Communists were the most willing to submerge social objectives to the need of a United Front and the only group willing to specifically designate Greece as part of the British sphere of influence after the war.[3]

At the Yalta conference in February 1945, Stalin made it clear that 'he had no intention of criticizing British actions there or interfering in Greece'.[4] Churchill indicated that he 'was very much obliged to Marshal Stalin for not having taken too great an interest in Greek affairs'.[5]

In Italy and France, similarly, the Russian-directed Communist Parties played a key role in preventing radical change. From mid-1943 the areas of Italy under Allied occupation were nominally ruled by a government under Badoglio, appointed by the fascist Grand Council in place of Mussolini. But this government had no popular support anywhere in Italy. The mass of the resistance forces were adamant in their opposition. Not only the Socialists and the Communists, but also the liberal Action Party would have no truck with Badoglio. Then on 26 March 1944 Togliatti flew into Italy from Moscow. 'As matters moved towards a decisive resolution and Badoglio's days seemed numbered, the neo-fascist regime and Churchill found new allies: the Soviet Union and the Italian Communist Party.'[6]

Stalin's behaviour in Western Europe was to be matched by Western behaviour in the East. Western politicians made a great deal of noise and indulged in considerable rhetoric when Russian troops put down popular insurrections in 1953 and 1956, but gave no material aid to these uprisings. At late as 1968 the US refused a loan to the Czechs to assist them to overcome their economic difficulties, on the grounds that this 'might be construed by Moscow as a massive economic and political intervention in Eastern Europe'.[7]

Just as the regimes that replaced Nazi rule in Western Europe were established under the control of American and British capitalism, so the character of the regimes of Eastern Europe was determined by the rulers of Russia.

The Pre-War Regimes

The Russian armies found themselves occupying territories whose societies could never have survived in their old form on their own. The old ruling classes had demonstrated their bankruptcy and could mobilize no popular support for postwar reconstruction.

Already, before the war, the result was a lack of social direction and cohesion. Poland, Czechoslovakia and Hungary had only emerged as separate states in 1919. Everywhere extreme tensions threatened the unity of the various state structures – Poles or Czechs against Germans, Slovaks against Czechs, Ukrainians against Poles, Rumanians against Hungarians, Croats against Serbs.

The whole of Eastern Europe was trapped in poverty, a condition that increased immensely during the slump of the 1930s. The backward agriculture of the area was particularly severely hit. Existing national tensions within each state were exacerbated, and many of the existing nationalist governments began to be at least tinged with fascism. Against this background the dominant political pattern became one of the increasingly unstable, right-wing governments.

A viable industrial capitalist base had hardly been created anywhere in the area. Where industry did exist, foreign capital invariably played a key role. Thus in Poland in 1937 40.1 per cent of the capital in joint-stock companies was held by foreign investors, and companies in which foreign capital predominated constituted 63.1 per cent of all joint stock companies.[8]

The position in other countries was similar. As little as 15 to 20 per cent of Rumanian shares capital was in indigenous hands,[9] while the proportions of foreign capital in Yugoslavia and Bulgaria were respectively 49.5 per cent[10] and 42.6 per cent.[11]

Private industry's weakness was reflected in the indispensability of the state in sustaining what industry there was. Poland, Czechoslovakia and Yugoslavia all illustrated the extent of previous state intervention throughout Eastern Europe.

In Poland 'The state took upon itself the role of pioneer and entrepreneur in many fields of the economy . . . Roughly half the bank credits flowed from government banks and agencies. Some of the leading sectors of the economy were almost completely owned and managed by the state.'[12] In Czechoslovakia the pre-war state, while not as important as in Poland, 'had a tradition of an active initiator, supporter, controller and entrepreneur',[13] directly owning about 10 per cent of industrial capital. In pre-war Yugoslavia the state owned not only the railways and the telephone system, but also about 25 per cent of the coal and 90 per cent of the iron ore industries. Central government and the local authorities between them owned about 60 per cent of the forest area, basic to the important timber industry. Finally the Yugoslav state controlled the iron and steel industry and armaments production, as well as having a large slice of sugar and cellulose production.

Czechoslovakia, alone of the Eastern European states, enjoyed any success in modern capitalistic terms. Industry did at least grow in the inter-war period, despite being hit by the slump, so that production was a third higher in 1937 than it had been twenty-five years before.[14] And only in Czechoslovakia could some sort of bourgeois democracy be maintained. But even this was destroyed by the Munich agreement of 1938, as German tanks rolled in with British acquiescence.

The war shattered these fragile social structures. Whether the pre-war ruling circles had chosen to align themselves with the Nazis, as in Rumania, Hungary and Bulgaria, or had put up some sort of resistance as the Czech and Polish governments did, by 1945 they were weakened and fragmented.

Poland was the country hardest hit by the war. Estimates suggest that as many as 20 per cent of the population perished.[15] The military élite which had been so central to the politics of the country before the war was virtually wiped out. The factories that had contributed the wealth of the already weak indigenous bourgeoisie were reduced to rubble. Forty-five per cent of pre-war Polish territory was absorbed into the USSR.

The old ruling élites of Rumania, Bulgaria and Hungary were completely discredited. The local populations had already paid a terrible price, in losses on the Russian front and internal terror, for their rulers' alliance with Hitler.

Even in Czechoslovakia, where the losses directly due to the war had been least, and where the allied armies' occupation was least prolonged, the bourgeoisie did not emerge from the war unscathed. It was evident to old-time politicians like Benes that the pre-war policy of links with the West had come to a disastrous end with Munich and must be replaced by Russian influence.

If the war decisively weakened the old political set-ups, it also accentuated the trend towards statification of the various national economies. In Czechoslovakia by 1945 60 per cent of industry and virtually the whole of the finance system were in German hands. Only the state was in any position to take over when the Germans fled.

The bourgeois president of Czechoslovakia, Benes, described how

> The Germans simply took control of all main industries and all banks . . . If they did not nationalize them directly they at least put them into the hands of big German concerns . . . In this way they automatically prepared the economic and financial capital of our country for nationalization . . . To return this property and the banks into the hands of Czech individuals or to consolidate them without considerable state assistance and without new financial guarantees was simply impossible. The State had to step in.[16]

The German defeat meant that *without* any large scale nationalization of local capital, the Czechoslovak government found itself in control of about three quarters of industry.

In Poland a similar situation arose, through state appropriation of former German property in both the pre-war Polish territories ('Old Poland') and in the 'new' territories annexed from Germany.

In those countries, too, which had allied themselves with Germany (Hungary, Bulgaria, and Rumania), the war had witnessed a considerable further infiltration by German capital.[17]

The result was that whoever, at the end of the war, controlled the state apparatus in these territories controlled industry, to dispose of it as they would. They could either maintain it in their own hands or return it to its pre-war owners. Those owners, in turn, could only regain their former power and possessions by ingratiating themselves with those who physically controlled state power. And the Russian army was the most important factor in disposing of that power.

The old ruling classes were in no condition to put up real resistance to Russian demands. All their protests and manoeuvres over the next two or three years availed them nothing. No significant section of the population had enough faith in them to back them against the Russians. The occupying forces and the local Communist Parties were able to determine with remarkable ease the contours of the society that emerged out of the post-war chaos.

The Communist Parties at the Close of the War

Almost all the Communist Parties of Eastern Europe were, by themselves, extremely weak at the time of the German forces' withdrawal.

The Hungarian Party had led a shadow existence during the years of dictatorship from 1920 onwards. Its leaders had spent most of the period either in prison or in exile in Moscow – where any of them who might conceivably have begun to question Stalin's authority was purged, along with founder of the party, Bela Kun, at the time of the Moscow trials.

The Polish Party had always been a minority by comparison with the Polish Socialist Party in the trade unions and the working class generally. It was effectively liquidated by Stalin in 1938, when he had at least twelve members of its central committee executed.

The party was only reconstituted in late 1941, and did not develop into a really viable political force until after the defeat of the German armies at Stalingrad. Membership in the middle of 1942 was reckoned to be about 4000. Nor did it have anything like a stable or independent leadership. In 1942 the leader of the party was murdered in mysterious circumstances by his 'number three', Molejec, who in turn was executed after a trial by a party court. In 1943 two more leaders were picked up and executed in suspicious circumstances by the Gestapo.

In Rumania, party membership in the middle of 1944 was estimated to be no more than a thousand. Once again the leadership had undergone a process of 'natural selection': all those who failed to exhibit the requisite submissiveness to Russian dictation had been weeded out (and often executed in exile) in successive purges. Thus one of the principal party leaders at the time, Anna Pauker, survived – while both her husband and her lover were purged.[19]

In Czechoslovakia the party had been rather stronger than elsewhere. Even at its lowest point in 1930 the membership was 24,000.[20] Its electoral support never dropped below three quarters of a million. But it was still not the majority party among the organized workers. It tended to be weak in the larger factories and never controlled more than 12 per cent of the trade-union movement.[21] Its leadership had been selected according to the usual criterion – willingness to accept Stalin's policies. Nevertheless, the party was more successful than others in maintaining an organizational framework through the period of German occupation, so that by the time of the Nazi defeat and withdrawal in May 1945 it had 27,000 members in the Czech areas alone.[22]

Despite their previous weaknesses, the postwar Communist Parties found themselves in strong strategic positions, given the collapse of the old society and, crucially, the Russian presence. How was this strength to be utilized?

When Marx spoke of the socialist revolution he spoke of the action of the 'overwhelming majority in the interests of the overwhelming majority': for the first time in history decisive social change was to involve the mass of the population acting in their own interests, and not a minority proposing to act for them.

Lenin too, speaking of the socialist revolution, stressed this role of self-conscious mass activity. In his writings of 1917 (above all in the oft-misunderstood *State and Revolution*) he emphasized that the socialist revolution cannot be accomplished without the destruction of the old state based upon hierarchy and authoritarianism. Thus, in 'The Task of the Proletariat in our Revolution', he wrote that in a 'parliamentary bourgeois republic . . . all the machinery of oppression – the army, the police, and the bureaucracy – is left intact. The Commune and the Soviets *smash* that machinery and do away with it.' (Lenin's emphasis).[23]

If the Communist Parties of Eastern Europe had been serious about their claims to stand in the tradition of Marx and Lenin, their strategy would have been clear. They would have led an agitation among the mass of workers against the old forms of society and would have attempted to increase their own influence by proving themselves at every point the most consistent and far-seeing section of the workers. They would have led mass struggles of workers, the culmination of which would have been the creation of direct organs of workers' power (workers' councils, the Soviets of 1917), which would have endeavoured to smash the old state and replace it by the power of the councils.

In fact, the policy of the Communist Parties was to do exactly the opposite. Immediately after the German surrender they entered governments in coalition with the anti-fascist bourgeois parties, the peasant and the socialist democratic parties. Their justification for joining these coalitions was *not* that they could carry through any sort of social revolution, but rather that 'Popular Democratic' governments would eradicate the last remnants of feudalism and establish normal 'bourgeois-democratic' regimes. In these coalitions the Communists were allotted seats as a tribute, not to the extent of their popular support, but to the influence of the Russian occupation forces. Thus they were no less important in the government in Poland or Hungary, where their popular support was very small, than in Czechoslovakia or Bulgaria, where they had some sort of mass base.

The Revolutionary Wave and the 'People's Governments'

In the three Eastern European states that had been allied to Germany, military defeat was followed by revolutionary upsurge.

This was most pronounced in Bulgaria, rather less in Hungary and Rumania. But the Communist Parties made no attempt to lead this wave of popular insurgency into an assault on the old order of society. Instead they united with representatives of the old order to destroy the spontaneous movement from below.

Developments in Bulgaria were typical.

> Reports on the Bulgarian forces of occupation in Western Thrace and Macedonia vividly recall the picture of the Russian Army in 1917 (wrote a Western observer). Soldiers' councils have been set up, officers have been degraded, red flags hoisted, and normal saluting has been abolished.[24]

The Russian leaders rapidly intervened to put a stop to this. Molotov declared:

> If certain Communists continue their present conduct we will bring them to reason. Bulgaria will remain with her democratic government and present order . . . You must retain all valuable army officers from before the *coup d'etat*. You should reinstate in service all officers who have been dismissed for various reasons.[25]

The Communist leaders did everything they could 'to stop extremists in the party agitating for sovietization of the country'.[26] The Russian army also acted to preserve the status quo.

> On several occasions when local Communists in the provinces tried to displace city officials and take matters into their own hands they were ordered by the Russian military authorities to return the jobs to old officials until orders were received from the Fatherland Front government in Sofia.[27]

'Order' was rapidly restored in the Bulgarian army. The Minister of War 'issued a stern order for troops to return immediately to normal discipline, to abolish soldiers' councils and to hoist no more red flags'. Bulgarian troops were placed under the supreme command of Marshal Tolbukhin who had 'no patience with Balkan repetitions of 1917'.[28]

At the same time as they curtailed the revolutionary movement, the Bulgarian Communist leaders declared very emphatically that they stood for the status quo and the maintenance of private property. Yugov, the Communist Minister of the Interior, declared in mid-1944: 'This government . . . has no intention of establishing a Communist regime in Bulgaria . . . There is no truth in the rumour that the government intends to nationalize any private enterprise in the country.'[29] Early in 1946 Dimitrov declared: 'The immediate task is neither the realization of socialism nor the introduction of the Soviet system but the consolidation of a truly democratic and parliamentary system.'[30]

In this period (from September 1944 to October 1946) the head of the coalition Fatherland Front government was General Kimon Georgiev. He had played a leading part in the military, semi-fascist *coup d'etat* of 1923, in which tens of thousands of workers and peasants had been massacred, and was the direct author of the military coup of 1934 that led to the immediate dismissal of the government, to terrible persecution of Communists, Socialists and Agrarians, and to the dissolution of the trade unions for the first time in Bulgarian history.[31] His supporters wielded such influence in the Fatherland Front government that a serious western commentator could remark that 'the composition of the government suggests that the group that has now taken over in Sofia is the famous Military League that took power by *coup d'etat* in 1934'.[32]

It was in this government that the Bulgarian Communists participated, this government to which both they and the Russians gave unstinting support while the revolutionary wave was forced back. Only later did they turn against the pro-western elements within it.

In Rumania a similar situation occurred. The government was constituted from March 1945 onwards by equal numbers of Communists and members of the ill-named 'Liberal' party, together with various other individuals. The 'Liberal' vice-president Tatarescu had organized anti-Jewish pogroms in 1927. After the rise of Hitler, the British Communist weekly, *World News and Views*, had described him as belonging to the 'right, pro-Hitler wing of the National Liberal Party'.[33] The Minister of Culture, Mihail Ralea, had been a minister under King Carol and an open admirer of the Hitler regime. The Minister of Cults, Father Burducea, had been one of the most notorious members of the Fascist Iron Guards. The Minister of Labour, Lotar Radaceanu, had been in Carol's totalitarian 'Renaissance Front'.[34]

What applied to the government applied to the rest of the

structure, too. Cambrea, who had commanded the Rumanian troops fighting against the Russians at Stalingrad, was promoted and made Assistant Chief of Staff of the Army. The new head of the Secret Police was a former active Fascist, Major Popescue-Argetoia. The personnel of the judiciary remained virtually unchanged, with only 20 new Judges out of 2000 being appointed.[35] When the Peasant Party leader Maniu was put on trial in 1947, the president of the court was the same individual who had been prosecutor at the trial of the Communist leader Anna Pauker in 1936 and who had later been wartime director-general of all prisons and concentration camps.[36]

Not that the Communist Party itself was much different. Rumanian Communist leaders have since admitted that whole sections of the Fascist Iron Guards joined the party.[37] As in Bulgaria, Rumanian Communist and government leaders made numerous statements expressing opposition to nationalization or Sovietization. For the first three years of the 'People's Democratic Government' capitalists who had collaborated with the Nazis were untouched. Patrascanu, the Communist Minister of Justice, drew up a law permitting 'industrialists, business men and bankers to escape punishment as war criminals'.[38]

Far from deploring such a situation, the Communist leaders actually welcomed and defended it. On 3 November 1946 Premier Groza declared: 'The King, the Church, the Army, the People and the Government are all one.' On the King's birthday, the Communist daily *Era Noua* said: 'The people of Rumania have faith in their king.'[39] Such was the monarchist ardour of the Communist leaders, that they attacked the Peasant Party leader Maniu as anti-monarchist when he and his followers withdrew from parliament: 'In fact Maniu's unparliamentary attitude is only a guise for his anti-dynastic policy' complained *Era Noua*.[40]

In Hungary the pattern was again very similar:

> Instead of nationalizing property on a broad scale, an act that would not have met with serious opposition in 1945, the Communists were instrumental in restoring all but the largest factories and mines to private owners.[41]

The Warsaw Uprising

In Poland, a revolutionary upsurge took place before the final German evacuation. The mass of the population of Warsaw rose up against the occupying German forces on 1 August 1944, as the advance guard of the Russian army approached to within fifteen miles of the city. Poorly armed, with home-made grenades and other improvized weapons, the people of Warsaw fought heroically, women and children joining their menfolk in the combat. Within two days the Germans had lost control of most of the city to the insurgents.

Although the military command of the uprising lay in the hands of members of the pre-war Polish army like General Bor-Komorowski, mass popular organizations, particularly the Polish Socialist Party (PPS) and the Peasant Party played an important role, and military units of these parties in the main resistance movement, the Home Army, retained their separate identity, while the forces of the extreme right were small and organized in a separate organization, the NSZ. The uprising was said later by followers of the Moscow line to be 'reactionary' or to have been premature, but at the time the Communist organization in Poland, the Union of Polish Patriots, itself put out calls for the insurrection.[42] The Communist paper *Armia Ludowa* stated: 'The armed uprising has found the support of the broadest masses of Warsaw's people, quite independently of who started it and for what purpose, and that is its strength.'[43]

The programme announced by the Polish Council of National Unity in the middle of the insurrection, on 15 August 1944 included 'Agrarian reform covering estates of over 50 hectares ... Socialization of key industries ... Participation of workers in the management of enterprises and control by workers of industrial production.'[44] The leadership of the Warsaw uprising was clearly no more 'reactionary' than the various monarchist and ex-fascist elements who proliferated at the time in the governments of Rumania, Bulgaria and Hungary with Russian backing.

Yet the Russian forces, so close to Warsaw, gave no help. It is an open question whether it was militarily feasible for them to advance into the city – a German offensive forced a temporary withdrawal of up to fifty miles along most of the front. But air support was certainly possible, supplies could have been dropped, resistance could have been mounted against the Luftwaffe planes that were bombing and strafing the insurgents.

As it was, the Russian forces stood back while the Germans put down the rising. After 63 days Warsaw fell. The city had been systematically destroyed, house by house, 240,000 of its inhabitants had been killed and another 630,000 deported. In this way the revolutionary insurgency of the mass of Poles was destroyed *before* the Russian troops eventually took the city early in 1945.

Revolution from Above

Yet in the whole of Eastern Europe a decisive social transformation was carried through in the post-war years. The Communists were not making a revolution of the sort talked about by Marx and Lenin. But neither were they in the 'People's Democratic' governments to serve the interests of their bourgeois allies. They collaborated with these to put down any independent insurgent movements from below. But at the same time they were preparing the ground, in co-operation with the Russian occupying forces, to destroy these allies as well – 'from above'.

In each government the Communists held only a minority of ministries. But the Russian presence ensured that they obtained key positions from the point of view of gaining overwhelming political control. Everywhere those ministries concerned with the repressive functions of the state – in particular the ministries of the interior and of defence – were taken over by party members. The Hungarian leader, Rakosi, later admitted,

> There was one position, control of which was claimed by our Party from the first minute. One position where the Party was not inclined to consider any distribution of the posts according to the strengths of the parties in the coalition. This was the State Security Authority . . . We kept this organization in our hands from the first day of its establishment.[45]

The old state machine was not destroyed, it was handed over wholesale to those Communist leaders whom Stalin trusted. Its instruments of repression provided the keys to control over the rest of society.

Czechoslovakia provides a good example. Here the Communist Minister of the Interior ensured that all the major posts under his control were held by party members. The old police force was reorganized under Communist officers, so that, for instance, four of the five chief officers in the Prague headquarters of the Security Police were party members, along with twelve out of seventeen regional directors of the Police, while in the directing office of the Security Police Corps, nine out of thirteen officers were in the party.[46]

This system of control over the old repressive apparatus enabled the Communist leaders to begin eliminating from the rest of the state machine, and from the various political and mass organizations, those who ever refused to accept their dominance.

The speed at which the state machine and the mass organizations were purged varied from country to country, but its results were similar everywhere. A bureaucratic instrument was created which subordinated to itself all other social forces. Those who controlled its levers were increasingly able to dominate both their 'allies' in the government and the mass organizations outside it. Arrest and trial of leading figures on trumped up charges were used to intimidate activists at all levels. Those outside the apparatus were given the choice: succumb to the Communist leaders or face an unpredictable terror.

The Fate of Peasant and Socialist Parties

Two sorts of mass organizations constituted obstacles to the Communist Party takeover: the peasant parties and the non-Communist socialist parties.

The peasant parties of Eastern Europe varied enormously. Because of the heterogenous nature of the rural populations—extending from virtually landless labourers to capitalist farmers employing hired labour – and also because of the tendency for the real leaders of the peasant parties to be sections of the urban middle class, a single party could contain both progressive and reactionary elements at one and the same time. The parties also varied widely between countries.

The attitude of the Communist leaders to the various elements in the peasant parties was not determined by their 'progressiveness', however, but by a quite different criterion: the degree to which they could put forward independent policies and achieve an independent following. Where they enjoyed any independence, the line of the Communist Party was one of hostility and the state machine was used to weaken and fragment them.

The Rumanian Communist Party participated in a coalition with the arch right-winger Tatarescu, while persecuting the opposition party led by Maniu, censoring its press and eventually putting its leader on trial. In Poland the Communist Party supported the creation of a puppet leadership for the Peasant Party under the chairmanship of Andrzej Witos, who had supported the reactionary 'colonels' regime' in the interwar period. The real leader of the Peasant Party, the bourgeois democrat Mikolajczyk, was thus forced to form his own party, the PSL. Though Mikolajczyk was a member of the coalition government, tens of thousands of PSL members, including leftists like Baginski and Mierzwa[47] were arrested. In Hungary, the Communist leaders demanded the expulsion of a number of outspoken anti-Communists from the Smallholders' Party (which had half the seats in the government). When the Smallholders rejected this, the Russian Command in Budapest intervened directly, threatening to increase the level of reparations. The Smallholders then acquiesced.[48]

What applied to the peasant parties applied in equal measure to the socialist parties, in particular to the most important one, the Polish Socialist Party (the PPS). In a country where the Communist Party had been small before the war (and defunct for four years after 1938) the PPS had both dominated the labour movement and moved sharply towards the left to the extent of raising the slogans of 'social revolution' and 'dictatorship of the toiling masses'.[49] With years of experience of underground activity, it had survived the period of German occupation, building in the process a party militia on a territorial and factory basis which played an important role in the Warsaw Uprising.[50]

After the war, the PPS continued to gain majority support from the industrial workers. In 63 elections to shop committees held in the largest industrial district in Poland in 1945, the PPS gained 556 seats (64 per cent) as against the Communists 193 (21 per cent). It also had the support of two thirds of the delegates at the Congress of the Polish TUC in November 1945.

The Russians and the Communist leaders tried to break the

independence of the Socialists. A new leadership was imposed on the PPS at a non-representative congress in Lublin in September 1944, while most of Poland was still under German control. Two of the new 'leaders', Osubka-Morawski and Drobner, had not even been members of the PPS during the war.

The real leaders of the PPS emerged from the underground or from German prisons, to face harassment and even arrest by the police and the Russian forces. Puzak, Zdanowski, Cohn, Pajdak, Dziegielewski, Krawczyk, Wilczynski, Sobolewski, Oberski, Galaj and many others were imprisoned.[51]

The new 'official' leaders of the PPS tried to secure a unification of the party with the Communist Party. But they faced continual resistance from the rank and file. When the question of fusion was raised at regional conferences in Cracow, Katowice and other towns during 1946, it met with almost unanimous opposition. Adam Kury-lowicz, recently elected General Secretary of the Trade Unions, wrote in *Robotnik*:

> From all parts of the country fresh reports are coming in of injustices suffered by the workers. The elements alien to the working class behave in an arbitrary fashion and act like 'bosses'. They hire and fire workers without taking into account the opinion of the workers of the plant, scorn-ing the laws, conquests and social rights of the workers. A clique of self-seeking politicians is being formed.[52]

The Socialist Party Congress, in December 1947, refused to vote for unification. However, three months later Cyrankiewicz, a member of the leadership, declared that the merger of the parties would be carried out. 82,000 members were expelled; twelve members were removed from the Central Executive Committee and twelve from the Supreme Council. Kurylowicz was removed from his posi-tion in the unions.

Elsewhere in Eastern Europe the pattern was similar: on the one hand threats to the social-democratic leaders of the established workers' movement; on the other, the offer of positions in a new and rapidly expanding bureaucracy if they would collaborate with the Communist Party and the Russian occupying forces.

In Eastern Germany in 1945, for instance,

> individuals who commended themselves to the local Soviet commanders were given positions of responsibility on the

spot, regardless of their record, provided they were not obvious National Socialists. In this way a whole new cadre of mayors, *Landraete* and police officers was appointed . . . the minor war criminals and Nazis had an easier life in the East than in the West. . . .[53]

In 1946, a number of leaders of the Social Democratic Party agreed to merge their party with the Communist Party in the Russian-occupied zone. The party leader most prominent in pushing this line was Grotewohl, although he had opposed such a merger only four days previously. He was rewarded with a top position in the new regime.[54]

Nevertheless, the Social Democrats rather than the new Stalinist Party, the SED, retained the allegiance of many of the workers. In the elections of 1946 the SED failed to get a majority, and in Berlin only got half as many votes as the Social Democrats.

The Russian occupying forces and the SED leaders set out to overcome their weakness – not by class agitation (they opposed any strikes or wage agitation, although industry remained privately owned in 1946), but by a mixture of bribery and threats. Those who joined the SED were given special ration cards by party headquarters.

There were many cases of political opponents of the SED, who while being slandered almost daily in the Eastern Zone, received gifts from time to time from the SED, combined with offers of a good position in the SED itself.[55]

At the same time many ex-social democrats were arrested for 'social-democratic agitation', including some who were formerly members of the SED. In the prisons they found that their conditions were no better than those of ex-Nazis; and a 1948 general amnesty that freed minor ex-Nazis, left social-democratic workers languishing in their cells.[56]

After such policies had been implemented for a period of three years, the Communists effectively controlled every aspect of political life in the Eastern European countries. By now the 'coalition' governments were coalitions between the Communist Party leaders and their shadow. Those who opposed the hold of the Communist Party, whether they came from the old bourgeoisie or the working-class movement had either been bought off with bureaucratic posts or eliminated.

The Fate of Peasant and Socialist Parties   39

The Growth of the Communist Parties

Bribery, intimidation and terror alone were not sufficient to dominate society. Human material for staffing the mushrooming apparatus was needed. Only if a solid layer of the population identified themselves with Communist leaders would their rule have a secure base. What was required was the formation of a new social stratum bound to the policies of the new rulers by common interest and aspirations, sharing some of the privileges of those at the top of society and aware of the gulf between themselves and those at the bottom.

The Communist leaders set out to build up mass, bureaucratically centralized parties, on the lines of the Stalinist party in Russia, organizations which could be employed to monitor and control social life throughout the nation at every level. The method used was simple: they recruited everyone willing to join the Communist Party, and offered considerable advantages to those who did.

The doors of the party were thrown wide open to all those seeking admission.

> They applied pressures to those who refused to cross the line. Peasants needing tools or fertilizers quickly found they could get them much more easily by joining the party. Those eager to obtain more land soon found that the party membership card was the magic formula that alone seemed to clear the interminable red tape. Employees of Ministries and offices headed by Communist chiefs and their fellow travellers saw promotion evading them until they chose to sign the membership application blanks . . .This experience was shared by those who aspired to better or softer jobs in the nationalized factories.[57]

Only one thing was demanded clearly of anyone who joined the Communists at this point: a readiness to obey instructions from above. The Communist Parties grew at a rapid rate, taking in ever larger numbers of people who were bound to them by ties of relative privilege and identified their future with that of the Party. The Polish Party grew from 30,000 members to 300,000 between January and April 1945;[58] the Czechoslovak Party membership from 27,000 to 1,159,164 between May 1945 and the beginning of 1946;[59] the Rumanian Party from about 1,000 members to 800,000 between mid-1944 and October 1945.[60]

Careerism and opportunism were not the only motives drawing the mass influx into the Communist Parties. There were others. Clearly some, if not many, of the recruits were motivated by various degrees of idealism, or sentiments of generalized working-class solidarity. More significant, however, was a feeling among whole strata of the population that the moderate, statified, economic and social system for which the Communists were agitating at the time – with, for instance, full freedom (and even privileges) for organized religion, with positive encouragement for areas of private enterprise, with land belonging to the peasants, and so on – was the only way forward for any sort of national development. This programme appealed especially to all those who wanted to 'get on' in society, who had aspirations to mobility before and during the war, but had been unable to improve their situation because of the backwardness of the country and the disastrous policies of the ruling class.

As in many undeveloped countries today, sections of all social classes responded to such a vision. In the pre-war period the educated lower middle classes of the towns had often turned in despair to the fascist parties. Now they streamed into the Stalinist parties, seeing here hope for both personal advancement and for national development. But it was not only to the existing middle class that these parties offered a way forward. Similar opportunities were offered to thousands of manual workers too, who could join and rapidly be raised out of their class: in Czechoslovakia 300,000 were individually promoted from the workbench to bureaucratic positions in this way.

In summary: the Russian rulers were looking for local mass parties with which to gain total control over social life. To this end the Communist Parties were turned into giant machines for promoting social mobility. Hundreds of thousands of individuals were raised to positions of authority at every level and in every sphere of social life – positions in which they were utterly dependent on the will of the Communist leadership.

Slav against Teuton

In Czechoslovakia and Poland this process was aided by another policy, which the Communists and their coalition partners carried out without any sign of hesitation: that of 'racially purifying' the nation.

For more than 700 years there had been a German-speaking

population in Czechoslovakia, which by the early years of the twentieth century numbered about three millions. It was slightly more proletarianized than the Czech population as a whole – 61 per cent being workers in 1930. This Sudeten population voted overwhelmingly for either the Social Democratic or the Communist Party in elections between 1920 and 1930.[61] 'The ratio of Germans and Hungarians in the Communist Unions far exceeded that of the Czechs and Slovaks . . .'[62]

However, the failure of the Social Democrats and Communists in Germany to resist the rise of Nazism and to offer the German workers a socialist alternative to unemployment and fascism had its effects in Czechoslovakia. Industry in the Sudetenland was more severely hit than elsewhere in Czechoslovakia by the slump of the thirties, and unemployment among German speakers was about twice the national average. The appeal of pro-Nazi German nationalism grew among the Sudeten population, until in 1935 the pro-Nazi party polled 62-63 per cent of the Sudeten votes. Nevertheless 300,000 Sudetens continued to vote for the Social Democrats and about 120,000 for the Communists. After Munich 40,000 of these suffered heroically for their internationalism in Nazi concentration camps, where about half of them perished.[63]

In 1935, the official Comintern organ apportioned the blame all too clearly for the victory of the Nazis in the elections: 'The reason for this victory is the policy of the Czech bourgeoisie which has led to terrible poverty and misery and national oppression in the German districts . . .'[64] A Czechoslovak historian recently pointed out that: 'Until 1944 the leadership of the Czechoslovak Communist Party opposed the demand for population transfer'.[65]

But when the war ended this tune changed completely. Instead of calling for any kind of working-class unity between Czechs, Slovaks and German workers, they proclaimed quite clearly that:

> The new Republic will be a Slav state, a Republic of Czechs and Slovaks. We will deprive the Germans and the Hungarians, who have so heavily sinned against our peoples, of their citizenship and will severely punish them.[66]

The Communist Minister of Education was adamant:

> We do not know any progressive Germans, nor are there

any . . . We will purify Prague and the border districts, and we are in a position to do this because we have a great helper in doing this – the Red Army.[67]

With the Communists outdoing the bourgeois parties in chauvinism, this 'purification' was carried out very rapidly. As one bourgeois Czech politician who *approved* of that policy describes it:

> On May 17 the Germans were given smaller food rations ('the same basic food ration as the Jews received during the occupation' according to a government order of May 17). They had to wear special white armbands and were not allowed to use public means of communication. . . . In June all German schools were closed. Compulsory labour conscription was introduced . . . Practically all movable and immovable property was taken away from the Germans . . . The confiscation would make good wrongs committed on the Czech nation since the end of its independence in 1620. The Communist Party in particular emphasized the national movement and became the most nationalist party.[68]

This anti-Sudeten feeling might, of course, be explained as a spontaneous upsurge (although this does not explain why there was not, say, a similar 'spontaneous' upsurge among Czechs against the Slovaks, many of whom had collaborated with the pro-Nazi Tiso regime, or why there was not a similar upsurge of Yugoslavs against German speakers). But even if this were the case, any genuine marxist party would have fought against chauvinism and racism, explaining to the mass of Czech workers the reasons for the Nazi sympathies of many German speakers (as the Czechoslovak Party had done in the thirties). Instead, the Communists chose to fan the flames of chauvinism deliberately, to turn Czech worker against German worker (and Slovak worker against Magyar worker).

The German speakers were driven off the land and out of the factories. As one Stalinist writer put it at the time:

> Above all two problems stand out; namely the distribution to Czech peasants and agricultural workers of confiscated German land and property, and secondly the replacement of Germans by Czechs in industry.[69]

There was token recognition by the Stalinists that some Sudeten workers might have resisted Nazism and even suffered somewhat in doing so:

> The Czechoslovak Social Democrat and Communist
> Parties set up special offices to provide for the voluntary
> (sic) emigration of members of their former German sister
> parties. . . . Over 100,000 anti-fascists were transported to
> the Soviet and American zones in 1945-46.[70]

Thus those who had risked their lives to fight for socialism against the Nazis were rewarded by the 'socialist' parties in power with . . . more pleasant forms of transportation than was usual!

In whole areas of the country the Czechoslovak working class had been about half German speaking. The proportion of German speaking workers in the glass industry, for example, had been 60 per cent, in paper 58 per cent, in textiles 56 per cent and in mining 45 per cent.[71] As the Stalinist writer we quoted above put the matter: 'President Benes . . . emphasized that the transfer of the Germans means the loss of one million workmen . . .'[72]

Through confiscation and deportation, broad avenues of social mobility were created in the Sudeten areas of Czechoslovakia. Peasants without land could suddenly acquire it; those with land could get more. In factories, with half the workforce gone, there could be some promotion for nearly everybody. The unskilled could become 'skilled' overnight. At the same time houses, furniture and other property were suddenly 'created'. And those who redistributed the positions and belongings of one section of the working class to the rest were the functionaries of the Communist Party and the trade unions. It is small wonder, then, that the recipients were ready to join the party and, for a time, to show some allegiance to it; and small wonder, too, that the party could grow so rapidly and gain such influence in a 'racially pure' labour movement.

The hysterical, chauvinistic campaign against German (and Hungarian) speakers served the interest of the Stalinist leaders admirably. It provided an issue with which the bourgeois parties were in full accord. It enabled the Stalinists to take the forefront in carrying through 'national unification' while avoiding the key question: which class would control the country in the future. Above all it enabled them to divide the working class down the middle and to turn organizations of the working class into their opposite.

The role of the trade unions was no longer one of furthering the goals of a unified working class, but rather that of offering displaced Germans' places to Czech workers. 'It was chiefly the trade unionists who organized the work and supply of workers.'[73] Not only German speaking workers 'lost' their trade unions: so did the Czech and Slovak workers. Their trade unions changed their class goals:

> Today questions of labour disputes are no longer the main preoccupation of the trade unionists . . . Today they are talking about the standard of production, the state of various industries, the policy and measures for the increase of industrial output.[74]

Czech policy towards the Sudetens was matched in the territories taken by Poland from the Germans after 1945. Here again the Communist Party used the situation to strengthen its hold over the Polish immigrant population – with the Communist, Gomulka, as minister for the New Territories, the party gained support by distributing land, jobs and property.

Nationalization

By the end of 1947, whoever controlled the Communist Parties of Eastern Europe had de facto control over all the major institutions of those societies. Control over the security police permitted systematic intimidation of opponents, both in the bourgeois parties and in the labour movement; show trials, imprisonment without trial, torture and censorship were the chosen instruments. At the same time, offers of rapid, unexpected promotion enabled the creation of a growing body of loyal, disciplined recruits both among the ranks of the governmental bureaucracy and within society generally. Mass parties had been built, most of whose members were dependent on those above them for their relatively privileged positions.

Only when the levers of control were firmly in their hands, at the end of 1947, did the regimes of Bulgaria, Hungary and Rumania move on to extensive nationalization. Together with the other Eastern European states, their economies were internally restructured in the image of Stalin's Russia.

With one possible exception, the transformation of the national economies was carried out without mass mobilization or agitation. The nationalizations were a mere rationalization of a situation in which, as everyone knew already, the Communist Parties had succeeded in establishing monolithic social control. Only in Czechoslovakia did it seem that elements of a real workers' uprising were involved in the reorganization of the economy.

The Prague Coup – Workers' Uprising?

Even writers generally hostile to Stalinism have argued that it was a workers' movement that gave full power to the Communists in Prague in 1948.

> Unlike the other European upheavals, this bore the mark of a revolution from below, even though it was timed to suit Stalin's convenience. The Communists accomplished the revolution by their own strength, supported by the great majority of the workers; they had only to parade their armed militias in the street to block any counter action . . . Benes and Masaryk, overwhelmed and depressed by the evidence of mass popular support for the revolution – the streets of Prague were full of armed workers marching towards the seats of government – bowed to the victors.[75]

Although Isaac Deutscher's description of the pessimism and resignation of the bourgeois leaders is accurate, his talk of 'revolution from below' is not. Deutscher ignores an aspect of the situation far more fundamental than the 'armed workers' – the role of the armed police. The significance of the Prague coup was the issue that brought it to a head. It followed a ministerial crisis when the non-Communist ministers attempted to resist increased Communist Party control over the police.[76] But the ministers proved powerless against the Communist Party leaders, who were already in effective control of the state apparatus and able to use it.

The Ministry of the Interior moved police regiments to sensitive areas. The offices of the non-Communist political parties were placed under guard. The 6,000-strong border police – established in 1946 in the Sudeten areas – were so deployed as to be able to take over key points in Prague and Bratislava at short notice.

The media were also already under effective Communist Party control, through the Ministry of Propaganda. Non-Communist politicians, including the leader of the Social Democratic Party, were denied access to the radio, which broadcast non-stop support for the coup. The non-Communist newspapers were simply refused supplies of newsprint. As an additional precaution, and by way of a warning to any who opposed the coup, Russian troops gathered on Czechoslovakia's border, making it clear that they would intervene if necessary.

If revolution means turning the state machine upside down, there was no revolution in Czechoslovakia in February 1948. Rather, the state machine itself was used to remove the symbols of formal power from the non-Communist section of the government. Nor did any major change in property relations occur. Before the coup 80 per cent of industry was nationalized; afterwards 95 per cent.

There was a façade of workers' activity, but not an 'insurrection'. A congress of works councils was called – but just for one day, with uniformed policemen acting as ushers. Its delegates voted to support the coup, and were then sent home. They were not meant to run the country themselves. There was a general strike, but as it only lasted for one hour, it was hardly the decisive factor in the crisis. There were a couple of mass workers' demonstrations, organized from above, with the police, as well as other workers, beating up those who refused to participate.

More significant in the coup was the role played by the so-called workers' militia, whose unarmed members patrolled the streets of Prague during the decisive days and guarded strategic points.

But the workers' militia was in no sense an organization emanating from or belonging to the mass of the workers. It was dominated by a minority of Communist Party members in the factories, who were dependent on the Communist leadership for their relatively privileged positions. And during the coup itself, the militia was organized not from below but by the security police.

Josef Pavel, a party member with a senior position in the Interior Ministry, commanded the militia, while two other security police officials, Majors Duda and Paducha, were attached to it, to provide co-ordination with the police. It was the security police, too, who arranged the arming of some 6,550 members of the militia (a minuscule proportion, about 0.20 per cent, of all Czechoslovak workers). Remembering that some 300,000 workers were being promoted into privileged positions in the state machine by the Communist authorities, it is not difficult to understand why many of them should have given active support to the coup. But none of that amounts to the working class as a whole taking control of its own destiny.

Indeed, there are indications that in the period prior to the coup, increasing numbers of workers were turning hostile to the

Communist leaders. In April 1947, the Communist general secretary of the trade unions complained that in the first round for the election of Works Committee members, 35 per cent of the official Communist Party-nominated candidates had been voted down, although no other candidates were allowed. The chairman of the unions had a simple answer to this – he prolonged the life of the old committees by one year.[77]

Precautions were taken to ensure that the same discontent with officials did not get expressed in the elections of January 1948. The social-democratic paper *Pravo Lidu* complained afterwards that

> especially in the large industrial concerns, it is evident that all sorts of questionable practice was used, calculated to upset the democratic form of election . . . The meetings were usually called after working hours, when the majority of workers were leaving or had left . . .[78]

With 80 per cent of industry nationalized *before* the coup, Communist union officials could rely upon the co-operation of Communist factory managers in their efforts to keep tight control over the unions. Union officials and managers also worked together to mobilize for the mass demonstrations and the one hour strike in February.

Very few workers resisted participating in the demonstrations. The majority probably identified with the Communist Party's aims – just as many British workers support the Labour Party, even though it rarely fights for their interests. On the other hand they were moved by no massive enthusiasm. When the coup was over, they still had to clock into work, still had to submit to the orders of the same foreman, still faced the same relentless pressures to put out more effort. To that extent the coup had changed nothing.

The Prague coup was not a 'revolution from below' but a police manoeuvre, accompanied by a carefully prepared display of popular support. In that display the state machine played the key role ; the workers had a strictly walk-on part.

2.
The Russian Interest

Russia had divided Europe with America and Britain, and had set about establishing regimes there, to safeguard her interests. But what were these interests? After all, while Russian methods might not have been all that pleasant, their intentions might have been. A brief examination of Russian economic policies vis-à-vis her 'satellites' in the early post-war period is necessary.

The economic relationships between Russia and her satellites between 1945 and about 1954 can be examined under three headings: reparations, mixed companies and trade.

Reparations

In the inter-war years a central feature of Communist Party propaganda and agitation throughout Europe was the campaign against the reparations that the Versailles Treaty had imposed on a defeated Germany. The Communist argument was straightforward: the German people were being asked to pay for the crimes of their capitalist masters. This argument fully retained its validity after the Second World War. The German workers had been the first to suffer from Nazism: years before Hitler turned his attention abroad their trade unions and socialist parties were destroyed, their shop organizations smashed. More than 800,000 socialists, communists, trade unionists and others suffered in the concentration camps. In no sense could these be said to have benefited from the rapacity of German militarism in Eastern Europe.

Yet by the end of the war the line of the Communist Parties, under direction from Moscow, had been completely reversed. Reparations were not only justified, but demanded in ever larger quantities, now that the Russian bureaucracy itself stood to benefit. The Russian government demanded ten thousand million dollars worth of reparations from Germany. It took these in two forms: until mid-1946, by dismantling equipment and physically moving it to Russia; from then onwards, by running it in the Russian zone of Germany as Russian equipment, under special Russian-owned companies (known as SAGs) specifically set up for that purpose. About one third of East German industry (comprising virtually the whole of heavy industry) was owned and run by the SAGs until, with one exception, they were liquidated in 1954.

In Rumania the initial Russian occupation of the country was the occasion for immediate, large-scale looting. Between 23 August and 12 September 1944 the total value of equipment seized by the occupying forces was about 2,000 million dollars[1] and included the entire war fleet, most of the merchant marine, half the available railway stock and all the motor cars, as well as a large part of the oil industry's equipment. There are varying estimates of the real cost to Rumania of the reparations agreed under the armistice of 1944. The present ruler, Nicolae Ceausescu, gives the figure as 'over 100 million dollars'. Other estimates vary from $1,050 million to $1,785 million for the years 1944-48.[2] The latter figure would represent about 84 per cent of Rumania's national income for the period.

In Hungary reparations consumed something like 90 per cent of the working capacity of the metal working and engineering industries in 1945;[3] in 1948 reparations accounted for 25.4 per cent of budget expenditure, and in 1949 9.8 per cent.[4]

Even the countries whose rulers had not allied them to Germany in the war were not immune to massive Russian looting. Thus sixty big industrial enterprises from the Sudeten region and a number of enterprises in other parts of Czechoslovakia were dismantled and taken by the Russian army. 25-30 per cent of industry in the part of Germany annexed by Poland was moved to Russia, while in Old Poland and Lodz and Bialystok textile works suffered the same fate.[5]

In Hungary, Rumania and East Germany the populations were reduced to a pitiful condition by the combined effects of reparations and the devastation resulting from the war. The International Committee of the Red Cross reported:

It is difficult to convey the misery of the Rumanian people

in 1947 : famine prevailed in whole sections of the country, in some regions people were eating grass and the bark of trees and even clay . . . infant mortality actually reached a rate of 80 per cent.[6]

In Hungary the food shortage was so serious that the ration amounted to no more than 850 calories per person per day.

The extraction of reparations tied in with the policies of the local Communist Parties in various ways. While the Russians were still demanding reparations on a massive scale, the local CPs did not push for nationalization. Apparently, the Russian leaders felt their robbery would be too obvious if they took property 'belonging to the people'. Hence those states paying reparations were the last to nationalize. East Germany, which paid reparations for the longest period, was the only Eastern European country to retain anything like a visible private sector into the early 1950s. Furthermore, the fact of reparations, together with the ability of the Russians to raise them if they so wished, was a weapon that could be used against any non-Communist government ministers who began to question Communist policies too strongly.

Mixed Companies

In addition to reparations, the Russians established companies in which they shared control with the local capitalists or the local state, as a mechanism for pumping resources out of the satellites into the Russian economy.

The way in which these 'mixed companies' worked was most clearly revealed after Tito's split with Moscow. In Yugoslavia in 1947 two of these 'mixed companies', 'Juspad' and 'Justa', were set up for transport. In theory the capital for these companies was to come equally from both participants. In practice, while the Yugoslavs had paid up 76.25 per cent of their contribution after fifteen months, the Russians had paid only 9.83 per cent of theirs. Yet Yugoslavia got only 40 per cent of the services from the companies. Moreover, Juspad charged the Yugoslavs 0.40 dinars per kilometre-ton moved, as against 0.19 dinars to the Russians.[7]

Elsewhere in Eastern Europe such companies were set up without the Russians having to pay a penny. German-owned capital passed straight to the Russian state in Hungary, Rumania and Bulgaria. The fact that much of this capital had previously been more or less stolen from the local population by German militarism was beside the point. Effectively, German booty became Russian booty. Sovrompetrol, for instance, which owned the lion's share of Rumania's oil fields was set up in this fashion. Similar companies covered the whole spectrum of industry in both Hungary and Rumania, although they were more important in the latter.

Trade

The final weapon used by the Russian rulers for pumping resources from Eastern Europe to the Soviet Union was trade. This aspect was particularly marked in the early post-war period (up to the mid-fifties). The method of exploitation was quite simple: Eastern European goods were bought at below world market prices, at times even below cost price, while Russian goods were sold in Eastern Europe at above world market prices. The most obvious, and probably the most important, single instance of this process concerned the buying of Polish coal in the early post-war years. The Poles agreed to sell the Russians 65 million tons of coal over a seven-year period at a price which just about covered the transport costs – at a time when Denmark and Sweden were offering to pay between 12 and 16 dollars a ton for identical coal.[8] It has been estimated that the Russian government made about 900 million dollars out of this agreement – though in 1956, with Poland in ferment and then the Hungarian insurrection, the Russians expediently 'compensated' for over half of this excess profit by writing off Polish debts to the value of 525 million dollars.[9]

There are various other significant examples. After the Tito-Stalin split, the Yugoslav Communist paper *Borba*, reported that Yugoslavia had received 45,000 dinars a ton for molybdenum sold to Russia – although this had cost 500,000 dinars a ton to produce.[10] Again, in 1948 the Russians bought four-fifths of the Bulgarian tobacco harvest at such a low price that they were able to resell some of it on the world market, undercutting the Bulgarian price by 35%.

In 1956, the Russians themselves indirectly admitted that relations between their satellites and themselves had been far from equitable, both by redressing some of the balance as far as Polish coal was concerned and by declaring:

> There have been many difficulties, unsolved problems and downright mistakes, including mistakes in the mutual relations between socialist countries – violations against the principle of equality in relations among the socialist states ... The Soviet government is prepared to discuss ... measures ensuring further development and strengthening of the economic links between the socialist countries in order to remove any possibility of violation of the principle of national sovereignty, mutual benefits and equality in relations.[11]

To impose such trade terms, the Soviet rulers did not need direct political control over the content of each and every trade deal. All they required was sufficient overall control to direct the general pattern of trade. This condition was met by early 1948, through the complete consolidation and formalization of 'Communist' rule.

In the first years after the German defeat, devastation throughout Europe had precluded the immediate re-establishment of traditional patterns of trade. There had been an initial upward surge of trade between the East European economies and Russia. However, in 1946 and 1947 this began to decline, as pre-war patterns of trade began to re-assert themselves. But all this changed drastically in 1948, after the local Stalinists had taken complete political control: a series of long-term trade agreements was signed with the USSR. The following table shows the overall pattern:[12]

East European trade

	Imports			Exports		
	millions of dollars at 1938 prices					
Trade	1938	1947	1948	1938	1947	1948
Between USSR & E. Europe	7	97	169	14	75	128
Between E. European states	147	87	186	147	87	186

One very important fact emerges from these figures. Trade between the East European states after 1947 rose only a little above its pre-war level. On the other hand trade with Russia expanded enormously by comparison with anything that had taken place before, until by 1954 it accounted for 42 per cent of East Europe's trade (compared with a 31 per cent share taken by trade between these states themselves).[13] In other words, political control over the regimes of Eastern Europe enabled the Soviet Union to force itself on them as their major trading partner, and thus to dominate economically in any particular trade bargains: the Russians could choose to buy a particular commodity from one of a variety of partners, whereas each satellite producer had much less choice of purchaser.

A corollary of this was that, until the late fifties, there were few serious attempts at integrating the different Eastern European economies. The Russians regarded any such integration as likely to weaken their dominant position in trade bargaining. They were bitterly hostile, for instance, to Tito's plan for a Bulgarian-Yugoslav-Albanian Union.

Conclusion

Stalinist policy in Eastern Europe up to about 1954 was above all centred on siphoning off as substantial a portion as possible of the resources of the area into the Russian economy. The actions of the Russian occupying forces, and later of Russian trade negotiators, were constrained, not by considerations of 'socialist internationalism', nor by any concern with the welfare of the local populations, but by a drive towards the crudest sort of physical exploitation.

In the mid-1950s, however, the scale of Russia's direct exploitation of Eastern Europe declined. The Russian leaders were shaken by the forces released after Stalin's death. They feared that, if too heavy a pressure were applied, this could provoke revolutionary upheaval throughout Eastern Europe and put their overall rule in danger. They were also concerned to strengthen the local ruling groups – and to strengthen these groups' attachment to themselves – by making a whole series of concessions. The mixed companies were wound up and more realistic prices introduced into trade transactions.

This was not, however, the end of economic subordination. The Eastern European states were still expected to develop their economies in accordance with the needs of the Russian bloc as a whole. The Russians argued, for instance, that Rumania should slow down its rate of industrialization and instead concentrate on providing raw materials needed by the rest of the bloc. This was one major factor leading the Rumanian rulers to assert their independence from the rest of the bloc in the early 1960s.

In the late 1960s, the rulers of Czechoslovakia faced a powerful case for strengthening economic ties with the west. They needed modern industrial equipment which it was difficult to obtain elsewhere. But after the Russian invasion of August 1968 the trend was in the other direction. 'Unobtrusively and without much publicity the Czech economy is now being integrated into the USSR to become more and more an industrial complex for the processing of Soviet raw materials.'[14]

Similarly:

under Soviet diplomatic pressure the Hungarian government rejected last year (1971) the Japanese offer to build a factory for the assembly of Honda cars. A special Soviet-Hungarian committee for cooperation in the motor industry, set up later in 1972, determined Hungary's participation in the production of the Soviet Fiat. According to the agreement, during the next four years Hungary will supply 18 types of component for this car.[15]

It is not that the Russian rulers have any particular animus against trade with the west as such. Indeed, they have recently been making massive efforts of their own in that direction. What they do insist is that they themselves shall take the initiative in this matter. Otherwise, they fear, their overall ability to tailor the East European economies to their own needs will be impaired.

At the same time, they continue to demand that the rulers of Eastern Europe help them with one economic burden in particular: that of arming them for their military rivalry with the west.*

In the late 1940s Russian imperialism in Eastern Europe involved crude robbery. Today it has changed its forms. But the Russian rulers still regard the industry of Eastern Europe as at least partly their own property, to be kept available for the pursuit of their interests. When the local population – including the local Communist rulers whom they themselves once put in power – have protested, they have used force to restore 'order'.

*The scale of arms spending in East Europe does not seem to be as high as that in the USSR, being closer to the West European level; but it does represent a diversion of value produced by East European workers to those who control the Warsaw Pact.

3.
From Control to Subjection

The period up to 1948 saw the national Communist Parties of Eastern Europe gradually permeate and penetrate the existing state structures. From initial weakness, they had, with the backing when necessary of the Russian forces, gained control over all spheres of social life, bribing or terrorizing their opponents in the process. The ousting of non-Communist politicians from positions of nominal power in 1947 and early 1948 was merely the culmination of this.

We have emphasized (in Chapter 1) that it was in no sense revolutionary action that gave power to the East European Communists. On the other hand, the Communist takeover did not encounter any serious resistance from organized workers. Indeed, in some cases at least, large sections of the factory workers gave passive support to the new rulers.

The reasons for that passive support are not hard to find. The period in which the new Communist bureaucracy tightened its hold over these countries was a period in which the immense physical hardship occasioned by post-war dislocation was gradually overcome. Production and living standards rose once again to pre-war levels. The condition of the peasantry was improved either through land reforms or by re-division of the land previously owned by German speakers. Many individual workers and peasants experienced a rise in the social scale, to well-paid and prestigious posts in the new bureaucracy. Moreover, the policies of the growing bureaucracy – in particular 'nationalization' – seemed to correspond to the labour movement's traditional demands. In 1947 and 1948 the immense difference between 'nationalization' by a bureaucracy increasing its control from *above* and 'nationalization' by the mass of workers increasing control from *below* was apparent to only relatively few workers.

Finally, most of those who had the first taste, before 1948, of the new instruments of state control – the rigged trials, the expanding powers of the police, the growing apparatus of intimidation and terror – were just those sections of society who were traditionally opposed to the demands of the workers. Their fate excited little practical sympathy in the factories.

From the beginning of 1949 onwards, however, this picture of mass acquiescence in the Stalinist takeover was changed radically by two parallel and related developments throughout Eastern Europe.

The Purges

In the summer of 1948 the terror apparatus which had previously been directed against other sections of society, turned upon the ruling stratum of the Communists themselves.

In June of that year Tito broke with Stalin, and Yugoslavia was expelled from the Stalinist international organization, the Cominform. Immediately a wave of purges began throughout Eastern Europe, aimed at removing from positions of influence all those who might conceivably be tempted to sympathize with Tito. Not only were such Communists deprived of effective power: within a few months large numbers found themselves denounced as 'fascist spies' and agents of western intelligence services.

In Poland, Gomulka, general secretary of the Communist Party and vice-premier, along with Kliszko, Spychalski and at least four other ministers, were arrested and imprisoned.

In Bulgaria, the acting Prime Minister, Kostov, who had been a party member for thirty years, ten of them in prison, was brought to trial and executed for 'having been an agent of the Bulgarian police since 1942'. Ten out of sixteen Communist ministers and six out of nine members of the politbureau were dismissed – the majority as 'fascist agents'.

In Hungary another lifelong Communist from the pre-war period, Laszlo Rajk, Foreign Minister and ex-Minister of the Interior, came to trial together with other leading Communists and was executed as a 'fascist spy'. Later Kadar, Rajk's replacement as Minister of the Interior, was likewise imprisoned and tortured, although not executed. In Czechoslovakia the purges began about a year later than elsewhere, but were as far-reaching.[1] In November 1952, ten government ministers and the secretary general of the Czech Communist Party, Slansky, were sentenced to death. The final speech of the Czech prosecutor summed up the charges:

> Thanks to the vigilance of the working masses and the Communist Parties we have unmasked and rendered harmless the traitorous gangs of Laszlo Rajk in Hungary, Traicho Kostov in Bulgaria, Kochi Xoxe in Albania, Patrascanu in Rumania, and Gomulka in Poland.

The effects of the purges were felt not only among the leading Communists who were put on public trial, but also by the hundreds or even thousands more who faced secret execution, and the tens of thousands who were imprisoned without trial. At the same time, hundreds of thousands suffered expulsion from the Communist Party and loss of their jobs. Between September and December 1948, 30,000 members were expelled from the Polish Communist Party. In August 1948, 100,000 were expelled from the Czechoslovak Party and half a million were reduced from full to candidate membership. In 1949-50, 92,500 members were expelled from the Bulgarian Party.

Whole sections of the bureaucracy that had just taken power found themselves at best forced back into menial occupations or, worse, into labour camps, to imprisonment, torture or death. They were joined in their various punishments by hundreds of thousands of people from every other section of society: members of the old ruling classes, large numbers of peasants or artisans who had collided in one way or another with the regime, workers who refused to accept higher work loads or lower wages.

In turning against sections of the bureaucracy itself, the apparatus of purge and terror aimed chiefly at those who had independent roots inside the local society. In each country it was the overwhelming majority of the leaders of the underground struggle against the Nazis who were executed or imprisoned, whilst those leaders who had spent the war, and often many years before it, in Moscow were left in sole command. In Poland, Gomulka went to prison, Bierut remained in command ; in Hungary Rajk was executed, Rakosi stayed in control. The same happened elsewhere. Precisely those members of the Communist leadership who were not completely dependent on Moscow for their positions of power were eliminated. Stalin's logic was simple: Tito was the only Communist leader in Eastern Europe to have come to power independently without Russian support. He had had the strength to break with Moscow. Where Tito led, other leaders with local roots might be tempted to follow. Therefore, all such leaders must be removed. The Eastern European bureaucracies must be made absolutely dependent on the Russians for their positions, and utterly unable to resist Russian demands.

The purges and show trials cut any threads of continuity with the parties which had fought, in however distorted a manner, for working class demands in the pre-war period. Thus, by 1953, in Czechoslovakia – which had had by far the largest pre-war Communist Party – only 1.5 per cent of the members had held party cards since before the war.[2]

Power within the party was openly wielded from the top downwards, as the Czech party paper announced:

> Control within the party from top to bottom, in central organs, in regional aid district committees, and in primary units is just as important as it is in the People's Committees, in the state apparatus, in the economy and in the mass organization.[3]

Although it was claimed that more than fifty per cent of the party members were 'workers by origin or occupation', only a special category of workers was allowed into the party after May 1947: 'No one would be accepted but shockworkers who had been exceeding their norm of production for at least three consecutive months.'[4]

And, to ensure that even these rate-busters did not exercise any degree of control over the party from below, the secret ballot was abolished in party elections in 1952 because: 'Experience has shown that by instituting such secret ballots a number of organizations could be misused to elect candidates who offered no guarantee that they would fight for the correct policy of the party'.[5]

Economic Changes

The purging of the Communist Parties was accompanied by other changes that had a much more profound impact upon the mass of the population. The whole direction and pace of economic development was changed in such a way as to cut deeply into living standards.

Up to 1948, Eastern Europe had experienced rising living standards and a general recovery from wartime devastation. Rising industrial production had not been at the expense of general living standards, but, on the contrary, had tended to raise them.

But the Russian rulers had long identified their interest as being 'to catch up and overtake' the West, not in every sphere of production but in certain crucial areas related to military considerations, in particular in heavy industry. In Russia itself from 1929 onwards there was enormous growth in heavy industrial and military production, an expansion achieved at terrible cost to the mass of Russian workers, peasants and slave-labourers, whose living standards fell as production of food and consumer goods was ruthlessly subordinated to the drive for industrialization.

Once complete Stalinist control had been established in Eastern Europe, the same pattern of 'planned growth' was imposed on these countries too. A writer in the Czechoslovak party journal *Nova Mysl* described the process in 1968:

> The Cominform conference held in November 1949 . . . demanded in no uncertain terms that the socialist camp withdrew completely from the capitalist camp . . . The unification of the socialist camp required the unreserved subordination of politics, economics and ideological activity in each country to the needs of the camp as a whole …During the cold war the army and security services grew in importance. Their influence shaped the political attitudes of the period . . . The military made demands on resources that no-one had the courage to refuse.[6]

Five-year plans were introduced that aimed at a massive increase in total production. In Hungary a production growth target of 86 per cent for the five-year period from 1 January 1950 was planned, along with a 35 per cent increase in workers' living standards. In 1951, following the general increase in international tension and consequent increased military pressures on the Russian bureaucracy's resources, these figures were upped to 200 per cent and 50-55 per cent respectively.[7]

Total production certainly rose, whether Eastern or Western estimates are taken.

Claimed industrial growth (1937=100)[8]

	1948	1950	1953	1955
Czechoslovakia	107	143	210	243
East Germany	—	111	117	210
Poland	148	231	—	478

In Hungary a 210 per cent increase in industrial production in five years (1949-53) was claimed, in Poland 158 per cent, in Czechoslovakia 98 per cent, in East Germany 98 per cent, in Rumania 144 per cent and in Bulgaria 120 per cent.[9] Gross capital formation as a percentage of GNP rose everywhere to something over 40 per cent in the cases of both Poland and Czechoslovakia,[10] compared with a figure of about 20 per cent for the states of Western Europe.

Within the framework of 'planned growth', most of the plan targets were ignored. Only heavy industry was expanded, while the targets for growth in popular consumption were simply abandoned. Capital expansion was achieved at the direct expense of the mass of the population's standards of living.

It is always difficult to measure changes in living standards. But there can be no doubt about one thing – between 1949 and 1953 living standards fell throughout Eastern Europe. Thus Zauberman[11] has calculated the real earnings of industrial workers as follows:

Index of real incomes

	Pre-war	1950	1953	1955
Czechoslovakia	100	96	84	108
East Germany	100	46	89	109
Poland	100	85	72	80

Peter Kende (who worked on the Hungarian party daily paper until 1956) calculated that Hungarian workers suffered a ten per cent fall in total real incomes (including welfare benefits etc.) between 1949 and 1953.[12] Ivan T. Berend, of the Hungarian Academy of Science, has written recently that 'the real value of wages diminished in Hungary by 20 per cent during the period of the first long-term plan'.[13] Simultaneously there was continual pressure on workers to speed up their pace of work. Work norms were continually raised,[14] while real living standards fell. Where the Communist leadership, in a bid to gain support, had made concessions to the workers in the previous period, now these concessions were rapidly withdrawn. In Czechoslovakia, for instance, the premier declared in February 1949 that the five week annual vacation given to workers in 1947 was 'an unreasonable measure with which we jumped ahead of our times'. One month later workers' holidays were halved. In a similar way, the statutory five-day week was abolished (and not revived until 1968).

But these pressures on the working class did not succeed in raising productivity. The workers demonstrated a growing resentment against the system, resisting the speed-up in a host of informal and more or less individual ways.

The clearest index of this was the rising level of absenteeism from work. One Czech leader wrote in October 1949 that:

> one of our greatest shortcomings is absenteeism . . . Missed worktime, paid and unpaid, shows a constant increase. While total work hours increased by 2.7 per cent last year, absenteeism rose by 21 per cent . . . In comparison with 1947 absenteeism rose by 26 per cent in 1948 and by 37.3 per cent in this year.[15]

The Hungarian leader, Rakosi, complained in similar terms, pointing out that days lost through sick leave in Hungary in 1949 were two to three times higher than before the war.[16]

At the same time the actual quality of what was produced fell. Rakosi complained, for instance, that the percentage of waste in the Manfred Weiss iron foundry, the second biggest metal factory in Hungary, had risen from 10.3 per cent to 23.5 per cent.[17]

Despite an ever-increasing battery of punitive measures developed to combat this kind of workers' resistance – in Czechoslovakia, deduction from annual holidays of days lost through absenteeism ; in Poland, wage cuts of 10-25 per cent for the same offence ; in Hungary, threats of forced labour camps[18] – the bureaucracy had few successes in its struggle to raise productivity.

The total increase in production that did occur was dependent upon quite another factor. Production was raised by increasing the total number of workers. To achieve this expansion of the size of the working class, the bureaucracy carried through a series of measures. Some were fairly straightforward: thus in Czechoslovakia 30,000 governmental clerical workers were sacked and forced into industry. But only one source could provide the overwhelming majority of the new workers – the countryside.

Large numbers of peasants had to be persuaded to abandon their own land (which often they had only just acquired as a result of post-war land reform) and migrate to the towns ; and those remaining on the land had somehow to be persuaded to sell increased quantities of food to feed the growing urban population. Since industry was not producing the kind of light industrial goods that the peasants could buy in exchange for that food, 'voluntary' market forces was not expected to produce the desired outcome. So the various governments tried to attain their goal through 'collectivization' campaigns: raising taxes, setting quotas of produce that had to be sold to the state at low prices, and pressurizing the peasants to abandon individual farming and enter 'co-operatives'.

In this way, 'partly by persuasion, partly by economic pressure and partly by forcible police methods' the number of families in 'co-operatives' grew, in Hungary for instance, from 21,000 in December 1949 to 300,000 by the end of June 1953. At the latter date 55.5 per cent of agricultural land was in state, municipal or co-operative farms, as against only 44.5 per cent in private plots. The immediate post-war agricultural reform turned this 'land of large estates' into a land of small-holders; now once again it was a 'country of large estates',[19] this time, however, controlled by the state hierarchy rather than by a few large landowners and the bureaucracy of the Catholic Church.

This 'collectivization', it must be stressed, did not improve agricultural production – everywhere the result was stagnation and even a fall in total agricultural output. But 'collectivization' did free large quantities of manpower from agriculture for urban industrial production, and it did put a larger surplus of agricultural produce into the hands of the state.

The Pattern of Economic Development

All these measures – the forcing down of urban living standards, the driving of peasants from the land, the elimination from the Communist Party of all those with roots in past popular struggles – had one central purpose: forced industrialization in conformity with the needs and demands of the Russian rulers, who imposed upon Eastern Europe a pattern of economic development more or less a carbon copy of Russia's own. The emphasis was on 'the maximum development of each country's socialist industry as the leading branch of the national economy, with priority given to the output of the means of national production . . .'[20]

In practice this meant that each East European country was to attempt to build up a few key industries, the so-called 'leading links' industries – those developing sources of energy, metal industries, engineering, chemicals, and building materials. On a supranational scale, however, there was virtually no attempt to co-ordinate the economies of the different states.[21] Each national economy was subordinated to the needs of the Kremlin, and each had to attempt independently to satisfy those needs.

This pattern of independent development of heavy industry in each separate country appealed very much to whole sections of the local bureaucracies. Within it, their own national importance also appeared to grow. But the real motive force lay elsewhere: in the determination of the rulers of Stalinist Russia to subordinate economic life throughout their empire to their over-riding need to accumulate ever-greater quantities of capital in competition with the West. With the breakdown of the wartime alliance against Germany, this goal became ever more pressing for the Russian leaders. They matched the Marshall Plan's consolidation of western capitalism in one half of Europe with their own form of consolidation in the other half.

To obtain the resources needed for accumulation under the new conditions of intensified cold war competition, they destroyed every remnant of the old workers' parties. They lowered living standards, they began to expropriate the peasants; they used murder, torture, imprisonment and the labour camps to intimidate all potential sources of resistance, whether from workers, from peasants, from remnants of the old ruling classes or even from sections of the new bureaucracy itself.

1952 or 1984?

The end product was a group of societies, rigidly and hierarchically organized, in which a monolithic bureaucracy and police apparatus continually fragmented other social forces; where political debate amounted to the dull, uniform reiteration of platitudes that were patently untrue; and where cultural life became a deadening apology for those same platitudes. Life within the bureaucracy was characterized by cringing fear, and at the same time cynical enjoyment of enhanced privileges. In the factories the joyless toil to accumulate was intensified without even the marginal protection obtainable in the advanced west from trade-union organizations. In every sphere, spies and informers, motivated by a desire for material gain or just petty spite, could be relied upon to betray those who tried to resist the system by collective organization from below.

Societies where a bureaucracy combines control over the state with control over the means of production have existed before in history. Using terror to fragment and dissolve all opposing social forces, the rulers of such societies have managed to preserve their dominance unchallenged for decades, if not centuries. To many observers, the Russian Empire in the early 1950s – with the still more efficient techniques that modern technology gave it – seemed to be guaranteed an even greater durability.*

Most observers deduced from the apparatus's total control over political life, the conclusion that extensive social change was impossible; but they ignored a truth proclaimed by Marx and Engels in relation to bourgeois society a hundred years before:

> The bourgeoisie cannot exist without constantly revolutionizing the instruments of production, and thereby the relations of production, and with them the whole relations of society. Conservation of the old modes of production in unaltered form, was, on the contrary, the first condition of existence of all earlier industrial classes. Constant revolutionizing of production, uninterrupted disturbance of all social conditions, everlasting uncertainty and agitation distinguish the bourgeois epoch from all earlier ones. All fixed, fast frozen relationships, with their train of ancient and venerable prejudices and opinions are swept away, all new-formed ones become antiquated before they can ossify. All that is solid melts into air, all that is holy is profaned, and man is at last compelled to face with sober senses his conditions of life and his relations with his kind.[22]

The political structures of Eastern Europe appeared similar to those of societies that survived for centuries without great social convulsions. But the states of Eastern Europe share one feature above all with the bourgeois society of Marx's day, a feature which distinguishes them from all preceding forms of society – and, indeed,

---

*This, of course, was the pessimistic view of Orwell in *1984*, as well as of such writers as Karl Wittfogel in *Oriental Despotism*.

from genuinely socialist societies for that matter. That distinguishing feature is the continual necessity to accumulate capital, and hence 'the constant revolutionizing of the means of production'. That necessity has an inherent dynamic which was bound, eventually, to burst the rigid, monolithic and bureaucratic political structure. And when that happened, the very oppressiveness of the old structure was to ensure enormous social upheavals.

2.

Revolt and Revolution

4.

1953: The German Workers' Revolt

On 5 March 1953, Joseph Stalin died. Those who had been his accomplices for twenty-five years paid homage in glowing terms to 'Lenin's comrade in arms and continuer of genius of his cause, the wise *vozhd* and teacher of the Communist Party and the Soviet people . . .'[1] Nikita Khrushchev presided over the organization of a massive state funeral at which Malenkov, Beria and Molotov delivered speeches in praise of the memory of their former chief.

Stalin's death brought genuine grief to working-class militants, both in the west and in the third world. Typical of the response of the Communist movement was an article by Palme Dutt in *Labour Monthly*[2] in Britain, which described Stalin as

> the symbol and champion of the oppressed and exploited over the whole earth, the main target of the hatred of imperialist oppressors and exploiters, the tireless fighter for peace, the shield and bulwark of humanity from the horrors of a third world war.

Palme Dutt himself knew something of the truth about conditions in Stalin's Russia. But millions of ordinary socialist militants could read such words and agree that:

> the whole world – with the exception of a handful of evil maniacs – mourned the loss of Stalin . . . The genius and will of Stalin, the architect of the rising world of free humanity, lives on forever.

But among the workers of Eastern Europe feelings were rather different. Early in June troops had to be brought from Prague to disperse demonstrations against a currency reform in the streets of the

Czech industrial centre of Pilsen. A few days later, a full-blown insurrection developed in East Germany.

The Uprising

It began quietly enough on the Friedrichshain hospital building site in East Berlin. About sixty building workers stopped work and held an impromptu meeting on 15 June. After some discussion they drew up a letter signed by each of them. It protested at increases in work norms which meant that if they did not increase their output by more than ten per cent, their wages would fall by a third or more.[3] A similar decision was taken by workers on the Friedrichshain police barracks site and on block 40 of the Stalinallee construction site.[4]

Pressure for imposition of the new norms had been growing for some months. The central committee of the Stalinist Party in East Germany, the SED, had called a month before for 'a rigorous economic regime and thorough carrying out of all to do with the decrees concerning the aim of accumulation'. It argued that the norm increases were necessary because 'accumulation can only be achieved through continual advance of labour productivity'.[5]

Resentment at this decree was widespread – particularly among building workers who had been looking forward to the larger wages they could take in the fine weather and longer daylight hours of the summer months. The next morning, 16 June, they assembled outside Stalinallee block 40 and the hospital site in Friedrichshain. Fearing that the members of any delegation they sent would be victimized, they decided to march together to the government offices.

At the Stalinallee site,

> one worker indicated that the time to act had come. Another demanded that all those who agreed should gather on the right. The whole workforce moved to the right. A few moments later the 300 workers from block 40 set off in motion.[6]

The two groups of marchers toured the other sites, calling them out, before going to the union offices in Wallstrasse and the ministry building in Leipziger Strasse. By now the whole of the Stalinallee complex was closed down and the demonstrators, it is estimated, numbered some 10,000.[7]

The then pro-Rector for Student Affairs at the University, Professor Havemann, saw the beginning of the demonstration:

On the morning of 16 June 1953, I was in my flat on the seventh floor of the building in Strausbergerplatz 9 and just eating my breakfast when, suddenly, unusual and strange noises reached me from the square. The whole square was at the time a single building site. Most of the buildings were incomplete and one of the two skyscrapers, to which I was later to move, did not yet exist while the other was in the course of construction. Many kinds of noises could have come from such a large building site which was only part of a still larger building site, the Stalinallee. But this was not the noise of cranes or the screeching of building lifts, no sort of technical noise. It was human voices. I went to the window and saw how a small procession of building workers had formed behind a crudely painted banner on the square and had just began to move. I read: 'Down with the 10 per cent rise in the norms!' It was a moving sight, for the small procession grew in a moment into a huge demonstration. They came running from all sides in their working clothes, attracted like iron filings to a magnet. When I left home to go to the University, the procession had already left the Strausbergerplatz and was proceeding eastwards to the other larger building sites in the Stalinallee.

I went to the main building of the University to discharge for a few hours my duty as pro-Rector for Student Affairs; that is, to read documents, append my signature and listen to oral reports from my colleagues. I was just about to go again when the procession of building workers reached Unter den Linden, in front of the University. It had grown mightily and, apart from building workers, many young people who were not wearing working clothes, were to be seen in it. They had enthusiastically joined the protest march. They shouted in chorus: 'We are workers and not slaves! Put an end to the extortionist norms. We want free elections!' And, always loudest of all, the sentence 'We are not slaves!'[8]

Another spectator, Heinz Brandt, at that time secretary of the SED organization in Berlin, described the development of the demonstration as follows:

When I reached the demonstration it had already advanced to the Alexander Platz, the centrum of East Berlin, and had increased to several thousand people. It was constantly being swollen by streams of workers, clerks, officials and passers-by. For this reason it moved forward very slowly but with unwavering will and elemental power. The procession had a natural inner discipline. This was not the soulless order of the compulsory processions. Voices were raised against the norm-exploitation, against the government, for free elections, against the party and in particular against Ulbricht. 'We want to be free men, not slaves' was heard again and again.

A spontaneous and explosive unity of purpose had sprung up between the demonstrating workers and the population. People shouted and waved encouragement from the windows of blocks of flats and office buildings. A great fraternization began in the streets. The slogan: 'To the government, to the Leipziger street!' spread like wildfire in all directions.

'The people's police' directing the traffic stood by confused and helpless in the sea of people who as yet neither understood nor quite believed what had happened. It was quite obvious that the demonstration was quickly developing into a general uprising.

The building workers had thrown a spark into the mass. The spark burst into flame. It was like Lenin's dream come true, only this mass action was directed against the totalitarian regime ruling in Lenin's name and headed by those who called themselves Lenin's followers . . .

The party and state officials were overwhelmed by the events and increasingly paralysed. Something monstrous was going on before their eyes: *the worker was rising against the worker-peasant state.* They were petrified because – themselves victims of a mass-deception – they had taken fiction for reality. They were dumbfounded and unable to act. A small, numerically insignificant layer went over immediately to the workers. The overwhelming majority, however, furious and disoriented by the incomprehensible failure of all hitherto valid principles, and in deadly fear of this revelation of the real mood of the people and the elemental power of the masses, fell into a helpless passivity . . .

The mass movement, on the other hand, was absolutely spontaneous, without central leadership or organization. The desire to sweep away the existing state of affairs was general but the ideas as to what should follow were uncommonly at variance, hazy and confused – except for the elemental wish for free elections. But from the outset the movement was directed with spontaneous discipline against the SED and the government, and avoided any direct conflict with the occupying forces . . .

The procession continued to grow every minute, spreading over the entire Leipziger street to the square in front of the government building.

The 'worker-government' had hurriedly barricaded itself against the workers. The iron gates were locked against the demonstrators. In vain did the workers demand in chorus that Grotewohl and Ulbricht should speak to them. The window and balconies remained empty.[9]

Havemann's account of the meeting in front of the House of Ministries catches the crowd's feelings very well. On a table stood a building worker, not speaking, but conducting the demonstrators' choruses: 'We want to talk with the government. Pieck and Grotewohl! Pieck and Grotewohl!' Heinz Brandt got on the table, and was finally given a hearing.

'I am instructed to inform you about an important decision of the Politburo,' Heinz shouted as loudly as he could, 'the ten per cent rise in norms is cancelled.'

The response of the crowd was a remarkable roar of triumph, mingled with joy, anger and laughter. It was not long before the aggressive tones prevailed:

'Where is the Government?'

'Away with the Government!'

'We want free elections! We want freedom!'

Then I was able to climb onto the table. The elderly building worker, a sympathetic, broad-shouldered fellow, got order for me, too, and a hearing from the men.

'We all want peace, freedom and a better life,' I cried. It became quieter because, evidently, they did not know for whom I was speaking. 'We want free and secret elections for a government in the whole of Germany – free, equal and secret elections.' My words received applause. Then I had to make a transition:

'But you know, our Government has proposed all this to the West German Government. Grotewohl wants free elections in the whole of Germany. What do we want here? We must go to the West. It is there that the dividers of Germany are. It is there that we must demand free elections . . .' I received no further applause. Again there arose a roar against which no voice, however strong, could make itself heard.

Comrade Robert Naumann climbed on to the table after

me. He was announced as 'Professor from Humboldt University'. But there was a great deal of murmuring as he cried in a voice that was far too low:

'Yes, I am a Professor from the University . . .' There was laughter. 'But I am a worker like you! Listen to me because I am one of you.' The roar of the crowd completely drowned him. Some called out: 'A Professor!' and laughed.

At this point the grilled gates of the House of Ministries opened. Comrade Fritz Selbmann, Minister in the Grotewohl government and a member of the Politburo, made his way to the table and climbed on to it. Very soon quiet prevailed. Loud voices cried: 'Quiet! A Minister is here! Fritz Selbmann is here . . .'

Fritz was very popular with the workers. With his natural manner and his gauche elegance he always looked like a proletarian in his Sunday best – something the workers could clearly see was different from the elegance of a 'fop'. In his speeches he combined coarseness with crude airs, seriousness with broad jokes, and all this showed that, in spite of his high government office, he had remained a proletarian.

His powerful voice filled the square:

'You have heard that the new norm rise has just been cancelled. It was just too much. But we must get together to talk. The norms will be raised, that's obvious, but not at your expense. We shall have a new technology and with this you will get as much done with your little finger as is done today with two hands . . .' Once again there was murmuring. 'We are your Government. We are not capitalists as in the West . . .'

'Where is the Government?' someone shouted. Another cried: 'Funks! Cowards! Why don't they come if they are workers?'

Everything else was drowned again in a menacing roar. Selbmann wrung his hands in despair. Finally, he gave up. No one else climbed on to the table. We waited. All that was to be heard from time to time were choruses calling for the Government and saying: 'We are workers and not slaves!'

Then a worker issued a call for a general strike. If Ulbricht and Grotewohl had not shown up in half an hour, the workers should march away and spread the strike. This they did. Loudspeaker cars appeared, attempting to explain the party leadership's position. The crowd seized the cars and marched with them, broadcasting that all workers in Berlin were to join a general strike the next day. Havemann went out with a loudspeaker van to argue the party's case again, but not for long:

> When the procession came, I gave it a friendly greeting with the powerful voice of my two loudspeakers which were attached to the roof of the van. Our windows were firmly closed because of the inevitable interference caused by the so-called acoustic feedback and we were insulated against noise from outside; so I could only just hear my voice through the loudspeaker and sometimes not at all. I merely saw the way the procession reacted to my words. In a moment my van was surrounded by a crowd of hefty young men. Unfortunately, there was a pile of bricks on the pavement in the immediate vicinity of the van. The first bricks hit my loudspeaker: its tone became hoarse and rattling. Then a brick broke the windscreen. I heard the people brawling and shouting. They formed a chain on both sides of the van and began to sway it. The rocking became more severe. It would not be long before the postal van, which was high off the ground, tipped over. As I had no desire to tip over with the van, I opened the door and I jumped among the astonished people. They laughed and had no thought of touching a hair of my head. They left the van and ran to join their procession which was still making its endless way along Wilhelm Pieck Strasse. After a while we were quite alone in the street, with our damaged vehicle.[11]

The rulers of East Germany were bewildered by this turn of events. The SED politburo spent hours discussing what to do, but to little effect. It issued a statement that meant all things to all men; it spoke of the need for higher production and higher norms if living standards were later to rise – workers who accepted norm increases would be able to have wage rises in the near future; yet it concluded 'norms may not and cannot be pushed through with administrative methods, only through free will'.[12]

Next morning not only East Berlin but the majority of the industrial cities of East Germany were in the grip of a general strike. More than 250 centres in the country were affected. Grotewohl, the East German President, later admitted that 300,000 workers were involved in strikes.[13]

The main centres of the strike and of the demonstrations that accompanied it were the older industrial areas: there were 121,000 strikers in the mid-German industrial area of Bitterfeld, Halle, Leipzig and Merseburg, 38,000 in Magdeburg, 24,000 in Jena, 13,000 in Brandenburg, 10,000 in Goerlitz.[14] 'Those areas that struck were already "red" areas in the Weimar republic.'[15]

In each case the strike movement spread outwards from the big factories – for the Leuna works (employing 28,000), the Buna works (18,000) the Farbenfabrik Wolfen (12,000) and the Herringsdorf works (12,000).

Only one major heavy industrial centre, Stalinstadt, near Frankfurt am Oder, did not join the strike. This was a new industrial area, with none of the traditions of struggle from the pre-Nazi period that existed elsewhere. What is more, its workers were relatively privileged.

Elsewhere, in Dresden for instance, demonstrations were suppressed at an early stage, or the strikers permitted themselves to be talked into returning to work by local functionaries.

One feature characterized the strikes and demonstrations everywhere. 'The middle class, bourgeois and intelligentsia kept almost completely out of the events.'[16]

In Berlin itself, more than 60,000 workers joined the strike. Heinz Brandt has described what happened at one factory:

> When I arrived that morning at the Bergmann Borsig Works nobody was working: the workers stood around discussing the events and organizing minor meetings. The most determined workers in the various shops tried to make contact with each other so as to organize a rally of all the workers at the plant. I instructed the party secretary (who considered that things were still 'calm' at the works) to summon the workers by loudspeaker to the large auditorium of the Cultural Centre. My suggestion to elect a works-committee on the spot was accepted. An elderly, experienced social democrat was elected chairman of the committee. About twenty of the workers spoke at the meeting. It was an elemental discussion of the SED regime, in particular many examples were cited of legal insecurity and the arrest of workers from their ranks. A resolution empowered the elected worker-council to represent the economic and political interests of the workers, with the principal aim of the re-unification of Germany and the preparation of free, democratic elections. Towards the end

of the meeting a worker mounted the platform and called upon all workers to meet at noon at the gates of the factory to demonstrate in the town, similar demonstrations having already been started everywhere else. The newly elected council retired for a constituent session, formulated the most important local and general demands, and decided to take the lead in the strike demonstration. This strike demonstration, however, did not get very far . . . The demonstrators were forcibly dispersed and the 'trouble-makers', among them the social democrat chairman of the council, arrested and beaten.[17]

The morning of 17 June began in a similar manner in most of the other factories of East Germany. Workers struck, elected strike committees, and then marched towards the city centre, with demands such as 'Down with the norms' and 'More bread and meat'. When the demonstrations reached the centres of the cities, the slogans tended to become more political – 'We want to live as men', 'We don't want to be slaves', 'Free the prisoners', 'Down with pointed beard' (Ulbricht), 'Free elections'. At this point other sections of the population, youths and housewives, joined in. The demonstrators began attacking prisons, releasing the inmates, burning party buildings, even lynching the police in some places.[18]

10,000 workers from the giant Leuna works, singing revolutionary songs, marched into Merseburg where they met thousands of workers from the Buna plant, stormed into the police station, ransacked the party offices, and broke into the jails to release prisoners. At Halle 8,000 men from the railway works seized control of the SED headquarters, the council offices and the prison. In Magdeburg, demonstrators freed prisoners from the police building, while in Brandenburg they beat up 'peoples' judges' and the public prosecutor. In Rathenow, an informer was beaten so severely that he later died from his injuries.[19]

By mid-day it was clear that the East German regime alone could not cope with the situation. Its functionaries had lost control in the factories. In the streets, its police were in no state to control most of the demonstrators: some were discussing with the workers, others had joined the demonstrations. Only the specially trained elite force, the garrisoned Peoples' Police, sided with the regime.

Already, the previous night, some 25,000 Russian troops and

300 tanks had moved into Berlin. Now martial law was proclaimed. An order was issued banning demonstrations, making any group of more than three people on the street liable for arrest and trial, and banning even normal traffic from the roads at night. At the same time the tanks and troops moved in to break up the demonstrations and arrest the workers' leaders.

The workers fought back with considerable heroism. Fighting with nothing but bottles, crowbars and sticks, they tried to force the tanks back. But against an overwhelming military force such resistance was doomed. The rising was crushed, its leaders imprisoned or executed.

No one knows how many died from Russian bullets or in the repression which followed. The East German authorities claimed a figure of nineteen; the West German government put it as high as 267. In any case it is clear that 'law and order' was restored only with the most savage of methods. 1300 were brought to trial; four were sentenced to life imprisonment and six to death.[20]

Nevertheless, the shooting of unarmed workers on the streets did not immediately quell all resistance. Three weeks later there were still reports of sit-down strikes in East Berlin demanding the release of arrested strike leaders, for higher wages and lower prices, for a change in government and for free elections.

Neues Deutschland of 8 July still complained that 'mischief makers were seen in factories, on building sites, in trams, buses and public places attempting to spread unrest . . . with such lies as the spreading of sit-down strikes'.

The government ignored the political demands articulated during the uprising. But it felt sufficiently worried to bow to many of the economic demands, at least for a time. Reforms already in the pipeline were speeded up. Large stockpiles of food and clothing materials were made available for sale. Early in July the wages of the lowest paid workers were increased and wage reductions dating from January 1953 were cancelled. It was announced that the policy of building up heavy industry at the expense of consumer industry had been a mistake and would be rectified. The trade unions were told that 'at present' their main task was to represent 'honestly and conscientiously the workers' interests in the struggle for better conditions'.

Once order had been re-established, however, many of these concessions were revoked. The increased norms that had produced the initial demonstrations were eventually reimposed. Three months later trade-union bureaucrats who had taken seriously the earlier instructions to stand up for their members were reprimanded by Ulbricht. The Minister of Justice, Fechner, an ex-Social Democrat, who had been rash enough to remark that the right to strike was embodied in the constitution, was removed from office for 'activities hostile to the republic'.[21] And even the increased emphasis on consumer goods production turned out to be at the expense of the workers – it was to mean replacing a two shift by a three shift system in these industries.

The Real Causes

The official explanation for the rising was simple: it had been 'an attempted coup d'etat and fascist putsch'. Ulbricht claimed that fascist provocateurs in 'Bonn and New York' had 'appointed 17 June as X-day'.[22]

The West German government also did its best *after the event* to encourage the myth that the rising had been pro-western in its aims. In the Federal Republic 17 June was made a national holiday and East Berliners were offered free food if they went into West Berlin to get it.

But *during* the rising, the western powers and the West German government did nothing to encourage it. After the first strikes on 16 June the West German minister for all-German affairs made his government's attitude clear. No one in the East, he insisted, should 'carry out rash acts' and people should 'keep away from dangerous actions'.[23] In line with this approach, West Berlin police were posted along the border to intercept any movement from West Berlin into the East. The British and French military authorities took similar action – for instance, preventing East Berlin workers in outlying factories from using a short cut through the French sector on their way to the city centre.[24]

When the Russian tanks started attacking the strikers in Berlin, 'strike leaders ran to the British and American authorities, to West Berlin police and trade union headquarters, begging for support, for arms. They were everywhere firmly refused.'[25]

The only positive role played by the West during the rising was that played by the West Berlin based radio station, RIAS. This broadcast news of the strikes on 16 June and of the call for a general strike next day, so that industrial centres elsewhere in East Germany got to know what was happening in Berlin. But the station, in line with official western policy, certainly did not encourage a rising. The programme director told strikers 'to demand what is reasonable' and 'it was decided that a broadcast by the strikers themselves would be carrying the station's anti-Communist policy too far'.[26]

The leaders of the SED themselves admitted in the first few weeks after the rising that explanations solely in terms of 'western agents' were not sufficient. The government spoke of 'dissatisfaction' among the population which had provided 'inflammable material for western agents'. Grotewohl conceded that much of the 'guilt for the events of the last few days lies with us'.[27]

Further evidence to the same effect was provided by a purge of the SED carried out later in the year. SED members in the major factories had joined in the demonstrations, and even played a key part in organizing them.[28] The party leadership blamed this on 'Social Democrat elements' who had joined the SED at the time of the forced amalgamation of the Communist and Social Democratic Parties in the Russian zone after the war, and it instituted a purge. However, a third of those purged had been members of the old German Communist Party prior to Hitler's accession to power in 1933, that is twenty years before! In East Berlin 68 per cent of those purged were former Communist Party members, in Halle 68 per cent, in Leipzig 59 per cent, in Magdeburg 52 per cent.[29] In short, a large proportion of the SED members who supported the rising in its major centres were old time revolutionaries, workers who saw the fight against the Ulbricht regime as a continuation of the old fight for workers' power that they had waged against the Weimar Republic and against Hitler.

The real roots of the discontent lay not with 'western agents' but with the miserable living standards of the mass of workers. In 1950 real wages were less than half what they had been in 1936.[30] In 1951 and 1952 living standards were further threatened. The government, in pursuit of its goal of accumulation, raised the output of iron and steel and heavy machine goods. But this it could only do by cutting down consumer goods production, and taking punitive measures against handicraft producers, farmers and the remaining sections of private industry. These in turn led to a further fall in the output of food and consumer goods. Peasants fled from the land to West Germany, so that the supply of milk and of the staple food, potatoes, was well below target.

Even then, immense economic problems faced the party leadership. Exports lagged behind imports. The 1952 plan was not fulfilled, although expenditure on it was above target. When it became clear that the plan for the first quarter of 1953 could not be fulfilled either, the party leadership requested help from Russia, but they were refused.[31] The increased work-norms were their way of finding the resources to solve their economic problems – by increasing the rate of exploitation of the workers.

The East German uprising was a quite simple reaction to the combination of falling living standards and continual speed-up. However, that alone does not fully explain why it took place when it did. These economic conditions had existed for some years. Another factor served to translate discontent into rebellion: an open division at the top of East German society during June 1953.

The Bureaucracy Split

Stalin's death was followed by a bitter struggle for power between those who had served immediately under him for the preceding twenty-five years. In part the issues were personal: fear on the part of each of Stalin's former lieutenants that one among their number would arrogate all power to himself and use it, as Stalin had done, to eliminate rivals. Each of them had murdered and terrorized at Stalin's command. Each might now do so for his own ends. Especially dangerous was the sinister Lavrenti Beria, who commanded a vast army of secret policemen, and whose apparatus penetrated into every area of Russian life.

But more deep-rooted political and social issues were also involved. The Russian leaders were only too aware that those at the top of Russian society were deeply isolated from those below. Successive purges within the bureaucracy had left the survivors fearing and hating their superiors; while outside the bureaucracy's ranks was a vast mass of people to whose feelings no one had access, a mass atomized by the continual activities of the police, but nonetheless an explosive force.

Stalin, in whose hands all power had been concentrated, had been able to bottle up these different pressures. He had acted as if oblivious to the fears and hatreds below, and had been content to use blind terror to enforce total control.

His successors were not able to continue in the same way. They were frightened that the massive police power Stalin had needed to maintain his rule could be turned against themselves. And they saw that certain limited reform must be granted and the basis of support for the regime broadened. However, none of them had any clear idea how this might be done. Their differing prescriptions for change fused with their mutual mistrust of each other to produce within the ruling group a succession of political disputes that were only settled as successive members of it were eliminated from power.

The result was a series of swings in policy and changes in personnel that almost shook Stalinist society to its foundations. In Russia itself, a series of reforms was implemented within weeks of Stalin's demise. The most recently discovered 'conspiracy' (the doctor's plot) was declared a frame-up and those allegedly responsible for inventing it were arrested. Whole classes of prisoners were released from the labour camps. Food prices were cut by ten per cent and more. Finally, it was announced in the summer that the previously all-powerful police chief, Beria, had been removed from power and executed as the leader of a 'gang of anti-socialist spies' who had infiltrated the state machine.

Such changes at the top gave renewed life to long-suppressed hopes among those at the very bottom of society. In Russia itself, half a million prisoners in the huge Vorkuta slave labour camp rose in revolt in July 1953:

> On 20 July 7,000 prisoners refused to work in the first pit. On 25 July all fifty (pits) were idle. The coal trains which had been crawling along in an unending chain had disappeared. 25,000 prisoners – the whole active mining population and half the total inhabitants of Vorkuta – had joined the strike . . . On 1 August 120 strike leaders were shot. And still the strike continued . . .[32]

The regimes of Eastern Europe were much less deeply rooted than that in Russia itself. They had only come into being five or six years before, and as satellites the effects of the division within the Russian leadership were greatly magnified in their circumstances. For three years after Stalin's death the rival groupings within the Kremlin were matched by rival groupings in many of the East European states, with devastating consequences. The East German leadership was the first to be drawn into these quarrels at the top, and its division into rival groupings meant that during June 1953 it was often giving the rest of the population quite contradictory sets of orders.

The SED party leader, Ulbricht, at first acted as if nothing had changed. He continued, after Stalin's death, just as before, subordinating consumption to the building up of heavy industry and eliminating his rivals from the party. He continued to sacrifice the interests of workers and peasants to accumulation and purged from the SED politburo and central committee his rival, Franz Dahlem, and it was hinted that he would be tried for 'links with the Slansky conspiracy'.

Then, without warning, the Russian High Commissioner for Germany, Semyanov, returned from a visit to Moscow and ordered the East German leadership to perform an abrupt turnabout in policy. They must now follow a much more conciliatory policy towards the rest of the population.[33] At the beginning of June a whole series of reforms were implemented, a mere ten days after the norm increases for workers had been decreed. Now it was admitted that 'the SED and government had made a number of mistakes . . . that impaired the interests of . . . the independent farmer, the retailer, the artist and the intelligentsia . . .' 'Grave errors' had been committed in tax collection, in certain agricultural measures and in depriving middle-class groups of their ration cards. These 'mistakes' were now reversed, concessions were made to small-scale private industry, to the farmers, to the universities and to the Church, and there was a drastic cutback in the plan for heavy industry.[34]

Ulbricht's personal position was no longer secure either. Between 9 June and 30 June his backing from the Russian leaders seems to have been minimal. Khrushchev later claimed that in this period Beria and Malenkov had 'urged the SED to liquidate the GDR as a socialist state . . .'[35]

Certainly, Dahlem's supporters in the SED leadership – men like Zaisser, minister of state security, and Herrnstadt, editor of the party daily, *Neues Deutschland* – thought that their hour of glory had come. They began to contradict Ulbricht's line more-or-less openly.

The reform package had not included any mention of the new work norms. This in itself created resentment among the workers, who saw themselves as the one section of the population whose demands had been ignored. However, it soon became clear that the rival groups within the party leadership interpreted the question of norms in different ways. *Neues Deutschland* of 14 June criticized the 'sledgehammer tactics' being used by party functionaries to impose the norms in the Stalinallee. The next day it repeated the message: 'The norms department is sadly mistaken if it believes that it can act with impunity against the interests of the building workers for long.'[36] By contrast, the trade-union paper, *Tribune*, insisted on 16 June that the norms had to be enforced.

In a Stalinist society, the sheer repressive power of the police apparatus is normally sufficient to put down strikes and demonstrations rapidly, and certainly to prevent them spreading. The isolation of the Czech workers' demonstrations in Pilsen earlier in 1953 was a case in point. However, the open split within the East German leadership over the question of the norms made it difficult for the repressive apparatus to function. The police were confused as to whether they should be preventing or permitting meetings and discussions over the norms. The disputes at the top provided a degree of political space, in which the workers could mobilize their own demands and develop their own slogans. Once they had mobilized, the East German police and army (as opposed to the Russian army) were powerless.

On 16 June, the divisions within the SED leadership meant that it was incapable of arriving at any policy for dealing with the strikes: it could neither make up its mind to give further concessions nor to unleash the police. Indeed, it was midnight before it issued any instructions to the local functionaries.

On 17 June, this confusion transmitted itself to bureaucrats at the local level throughout East Germany. The SED leadership later complained that functionaries had 'fallen into panic, had slipped into positions of capitulationism and opportunism in relation to the enemies of the party'.

But the confusion of the functionaries was not an accident.

It was the inevitable consequence of the splits at the top of East German and Russian society. And these splits were no accident: they flowed from the inner economic dynamic of state capitalist society, as the examples of Poland and Hungary three years later were to show even more dramatically.

5.
1953-56: Prelude to Revolution

Although Stalin's successors quickly and brutally put down the uprising in East Germany and the demonstrations elsewhere, they could not ignore the conditions that had given rise to them. Ten days after the Berlin insurrection Hungary's rulers were summoned to the Kremlin and ordered to introduce far-reaching reforms.

The Hungarian Communist leaders had previously been the most faithful followers of Moscow's line in Eastern Europe. They had provided more than their fair share of sacrificial victims in the 'anti-Titoist' purges. They had not hesitated to adjust their 'plans' for industry to the heightened war needs of the Soviet bloc. More than anyone else, they had striven to follow Stalin's path of building up heavy industry – they claimed a growth of industry to 210 per cent for 1949-53, compared with 98 per cent for Czechoslovakia (1949-55), 120 per cent for Bulgaria (1949-55) 144 per cent for Rumania (1951-55), and 158 per cent for Poland (1949-55).[1]

Now they were suddenly accused in Moscow of the most dangerous irresponsibility. Imre Nagy later reported that:

> Key members of the Soviet Communist Party . . . declared that the mistakes and crimes of the four-man Party leadership in Hungary . . . had driven the country to the verge of catastrophe, shaking the People's Democratic system to its foundations[2]

Khrushchev warned that unless changes were introduced 'we would be booted out summarily'.[3]

Forewarned by the events in East Germany and Czechoslovakia, as well as by increasing unrest among the peasants in Hungary's own Great Plains, Russia's leaders ordered immediate changes in policy and in the top government personnel. The effective ruler of Hungary, Matyos Rakosi, was retired from one of his positions, as prime minister, although he remained in charge of the Communist Party. The new premier was Imre Nagy.

The Hungarian 'New Course'

Nagy was in an unusual position within the Hungarian party, for he did not fit easily into any of the most obvious divisions within the party leadership. Like the members of the ruling clique around Rakosi, Nagy had been a pre-war exile in Moscow who had somehow survived the continual purging of the Comintern by paying undeviating lip-service to the official line and by keeping his head down. Certainly he seems at that stage to have expressed no scruples at the employment of Stalinist methods. His loyalty was not in doubt when, in 1945, he was given key jobs in Hungary's post-war coalition government, as Minister of Agriculture and, briefly, as Minister of the Interior.[4]

Later, when Nagy clashed with the ruling group in the party in 1949, his role was quite different from that of, say, Slansky or even Kadar. Nagy disagreed with Rakosi over the extent and nature of collectivization in agriculture, and was removed from office. But he was not seen as representing any real or potential threat to that leadership. While Rajk was executed and Kadar imprisoned and tortured, Nagy was made a Professor of Agriculture. He was even reintegrated into the party leadership early in 1951 and, the day after Stalin's death, delivered the eulogy before the Hungarian parliament referring to Stalin as 'the great leader of humanity'. Up to this point his disagreements with Rakosi had been tactical, concerned with the methods of implementing the overall, Russian-directed line, not over the basics of that policy itself.[5]

All this seemed to make Imre Nagy precisely the man Stalin's successors needed to introduce reforms in Hungary – although, it seems, he had another 'quality' that appealed to them, in that almost alone among the top Hungarian leadership, Nagy was not Jewish.

A week after his return from Moscow, Nagy announced the new programme of his government to an astonished nation. In a speech to the docile, handpicked parliament, he implicity repudiated the policies of his predecessors all along the line – and yet these predecessors still manned every position of any significance within the all-powerful Communist Party apparatus.

Nagy began by destroying any illusions his audience had about the stability of the country. He spoke of 'grave and responsible tasks if we are to make good the grave mistakes committed in the past by the government and restore law and order and assure full legality'. He admitted that the national economy was in an extremely bad state. 'The targets of the stepped-up plan exceed our abilities in many respects. Their implementation would exhaust our resources of energy and hinder the growth of the material basis of prosperity . . .' Furthermore, he admitted what everyone knew but dared not say: 'What is more they have lately led to a reduction in living standards.'

Nagy then announced various reforms. They were aimed on the one hand at overcoming the worst irrationalities of the previous years. Grandiose investment projects that had been drawn up without regard to cost, raw material availability or real need were cancelled. On the other hand the reforms were designed to reduce the hostility of different sections of the population to the government by improving living standards and reducing the level of police activity: peasants were given permission to withdraw from cooperative and return to private farming, increased investment in consumer goods industries was announced, the burden of overtime and Sunday work was to be reduced for industrial workers, and finally, the various internment camps were to be shut and 100,000 prisoners released.

In any society such a sudden and drastic reversal of policy would have a profound effect. In a society lacking any legitimate means for public discussion of political issues, the shock effect was inevitably intensified. The functionaries, all habituated to obeying directives without a murmur, suddenly found those directives themselves in question – from above. Clear and unambiguous lines for action no longer existed. The confusion was intensified because men who had been written off only a year or two previously as irredeemable 'fascist agents' began to re-emerge from prison, to be met in the streets, or even to be re-instated into government and party office.

The mass of Hungarian workers and peasants seem to have regarded the changes as a welcome improvement, but basically as emanating from forces outside their control and with which they should not concern themselves unduly. So, although certain governmental figures and in particular Nagy, gained considerable popularity among the peasants, the changes at the top did not release mass movements from below.

One section of society, however, did begin to mobilize on its own as a result of the reforms. Writers and journalists, many of whom had accepted the official view of the party with fervour, now found themselves compelled to question previously accepted truths. Slowly but surely they began to ask why they had been misled for so long and began, too, to formulate demands for the right to form independent judgements. Because they were professionally concerned with elaborating and propagating the established ideology, they reacted more sharply than other sectors of society when that ideology entered into crisis. They reflected the crisis of confidence among those who really held power, and transmitted the crisis to the rest of society.[6]

The 'New Course' could not fail to have a deep effect on the various classes of Hungarian society, an effect that was intensified by an additional factor of great importance: the sense of impermanence that surrounded the reforms. Reform had come despite the resistance of those who continued to control the apparatus of the Communist Party. Rakosi's supporters had acquiesced in the new measures because of direct pressure from Moscow. But they also knew that those ruling in the Kremlin were divided among themselves, and that Stalin's real successor had not yet emerged. So Rakosi's men bided their time, impeding the implementation of reforms without being too obvious about it. Their cautious resistance received the tacit support of tens of thousands of bureaucrats who had risen to positions of influence on the basis of the old methods and who feared changes.

As it turned out the 'New Course' was to last barely twenty months. Late in 1954 Malenkov, the Russian leader most identified with reform policies both in Eastern Europe and in Russia, was ousted. Nagy's fall could not then be long postponed.

In the intervening period there was fateful internecine struggle within the government and party apparatus. Nagy was able, with a formal majority, to carry through economic reforms, encourage private farming and consumer goods production, as well as to release prisoners and rehabilitate purged party members. On the other hand, Rakosi and his followers were able to tell party cadres that the 'New Course' would soon be reversed and that the economic changes were weakening the country without solving any problems – for example the balance of payments situation was still bad and the move from heavy to light industry was multiplying the number of half-completed projects.

It should not be forgotten that this division within the party over policy was a dispute between groups of men who had been accustomed to employ the crudest methods to solve such controversies in the past. It was barely three years since one of the factions in the dispute had been executing and torturing its previous opponents. The lives of the disputants might well be at stake in the fight over policy. As ex-prisoners began to re-enter and play some role in party life, usually on Nagy's side, fresh reserves of intense bitterness were brought to bear.

Yet what was involved was still no more than an argument about how a small and privileged section of Hungarian society was to rule the rest. No one questioned that power should lie with the top Communist Party leaders, or that these leaders should rule basically in accordance with broad directives received from Moscow. What was at issue was whether government should be characterized by the use of the stick or the carrot.

In January 1955, Moscow finally seemed to bring this debate to an abrupt termination. Once again, the Kremlin gave its full backing to Rakosi. Nagy was censured, removed from the party central committee, and in April from the premiership. Rakosi even sacked him from his post as Professor of Agriculture. At the same time those in the party apparatus who had backed Nagy, even out of the crudest opportunism, were demoted, and journalists who had supported him were sacked.

Fragments of opposition to Rakosi and loyalty to Nagy survived. This was particularly the case in governmental ministries where Nagy had had a direct influence on appointments and promotions, but was also true in particular areas of party life, where purge victims who had been rehabilitated under Nagy, men like Kadar, Losonczy, Haraszti, Ferenc Donath and Ujhelyi, now exercized a degree of influence. Just as Rakosi's supporters had been able to hinder the implementation of the 'New Course', so now Nagy's followers could resist, although to a lesser degree, its abandonment.

In addition, just as Rakosi had been able to operate with the realistic hope that a change of leadership in Moscow would favour his faction, now his opponents could work on similar assumptions. For

Stalin's successors had still not found their way to stability, even in the short term, either of policies or of the top personnel. 1955, for instance, saw the first attempts by Khrushchev to come to a rapprochement with Tito, a development hardly likely to encourage Rakosi, who had been the most bitter denigrator of Titoism in Eastern Europe.

Yet, for nearly twelve months, it seemed that the return to the past would be complete and that resistance to a renewal of Stalinist methods would be unsuccessful. When the writers' journal, *Irodalmi Ujsag*, published some criticisms of the new regime, the offending issue was confiscated and the editor sacked. When discontent among the writers continued, Rakosi prepared to clamp down in earnest. On 13 February 1956, he made his first move by arresting a dissident journalist.[7]

But Rakosi's renewal of repression was dogged by ill luck, emanating – like his previous good fortune – from Moscow. For the very next day the Twentieth Party Congress opened in Moscow.

The Twentieth Congress

It is difficult today to understand the ferment begun by the Twentieth Congress of the Soviet Communist Party, because it is difficult to understand the ideological monolithism that preceded it.

For nearly thirty years, Communists across the globe had been brought up to believe that the leadership of the CPSU could do no wrong. A mere examination of its statements was all one required to comprehend the truth about any aspects of the world situation. In such statements, and especially in the statements of 'Comrade Stalin', one could find the essence of the 'Marxist-Leninist' line. Of course, there was some difference between the situations in the so-called socialist countries and in the capitalist world. In the former, desire for promotion and privilege, or simply for survival, dictated that one follow the party line; while in the latter the line was accepted voluntarily by millions who were genuinely ignorant of the realities of life in Russia and of many aspects of Communist Party practice. But in either case the party line, monolithic and unquestioned, bound together into a single purpose the efforts and aspirations of millions of people.

The changes introduced in the first years after Stalin's death did little to break the boundless faith of millions. Within the overall

Stalinist vision, one had to admit, faults and aberrations could occur – but only on the periphery of the system, where a historical accident had allowed a Beria to work his way into a position of some power.

But on 24 February 1956, Nikita Khrushchev rose to address the assembled delegates to the Twentieth Congress of the CPSU, meeting in closed session. He spoke to destroy, to demolish carefully and deliberately the whole structure of myth and lies that had maintained a whole generation's unbridled faith in the old leadership of the CPSU. He set out to discredit Stalin once and for all. Using facts long known to the party leaders but never before admitted, bitter recollections, open derision and long-buried quotations from Lenin, Khrushchev assailed both the Stalin myth and the methods of crude terror associated with it.

In all this Khrushchev had one clear aim in view. He wanted to ensure that the millions of bureaucrats at every level and in every institution of the Stalinist apparatus who longed for a return to the old methods of Stalin's rule in all its crudity would be effectively discredited. Not because he, Khrushchev, had any moral scruples about such methods – after all, by using them himself, he had risen from nowhere to be boss of the Ukraine in the thirties – but because those methods were, on the one hand, a growing impediment to furthering Russia's industrial advance, and, on the other hand, served only to isolate the apparatus from other privileged strata in society and thus to weaken its rule. Besides, in the struggle for power within the apparatus itself, those who opposed Khrushchev were seeking to don the mantle of Stalin.

Khrushchev's aim, in short, was to destroy an ideological system associated with an apparatus of power no longer adequate to the interests of the class he aimed to represent. He was intent on reshaping the Russian ruling bureaucracy to take account of the realities of a society in which the most primitive tasks of industrialization had been accomplished. But this was impossible without first destroying every element of worship for Stalin and his methods. Khrushchev's chief difficulty was that he must destroy the old myths without undermining the power of those who ruled, for they had, after all, succeeded to Stalin's inheritance.

Subordinate Communist leaders everywhere found themselves suddenly tangled in a web they had helped to manufacture. The truths they had been retailing to their members for decades were now revealed as lies. Even worse, new truths had not yet been clearly defined. There was suddenly no easy way to deal with heretics in the party, or even to identify them: for all they knew today's heretics might be proclaiming Moscow's line tomorrow. Indeed, the safest thing for any Communist leader might actually be to encourage discussion, so as to accord with the apparent tenor of Khrushchev's speech.

Ideological confusion reigned for some months; and for those hectic months every Communist apparatus in the world, whether in power or miles from it, experienced considerable difficulty in maintaining inner-party discipline.

In Eastern Europe, two countries were most affected: Hungary, which had already undergone two radical changes of leadership in two years, and Poland. In both countries there was a sharp rise in internal dissent, both inside and outside the party, and increased demands for the Communist Parties to adopt a more independent stance vis-à-vis Moscow.

6.
1956: Poland - Aborted Revolution

Poland in 1956 was suffering from growing economic difficulties. As in Hungary, the policy of forced economic development – particularly in the period of heightened international tension at the time of the Korean War – brought massive problems for the leadership.

The industrialization plan involved identifying a few key areas of development, usually in the sphere of heavy industry, and concentrating all available spare resources on these. At the same time, the extra workers needed to build the development projects, along with the surplus food they would need, were obtained by encouraging 'collectivization' in the countryside.[1]

Between 1949 and 1955 unremitting pressure from above forced the Polish people to realize at least a part of this programme. Although only about 6 per cent of peasant holdings were affected by full collectivization, something like a million people moved to the expanding industries in the towns. Resources for these new industries and workers were found by holding living standards down: workers' living standards fell by up to 10 per cent during this period.[2] By these means, around 40 per cent of the National Product was used for gross capital formation (compared with an average figure of about 20 per cent for Western Europe).[3]

But the industrialization programme began to run into serious difficulties. Pressure from above brought massive investment projects into being, but that pressure did not and could not produce the raw materials needed to bring the projects to fruition. Production in the new plants tended to be in fitful bouts of frantic activity, often involving overtime and Sunday working, which were interspersed with long spells in which simple lack of materials forced factories to run at half speed. When the necessary raw materials were not available, the cost of providing them was carried by other industries, producing consumer goods and food, and/or by the Polish balance of payments.

The Polish party leaders themselves had, eventually, to admit to the chaotic state of the economy. They revealed, amongst other things, that coal output per miner had dropped 12.4 per cent between 1949 and 1955,[4] and that in the newly built Zeran car factory the models being produced were completely obsolete.[5] Only about half the new additions to the urban labour force had actually added anything to total production.[6] 'Machines and equipment . . . for projects long ago deleted from our economic plans continue to arrive to this day . . .'[7] Such equipment was being paid for 'by an adverse balance of payments in our foreign dealings', thus putting the state in the 'situation of an insolvent bankrupt'.

Even more serious than the developing situation in industry was the crisis in agriculture. Here the government's policies, whose aim had been to drive people into the towns and increase the surplus available to the state, were in practice destroying the peasants' incentive to produce, with the result that harvests were declining. The collective and state farms were highly unproductive: despite preferential treatment in the distribution of state credits, their output per hectare was only 83.3 per cent and 62.8 per cent respectively of the output figure for private farms.[8] The failings in agriculture in turn meant lower living standards for urban workers and greater discontent, as well as smaller food exports and further pressures on the balance of payments.

These economic difficulties put the stability of the state in question. In its early years the Stalinist regime in Poland had faced far more prolonged and bitter opposition than any other Eastern European Communist government. Elements from the Home Army and the right wing underground forces had harassed the regime militarily in its earliest days. Sections of the Socialist Party and the Trade Unions, as well as the organization with the largest single membership, the Peasant Party, had spoken out against increasing Stalinization.

The elimination of these centres of resistance had been aided enormously, of course, by the Russian occupying forces. But equally important to the new regime's stabilization was the real improvement in the material conditions of the mass of the people in the early post-war years. Industry revived, the former German territories were settled, and hundreds and thousands of peasants benefited from the division of large estates.

The programme of forced industrialization and collectivization turned mass acquiescence into covert opposition. Falling living standards led to resentment, and resentment to discontent. The thin layer of privileged bureaucrats became more and more isolated from the mass of the population.

This isolation was indicated by the changing social composition of the Communist Party. In the period from 1945 to 1955, while worker membership fell from 62.2 per cent of the total to 45 per cent, and peasant membership from 28 per cent to 13 per cent, bureaucrats and white collar workers increased their share of party cards from 10 to 41 per cent.[9] Such a process of isolation was bound to reach the point where some of these bureaucrats would sense the dangers of the situation and call for a halt.

As early as 1947-48 some leading communists had felt that an overhasty programme of industrialization and collectivization could be dangerous to the regime. Gomulka and a few others had argued within the party for a continuation of the earlier policy of concessions, particularly to the peasantry, so as to widen the narrow basis of popular support. They argued that the party's weak national roots necessitated a 'Polish Road to Socialism' rather than an exact replica of Russian development, with the bureaucracy slowly strengthening and consolidating its position before launching any major offensive against small property owners.

During Stalin's lifetime, such arguments were very dangerous. They implied that the East European regimes should worry about their own problems, rather than subordinate themselves to the Russian drive to 'catch up and overtake' the West in heavy industrial capacity and arms potential. Gomulka and his friends paid the price for their heresy: they were first removed from office, then imprisoned as 'traitors'.

By the mid-fifties, however, their views seemed more respectable. Moscow now looked to local Communist rulers to implement limited reform packages, so as to weaken local hostility to their rule. This was the burden of the various reforms within Russia itself. And a growing section of the Polish ruling bureaucracy showed itself ready to dance to Moscow's new tune, especially as the degree of economic disorganization became apparent and as popular discontent became more manifest.

A further impetus for change was provided in 1954 when a leading secret policeman, Swiatlo, defected to the west, and began broadcasting lurid details of the inner workings of the police apparatus. Even powerful and privileged party leaders were horrified by what Swiatlo revealed about the machination of the terror machine – a machine over which most of them had no control whatsoever and which might be turned against any one of them. Swiatlo revealed that the police even had a dossier on the party leader, Bierut, and that the politburo member in charge of the secret police, Jakub Berman, had himself been threatened in connection with the Field case (the 'conspiracy' for which Slansky had been hanged.)[10]

Bierut was forced to purge the UB (the Security Police), dismissing and arresting various subordinate functionaries. The Minister of the Interior, Radkiewicz, was transferred to a different post.

Over the next eighteen months further steps were taken towards 'liberalization' and 'democratization.' Many party members arrested during the previous purges were released, and censorship on the press was somewhat relaxed.

Intellectuals in Revolt

Anyone setting out to reform and liberalize a police apparatus enters on a highly risky enterprise, for the process tends to develop its own momentum. The police force is quite likely to collapse completely. The typical policeman is chiefly motivated by the desire to survive in his position, which – by comparison with those he polices – is a relatively privileged one. When state-directed terror is at its height, the precondition for the policeman's individual survival and promotion is whole-hearted participation in the terror. But under conditions of political uncertainty, when fellow-officers are suddenly being sacked for having ignored the constraints of legality, even a 'normal' level of police action may damage an individual's career prospects. The policeman who does not know who is going to win a political power struggle, may well decide it is better not to seem to take sides.

In 1955 and 1956 the Polish police apparatus functioned less and less efficiently.

As in Hungary a little earlier, the immediate impact on the mass of the population was small. They feared that the 'liberalization' would be temporary and that those who stuck their necks out might soon lose their heads. A Polish journalist described the feelings of many people at factory meetings early in 1956: 'People still do not believe in the sincerity of the present reforms and changes. They expect that one fine day someone will give the signal and everything will "go back to normal".'[11]

As in Hungary, it was not the masses who reacted most rapidly to the changes, but those standing between them and the ruling strata of bureaucrats, and particularly those whose jobs forced them to elaborate and expound the ruling ideology. The 'liberalization' produced a ferment among intellectuals, writers and journalists, similar to that produced in Hungary by the 'New Course'. The student and intellectual press became more and more free in its expression of opinion. The ideas it expressed were by no means clear-cut and unambiguous, nor were the motives of the writers and journalists in criticizing the ruling party line by any means all the same. Some merely wanted the ruling party to rule and hence to defend their own privileges more efficiently. Others were sincere socialists who had genuinely believed for a number of years that what existed in Russia was socialism, but who now began to recognize the realities of the society they had helped to build. This recognition often provoked intense feelings of guilt, and obsessive self-questioning; but it also led to begin exploring the roots of Stalinism and to seek out the basis of a genuine socialism in the writings of Marx himself. Other writers again reflected the aspirations of the factory manager who wanted greater freedom from bureaucratic interference in 'his' factory, or of the peasant who wanted to be left in peace to cultivate his own plot of land.

In the climate of 1955 and 1956, these diverse currents of aspirations, feeling and opinion were far from elaborated into clear and distinct programmes. One overall fear – of a revival of all the worst aspects of Stalinism – unified their various reactions; and in a situation in which the terminology of scientific socialist discourse had been hopelessly corrupted, the proponents of the various currents were not always aware of the differences between themselves. They could express common immediate demands with a single voice.

As they probed, these writers began to give vivid expression to the realities of society. They turned a mirror on Polish society, reflecting aspects of life that had been officially ignored or suppressed. And as time went on they did so ever more audaciously. The first significant move in this direction was made by the poet, Adam Wazyk – a pre-war Communist who had hitherto written 'odes to construction' and had been regarded as a 'poet laureate' for the regime. His *Poem for Adults* appeared in *Nowa Kultura* in August 1955.[12] In vivid terms it contrasted the official myth with reality:

> They ran to us shouting:
> Under socialism
> A cut finger does not hurt.
> They cut their fingers
> They felt pain
> They lost faith.

The poetry operated in a manner that appealed to an audience much wider than the author's fellow-literateurs, portraying life in 'People's Poland' in very sharply outlined sketches:

> From villages, from little towns, they go in wagons,
> to build a foundry, to conjure up a town,
> to dig a new Eldorado.
> A pioneer army, a gathered mob.
> They crowd each other in barracks, in hostels, in huts.
>
> They plunge and whistle in muddy streets:
> the great migration, dishevelled ambition,
> on their necks a little string—the cross of Czestochowa.
> With a storehouse of oaths, with a little feather pillow,
> bestial with alcohol, boasting of tarts,
> a distrusting soul—wretched from the bonds,
> half-awake and half-mad,
> silent in words, singing snatches of song—
> is suddenly thrust out from medieval darkness.
> A migrating mass, this inhuman Poland,
> howling with boredom in December evenings . . .
>
> The great migration builds new industry,
> unknown to Poland but known to history,
> is fed on empty words, lives
> wildly from day to day in despite of preachers—
> amid coal fumes is slowly melted in this slow torture
> into a working class.

This kind of writing was 'socialist realism' with a vengeance.

And while it annoyed party bureaucrats, it attained ever-widening popularity.

Through early 1956 the scope of discussion in the dissident journals grew. Though the terms were still veiled, not only the Polish regime but also Russian control itself began to be subjected to public criticism.

After the Twentieth Congress the slow trickle of criticism and debate turned into a flood. Now even the party leaders were forced to make cautious self-criticisms. Their confessions of past errors and their semi-public disagreements about future policy gave dissident writers new material for comment as well as additional room for manoeuvre.

Slowly but surely, reforms were introduced from the top, a process that was given extra momentum with the death, shortly after the Twentieth Congress, of the old party leader, Bierut.

A group of dissident young Communists had acquired control of a small student weekly, *Po Prostu* ('Straight Talk'). They turned it into the most outspoken vehicle of printed criticism of the old order and its circulation shot up to 90,000. *Po Prostu*'s writers provided graphic journalistic accounts of the situations and experiences of the different groups in Polish society. Jerzy Urban, for example, told what had really happened during 'socialist industrialization':

> During the recruiting campaign for industry and mining there existed near Warsaw a centre in which young girls who worked in the nearby factory were billeted. Terrible things happened there: dirt, hunger, misery, disease, prostitution, lack of care, mass attacks of hysteria, attempts at suicide. They did not let me write about these things in the name of 'higher goals' . . . I later visited the State farms near Zielona Gora. The youngsters lived there not like people, but like cattle. Somewhere on a wooden bed a young girl was dying of disease and hunger. She was fired because she developed tuberculosis. They did not let me write about that, again because of 'higher goals'.[13]

Other articles discussed the chaotic state of industry and 'the problem that does not exist' (i.e. Poland's 300,000 unemployed). Janusz Chudzynski drew a merciless portrait of the ruling group's privileges, contrasting them with the bleakness of the mass of the population's conditions, in *Behind the Yellow Curtains*:

> On the corner of Pulawska and Belgijska streets stands a

long queue of women. The wind is cold, blowing through coats and fur jackets . . . I look through the window (of the shop). Empty inside, bare hooks on the background of white tiles. The pre-holiday delivery of fresh and smoked meats has not arrived.

Across the way on the corner of Dabrowski Street stands an unstuccoed building. A separate drive for automobiles, several carelessly parked cars . . . Warsaws, Popiedas, Chevrolets, some sort of Cadillac or something of that kind . . . In each auto a chauffeur . . .

A lady in a silkskin coat and a green kerchief . . . opens the door covered with gold coloured drapes. I walk in right behind her, and maybe that is why the short, heavy-set man who holds back unauthorized persons from making purchases does not stop me . . .

Along the counter . . . chocolate, spices, all kinds of alcoholic drinks, canned goods; on the side many flowers. A door over which is artistically written 'fresh and smoked meats'. Behind the door, smoked meats, lard; on the counter – behind glass – bacon, much meat . . .

Boulevard Wojska, Boulevard Niepodleglosci, Nowag-rodzka, Rakowiecha, Nowowiejska and anywhere else – everywhere shops with golden or cream-coloured curtains . . . fencing off the well-stocked shops with heavy curtains from the eye of the passers-by . . .

But the people can see . . . And they speak many bitter words – and they are right.[14]

Half-hearted concessions to the urban masses were made, as the wages of the lowest paid were raised. The new party leader, Ochab, claimed there was no money for further wage improvements, but after a tour of Silesia had brought home to him the depths of discontent among workers in that area, he was forced to retract. He announced a 15 per cent wage increase for miners.

Discontent was not confined to the Silesian mineworkers. In every factory throughout Poland, workers' living standards had been falling while their work loads had gone up. There had already been strikes in Gdansk. In Warsaw workers had demonstrated in front of the labour exchanges. Fear of retaliation had kept the discontent from translating itself into action more widely. But now it was apparent that the terror apparatus was less and less effective, and that the regime was vacillating.

Insurrection Below

On 28 June 1956 the workers of Poznan moved as the workers of Berlin had moved three years earlier. A petition calling for improved conditions for one group of workers exploded into a strike; the strike turned rapidly into a mass demonstration involving many other workers; within hours thousands of demonstrators were battling against the political forces of the regime, destroying police stations, seizing arms, releasing prisoners.

The focal point in Poznan was the ZISPO factory, where discontent had been accumulating for years. Wages had fallen between three and five per cent since 1954. There had been repeated incidents of workers being overtaxed. The government had refused to pay for overtime at the full legal rate, while as a result of repeated shortages of materials whole sections of workers were never able to meet the norms necessary to earn production bonuses.

The ZISPO workers held a mass meeting to discuss their grievances on 23 June, a Saturday. They sent a thirty-strong delegation to Warsaw to put their list of demands to the authorities.

In the capital only two of the delegation's five demands were met. The government agreed to refund excessive tax deductions and to pay full bonuses, but rejected out of hand the demand for an immediate 20 per cent wage increase.

Back in Poznan the workers' anger was aroused by rejection of the wage demand; and it was deepened by a rumour (apparently unfounded) that members of the delegation had been arrested.

Early on Thursday morning, the night and day shifts from the ZISPO plant marched together towards the centre of the city. The 16,000 workers marched with banners whose slogans expressed their simple, immediate economic concerns: 'We want bread', 'We want lower prices and higher wages'.

In Poznan, which had not seen any sort of genuine demonstration for ten years, the spectacle of workers marching with banners expressing demands with an immediate appeal for the majority of Poznan's inhabitants was simply electrifying. People poured out of the factories, offices and shops to join in. By 10 a.m. a massive meeting of about a third of the city's population was taking place in front of the town hall, a meeting at which all the demonstrators' demands were being discussed. Even the propaganda secretary of the local party felt compelled to make a statement, only to be heckled and interrupted throughout his speech.

New slogans, no longer restricting themselves to economic questions, began to appear: 'We want freedom'; 'Down with false Communism'; 'Down with the Russians'.

The Poznan workers' spontaneous mass demonstration had suddenly given them an opportunity to influence events, an opportunity they might lose if they did nothing but voice their demands and then go home. What was needed was immediate direct action. A crowd attacked the city gaol, freed the prisoners inside, and seized the prison guards' arms. Another crowd destroyed the radio station used for jamming western broadcasts.

Faced with this sudden insurgency, the authorities could stand aside no longer. The whole power structure was being challenged. It was no longer a question of reforms being conceded from above, but of control being seized from below.

When the demonstrators moved on to attack the Security Police building, a fusillade of bullets cut into the crowd, killing men, women and children. The demonstrators replied with stones, molotov cocktails and, occasionally, small arms.

For a time the fighting seemed to be going in favour of the insurgents. Some sections at least of the local troops surrendered their weapons to the rebels. Two infantry lorries and three tanks which drove up were soon flying Polish flags, under the control of the workers. As the workers seized more police stations, they won fresh supplies of guns. A member of the Security Police was lynched. Trams and cars were transformed into barricades.

The government responded by pouring special units of the army (the Internal Security Guard) into Poznan. By the evening their superior armaments had given them control of the streets. Although sporadic fighting continued the next day, the insurrection was effectively put down.

Reforms

The bureaucracy still had sufficient forces to smash Poznan. It still retained sufficient reserves of credibility and support to keep enough troops loyal to win the fighting on the streets.

The state structure did not collapse as immediately and totally as it had done in East Germany (or as it was to in Hungary). The insurrection in Poznan had not spread to the rest of Poland.

At first the regime seemed content merely to put down the Poznan rising and continue as before. On 29 June the interpretation of the riots offered in the party daily, *Trybuna Ludu,* was classically simple:

> Enemy agents succeeded in provoking street disorders. Matters went so far that several public buildings were attacked, with casualties resulting . . . The organizers of this action, a broad and carefully prepared provocative diversionary action, will be punished to the full extent of the law . . . Poznan provocation was organized by enemies of our fatherland.[15]

In Moscow, *Pravda* repeated the same view: 'Imperialist and reactionary Polish underground agents . . . incited serious disturbances and street disorders . . .'[16] In line with their own interpretation, the authorities arrested 323 people and began to prepare to take legal action against them.

But a growing section of the ruling group saw Poznan as a warning; a repetition of Poznan might not be so easy to contain. Perhaps only massive concessions could pre-empt a much wider insurrectionary movement. After all, strikes were already occurring in Gdynia, Gdansk and Silesia.

So party leaders began to admit that there were more fundamental causes to the riots. They spoke of 'unquestionable existing grievances and dissatisfactions . . .' which the 'murderous provocateurs have taken advantage of'. [17] By 6 July the party daily was admitting that: 'The strike action of the Poznan workers . . . was to a considerable extent caused by bureaucratic distortions of the proletarian state.'[18]

By the time of the Seventh Plenum of the central committee in mid-July both the party secretary, Ochab, and the premier, Cyrankiewicz, were convinced of the need for an emergency economic programme, if they were to survive. Under this programme resources would be allocated immediately to increasing food and consumer goods production, thus raising living standards. Much greater freedom would be given to individual peasants and artisans, and 'workers' participation' in management would be encouraged.

They also began discussions with Gomulka about his reintegration into the party leadership. His imprisonment during the previous period was now an undoubted asset to him. He was untainted by any association with the repressive measures of recent years and his suffering gave him an aura of martyrdom. It provided the basis for a degree of popularity that the established party leaders could not match. They turned to Gomulka in an attempt to harness his personal popularity.

However, these moves encountered considerable opposition on the part of many other sections of the bureaucracy. A faction known as the 'Natolin group' emerged, made up of those most associated with running the police apparatus or the management of heavy industry, a grouping unified by fear that the reforms would mean a reduction in their personal power.

The Natolin group's fears were increasingly shared by the Russian leaders, who felt that the changes they had encouraged earlier in the year were now going too far. The Russian premier, Bulganin, warned that 'opportunist elements' were at work in the Polish party. With such powerful allies, the Natolin group seemed well placed to prevent further change, especially since the Minister of Defence in charge of the Polish army was a Russian general Rokossovsky.

The disagreement within the ruling group now widened into a real split. Initially, the reformers had seen the reforms as a means of preserving and stabilizing the rule of the whole bureaucracy. Now, however, their own futures were in jeopardy: six or seven years before, the Russians and the Natolins had not hesitated to murder and imprison their opponents in the party leadership, and there was no reason to suppose that they would not do so again. To survive, the reforming group had to take counter-measures.

They began by reinforcing those sections of the state machine under their control, to provide a counterweight to the army. The Internal Security Corps (which had put down the Poznan rising) was strengthened and put under the control of a staunch Gomulka supporter, General Komar.

At the same time they worked to increase their popularity outside the party. The writers, journalists and students were tolerated, and even encouraged in their agitation. When the workers involved in the Poznan rising came to trial, the state prosecutor refused to use evidence which had been obtained through torture and, in the end only three workers, found guilty of lynching a policeman, served sentences. The press freely reported what the Poznan workers said in defence of their actions.

Activities like these only antagonized the Natolin group and the Russians further. They decided the time for action had come in mid-October, when the reformers invited Gomulka to take over the party secretaryship and to remove the conservatives from the politburo. They drew up a list of 700 'progressives' to be arrested. Both Polish and Russian troops began to move towards Warsaw, and Russian warships appeared off the coast.

The reformers had little choice but to defend themselves. Komar's armed Internal Security Guard occupied all the key buildings in Warsaw, and were ready to defend them against the rival wing of the state machine. Units of the Guard blocked the approach of the army's tanks to the city, while on the border the incoming Russian tanks found the way barred by units of Polish border forces who made it clear, with warning shots, that only armed force would clear them out of the way.

Gomulka's supporters made additional preparations. The 'progressive' Warsaw committee of the party, led by Stefan Staszewski, organized a communications network outside normal party channels, linking the big factories, the University and the Polytechnic, the network being manned by radical journalists acting as messengers. Arms were allocated to the different factories and the organizers of the party committees were told to be ready to distribute them to the workers at very short notice.

The Gomulkaites were, in fact, threatening their opponents with a mass popular insurrection if the troop movements continued. What had been an argument over the best way to restore the stability of bureaucratic rule had degenerated to the point where a civil war within the state machine itself seemed inevitable.

It is important to note, however, that what was involved was the *threat* of popular action, not that action itself. At the height of the crisis, on the night of 18 October, when Russian tanks were moving towards Warsaw, the news was passed on only to a small key group of 'progressive' party functionaries. 'The workers were not alerted . . . Of 28 million Poles, perhaps a few thousand went to bed . . . with the knowledge that their strength was about to meet its test . . .'[19]

The next day almost the entire Russian politburo flew to Warsaw with the intention of ordering the Poles to drop Gomulka and retain the Natolins in key posts. But the reformers were adamant. There could be no going back. Gomulka met Khrushchev and continued to threaten him with a popular insurrection if the Russian leaders did not give way.

At 3 p.m. that afternoon mass meetings were held in all the Polish factories so as to have the workers in a state of mobilization if the Gomulkaites needed them. But the arms remained under lock and key and the 'progressive' functionaries exerted themselves to the full to prevent street demonstrations.

Finally, after several hours of angry debate, with Gomulka threatening to broadcast the news of the troop movements to the nation, Khrushchev backed down. The forces which had been heading towards the capital were ordered to withdraw and the Russian leaders flew back to Moscow. The central committee of the Polish party went on to appoint Gomulka as party secretary and to remove most of the Natolins from key positions.

However, Gomulka's position was by no means secure – *Pravda* was still speaking of 'an anti-marxist campaign which is shaking the foundations of the Democratic People's regime'.[20]

The tension inside Poland was greater than ever. Sections of the population were beginning to act independently of the 'progressive' party leaders. At Warsaw Polytechnic there was a massive, three day long, continuous meeting. On Monday, 22 October, there were riots in Wroclaw and the next day further stormy demonstrations in Gdansk. In Warsaw there were strikes at the giant Zeran motor works.

But the Russian leaders finally made their peace with Gomulka. On 23 October – the very day that revolution broke out in the streets of Budapest – Gomulka was guaranteed control over Poland. The next day he spoke to a meeting of 250,000 people, who were seething with excitement over the Hungarian events, and told them that the Russians had agreed to the new policies and to the new party leadership.

A wave of enthusiasm swept Poland at Gomulka's success. It seemed to many that despite the odds, the hold of Stalinism had been broken, without any eruption of mass violence. In the euphoria, many forgot Gomulka's own record as a faithful Stalinist apparatchik in the period before his imprisonment: they forgot that as First Secretary of the Party, before 1948, he had played a key role in establishing the hold of the secret police and in destroying the mass organizations of the Polish workers and peasants, the Socialist Party and the Peasant Party. Nor was the euphoria confined to Poland. It was widespread among liberal and social democratic circles in the West. The British left-wing paper, *Tribune*, for instance, wrote that leaders like Gomulka 'offered their countrymen a policy whereby they can begin to regain their national independence by themselves and without jeopardizing either the peace of Europe or Soviet Security'.[21]

Tribune had no hesitation in supporting Gomulka against those in Poland who were sceptical of his promises: 'Gomulka must prevent provocations against the Russians.'[22]

But illusions about Gomulka were not confined to the soft left. Even hardened critics of Stalinism like Isaac Deutscher and Ernest Mandel were confused. Deutscher spoke of 'something like a proletarian revolution from below' which had developed and 'adopted the Communist regime in order to free it from the Stalinist stigma'.[23] And Mandel believed that although 'Socialist democracy will still have many battles to win in Poland, the principal battle, that which has permitted millions of workers to identify themselves again with the workers' state (sic) is already won'.[24]

Few indeed were those who foresaw, at the time, that Gomulka himself would be the hangman of the 'October spring'. Only a few voices noted that 'while such illusions about Gomulka and his ilk exist, they quickly disappear under his rule'.[25]

Gomulka versus the Left

Yet the great turning point in the 'Polish Spring in October' had already been reached. From now on Gomulka's main attention was not directed towards the Natolin group, but to those who were demanding a much greater transformation than he was prepared to countenance.

His major aim now was to restrain all those forces that he himself had unleashed little more than a week before, for demands were now being made that were incompatible not only with control by the Natolin group, but with any form of bureaucratic rule.

Of course, the Natolin group was not eased out completely all at once. Problems remained. Some fairly hard bargaining with the Russians was still needed to get the final withdrawal of Russian troops, to strip Rokossovsky of all his powers, and to obtain some reimbursement for Russia's past exploitation of Poland. But Gomulka's real problem now was to re-establish control over a society whose state machine had virtually collapsed.

In his speeches Gomulka turned increasingly against the radical left. While Russian tanks were firing upon Hungarian workers, he urged the need to 'rebuff any attempts at anti-Soviet agitation'. 'Everyone should return to his job and work hard for a better future,' he urged.[26] When Russian troops went into Hungary the second time, Gomulka was even more bitter against those who wanted to open a second revolutionary front against the Russians in Poland. 'For the good of our country and for the peace of our homes we shall not tolerate any disturbance or rabble rousing.'[27]

Gomulka's message to the Polish workers was quite clear. The party leadership had been changed. Now the workers should stop participating in politics, go back to work as normal, and wait for the party apparatus to deliver the goods.

In line with this approach, all the slogans of the 'revolution' were given a new meaning. Gomulka translated them into a sense quite opposite to that they held for those who had mobilized around them. Thus, when Gomulka spoke of 'workers' self-government', he presented it not as a method for achieving workers' control over the process and fruits of production, but as a way to 'lower the cost of production'. In Gomulka's view, it could 'not remain indifferent to the problems of the excessive numbers of personnel'.[28] In other words 'workers' self-government' was to mean workers sacking one another!

In the October days Gomulka and the mass of Polish workers and peasants had confronted a common enemy. Both had wanted to see the end of the Natolin group and of complete Russian control over the Polish economy. But they had desired this single goal for different reasons. For Gomulka, what was necessary was to broaden the basis of popular support for the indigenous Polish bureaucracy, to increase the efficiency of the economy and to win a degree of national autonomy for Poland's rulers. This was impossible without breaking the power of the terror apparatus just long enough for the bureaucratic reformers to mobilize and to take over. But once the transfer of political direction was complete, new structures of authority had to be built and the rule of the bureaucracy once again safeguarded.

For the mass of Polish workers the immobilization of the old police apparatus was a precondition for their acting on their own behalf. At the same time they were bound to welcome any reforms that improved their own economic situation. But the workers had no interest in Gomulka's long-term aim, the reassertion of bureaucratic control. Although they might agree with Gomulka, even see him as representing their interests up to a certain point, in the long term they were bound to come into conflict with him. The development of that conflict is at the centre of Poland's history after October.

Between the workers and the bureaucracy stood various transitional strata, of which the two most important were the technocratic-managerial layer and the better-off section of the peasantry.

The various sections of the technocracy had played a very important role in the earlier stages of the reform movement. While this was particularly true of the writers, journalists and students, it was also true of many petty bureaucrats, lower-level managers and so on. Often these were able to maintain a degree of hegemony over the workers' movement in the factories. In the spring of 1956, their privileges gave them some security in expressing their political opinions. They could also offer workers a degree of protection against police interference.

This technocratic role was not a feature only of Poland in 1956. We shall see the same processes at work in Hungary and in the Czechoslovak events of 1968. It is, indeed, a paradox of all great revolutions that when the masses first begin to move into action, old habits of deference cause them to elect as their representatives those who were slightly above them in the old society. Trotsky describes this paradox at work in 1917. After the victory of the Petrograd insurrection in February 1917 the army

> found itself summoned to hold elections for the Soviet. The soldiers trustfully elected those who had been for the revolution against monarchist officers, and knew how to say this out loud: these were volunteers, clerks, assistant surgeons, young wartime officers from the intelligentsia, petty military officials – that is, the lowest layer of the new middle caste . . . The representatives of the garrison thus turned out to be much more moderate than the soldier masses. But the latter were not conscious of this difference; it would reveal itself to them only during the experience of the coming months.[29]

The technocrats were quite sincere in their opposition to the old regime in Poland. They had suffered under Bierut. Yet what they wanted from the 'revolution' was quite different from what the mass of workers wanted. For the technocracy what was wanted was an enlargement of their own privileges, a greater say in decision-making, an increase in their own job security (they, after all, had been most affected by successive purges), a relaxation of police surveillance. Once these gains had been achieved, the various technocratic strata tended to withdraw from the movement. There were exceptions, particularly among the intellectuals, but the majority now felt secure in their privileges, and lined up behind the reforming section of the apparatus. What they did not want was further disruption. So once Gomulka had taken over, those who had been the movement's leaders began to hold it back. They provided the new apparatus with much-needed ideological support at the time when its physical forces were almost inoperative.

The peasantry, or at least the better-off sections that usually gave leadership to the others, reacted in a similar manner. Prior to the political changes in October they were in clear opposition to the regime. However, once the changeover had taken place and they had been guaranteed their land as well as improved living standards, they were willing to come to terms with it. After 1956, despite disagreements over particular issues, they were to provide a mass basis of conservative support for Gomulka.

As with the peasantry, so with the major focus for peasant political aspirations, the Catholic Church. Prior to October the Church reflected its devotees' oppositional attitudes: thus, in August 1956 a million people took part in a pilgrimage to Jasna Gora, in passive defiance of the regime.

One of Gomulka's first acts on coming to power was to come to terms with the Church. Cardinal Wyszynski was freed from house arrest, and a month later Gomulka signed a new Concordat with the Church.

Some western commentators give the impression that the Church now constitutes the major source of opposition to bureaucratic rule in Poland. But from October onwards the Church in fact used its resources to marshal support for Gomulka against those who wanted to carry the revolution further. As the fighting continued in Hungary, Wyszynski's voice joined Gomulka's in calling on Poles not to behave 'rashly'. 'Poles know how to die magnificently. But, beloved, Poles need to know how to work magnificently.'[30]

Western commentators have quite rightly noted that 'by encouraging Catholics not to oppose his (Gomulka's) programme the church greatly contributed to the consolidation of his position among the people, if not within the Party'.[31]

When more or less free elections were held, support for the regime was assured because 'the country priest led the local peasants to cast their votes for Gomulka in the January 1957 election'.[32]

It is also worth noting that 'western interference' in Poland meant the same support for Gomulka: 'Radio Free Europe, as well as the Catholic Church, advised Poles to vote exactly as Gomulka outlined.'[33]

Following his assumption of power, in fact, Gomulka proceeded to build a bloc of social forces, led by the 'liberal' or 'progressive' wing of the bureaucracy. Behind it followed most of the technocratic groups, the better-off peasants, the church dignitaries, various petty-bourgeois elements, and the conservative wing of the bureaucracy, which now acquiesced in the reform programme. Excluded from this broad front were the working class and the poorer peasants, the classes whose labour provided the basis for the privileges of the others, and the dissident extreme left of the intellectuals.

Jacek Kuron and Karol Modzelewski have described what happened:

> The Eighth Plenum of the CC of the PUWP (the Polish Communist Party) was a victory of the liberal wing within the bureaucracy. This wing aimed at mitigating the social crisis and stabilizing the system by internal reform, economic concessions and by achieving hegemony; it aimed at taking the lead in the mass movement in order to contain it within limits safe for the system. A leadership was chosen which enjoyed popularity, and a platform of reforms and promises indispensable for the realization of the liberal bureaucracy's aims was put forward. Giving up collectivization and changing the agricultural policy met the demands of the entire countryside (though it most benefited the rich peasantry); widening the margin of private initiative corresponded to the aspirations of the petty bourgeoisie; the accord with the Episcopate removed an important factor of political tension and created new Political-propaganda possibilities (the electoral pact with

Wyszynski); the consistent post-October policy of increasing salaries and incomes of managers aimed at associating the technocracy with the system; criticism of the Six Year Plan and the announcement of a new economic policy gave rise to universal hopes for an improved standard of living. Above all, however, the national question brought popularity to the new leadership: the masses tended to regard the newly-won sovereignty of the Polish bureaucracy as their own. On the other hand, the working class was not even promised the wage increases that were later won. The fait accompli of the creation of Workers' Councils in the factories was recognized, but they were given no real rights and the new leadership of the bureaucracy, first secretly and later openly, opposed their development.[34]

The workers did not accept passively the new bloc of interests ruling against them. In a whole series of local confrontations they challenged the new alignment of forces, and began to see themselves as a class in opposition to the Gomulkaite apparatus.

But no class ever became conscious of its interests all at once in a single spontaneous act. Different sections arrive at this consciousness at different speeds, depending on their particular experience and traditions. A class only truly comes to act as a class against other classes if its most conscious elements join together to educate their fellows into the new world view and to lead them into action. In other words, the process by which a class becomes conscious of its interests involves a process of differentiation within the class as a whole and the creation of parties – whether or not they go by that name.

But under totalitarian regimes of the Polish variety the formation of any sort of effective party in opposition to the regime was impossible, at least until the crisis of mid-1956. The workers and intellectuals who were most aware of the conflict of interests between themselves and the 'liberal' wing of the apparatus had very little time in which to organize. A mass workers' party could only have been formed in the heat of the revolutionary struggle itself. But this was only likely to occur in exceptional circumstances, in which the experiences of workers throughout the country were so concentrated as to produce simultaneous reactions in different areas.

The massive growth of production in the preceding period meant that the regime had economic reserves with which to make concessions. Wages and working conditions improved considerably. The different sections of dissatisfied workers came into conflict with the regime at different times and were defeated separately. Thus the government was able to avoid forcing any sort of unified class opposition to its rule. Gomulka was clever (or lucky) enough in 1956-57 to avoid an immediate confrontation with the working class as a whole.

The October Left

There was no unified revolutionary workers' party in opposition to Gomulka. But there was a kind of substitute in the 'October Left', the grouping of intellectuals and others centred particularly around the journal *Po Prostu*.

At first these did not constitute a clear tendency in *opposition* to Gomulka. Kuron and Modzelewski write:

> The October Left differed from the liberal current, especially in its view of the workers' councils, in which it saw the basis for new production relationships and the nucleus of a new political power. But it was not a uniform movement. The Left did not separate itself off from the technocratic current in the workers' council movement (the demand that factories be run by the Councils did not go beyond the programme of the technocracy) nor from the political bureaucracy in the show-down on a national scale. It did not set itself apart from the general anti-Stalinist front as a specifically proletarian movement. In this situation it was evidently unable to formulate its own political programme, to propagate it in an organized manner among the masses, to create a party. Without all this it could not itself become an independent political force, and therefore it had to transform itself into a leftish appendage to the bureaucracy.[35]

The October Left was much more emphatic in its rejection of the Stalinist past than were the Gomulkaites. In November one of its leading figures, the philosopher Kolakowski, wrote a satirical piece for *Po Prostu,* 'What is Socialism?', rejecting out of hand a whole series of Stalinist practices as anti-socialist. Gomulka personally saw to it that this piece did not appear, and later commented '. . . when you read what socialism must not be, you find as well as correct ideas, a profound slander about the idea of socialism'.[36]

Yet at the same time, many of the left tended to see Gomulka as a representative in their viewpoint. *Po Prostu* carried an article on 28 October 1956 by S. Chelstowski and W. Godek, which claimed that:

> The speech of Comrade Gomulka has sketched out a positive programme for the future socialist transformation of the country, a transformation which accords with the will of the population and takes account of the difficult situation in which we find ourselves.

With that sort of politics, part of the Left not surprisingly supported the calls for 'order' and 'discipline' put out by Poland's new rulers.

> 'The Communist workers and students will smother false voices and hooligan excesses . . .'
> The present period poses for Communists new tasks: to maintain themselves at the head of the masses in the struggle to exterminate Stalinism completely in all areas of life, so as to construct in a peaceful fashion the Polish Road to Socialism. The Communists of Warsaw again stand in the forefront: they are liquidating groups of provocateurs who want to make trouble, they are explaining to the people of Warsaw the tasks of the present movement without allowing excesses likely to be more damaging than useful.

The trouble was that some at least of the 'hooligans' and 'provocateurs' saw further than the writers in *Po Prostu*.

While both Gomulka and sections of the 'Left' were talking of the need for 'discipline' and 'peaceful methods', Russian troops were moving into Hungary to smash the revolution there. Unless the revolt against Stalinism spread, the movement in Poland was inevitably doomed. Yet it was the 'discipline' and 'peacefulness' of Poland that left the Russians free to smash the Hungarians. At the time, many voices, even on the Polish left, congratulated the Poles on their 'careful moderation' in 1956. But later, as the gains of October receded further and further into the distance, that point of view became more and more questionable.

The confusion of the Left was an indispensable pre-condition for the restoration of bureaucratic rule. It meant that those who did attempt in the crucial days of October 1956 to continue the struggle on the streets were isolated and leaderless. It also meant that the apparatus had the ideological means to crush them. Following Gomulka's mass meeting on 24 October 'two processions of youths, each numbering more than 2000, met near the (Hungarian) embassy after marching through the city shouting anti-Soviet slogans'.[37] The ordinary forces of the state were in no condition to deal with this kind of incident. Only civilians, persuaded by arguments such as those quoted above, could act effectively to restore 'order'.

> Witnesses said that as the youths approached the embassy, men in civilian clothes wearing red armbands dashed into the demonstration and broke it up. The demonstrators said that the men punched and kicked them and beat them with rubber and wooden truncheons.[38]

Extensive support for the Hungarian insurgents continued in Poland. There were meetings backing them at the giant Zeran works, a demonstration by the Gliwice miners, talk of a strike at the ZISPO works. Hungarian flags were to be seen everywhere in Warsaw. After the final crushing of the Hungarian revolution, there were riots in Bydgoszcz and Wroclaw. In Szczecin demonstrators attacked the Russian consulate. According to *Glos Pracy,* 'crowds which cannot be described as hooligans are taking part in disturbances in many localities'.[39]

But the Hungarian insurgents needed more than sympathy. They needed a second revolutionary front to be opened in Warsaw if they were to stand any chance against the Russians. The opening of such a front demanded a conscious and coherent initiative from the left – and that was not forthcoming.

The Fight for Control

Skirmishes on the streets did not by themselves decide the issue. Just as important was a long drawn-out struggle for control within the various institutions of Polish society.

The new strategy of both wings of the bureaucracy was simple: to use Gomulka's ideological hegemony at the time of the October events to prevent new forces from really challenging the centres of power. When new institutions were thrown up despite this, the tactic was to deny them real power, gradually to wear down their supporters, and finally to infiltrate them with men who would support the bureaucracy.

Such methods were used, for example, among the youth. During the October events the old mass youth organization, the ZMP, collapsed. At the beginning of December, on the initiative of *Po Prostu*, a number of youth groups and Revolutionary Youth Councils came together to create a new Union of Revolutionary Youth (URY).

Its manifesto made it clear that the URY would not be a mere adjunct to the Polish party: 'We are partisans of the full independence of the Union. We don't want to be an annexe to any party . . .'

However, the Union did not stand in conscious opposition to the party either. Rather it wished

> to preserve the line of the Marxist Party of the working class in our actions, reserving for ourselves the right to interpret the line of the party and influence the decision on this line. We recognize the political role and importance of the leadership of the party, which is the directing force in our nation . . . We are also opposed to our organization receiving orders from the party.[40]

The party leadership, however, could not permit such an organization to survive in independence. Three weeks later the URY was merged with the debris of the official organization. The old leaders rapidly took over control, taking away the possibility of independent political action from thousands of young people, who dropped back into apathy.

The trade unions had hardly been involved in the October events. Their leader, Klosiewicz, was a member of the Natolin group. But when a carefully selected body of 120 'delegates' met to replace him in mid-November they were surprised to find themselves inundated by about a thousand workers elected from factory meetings, who took the meeting over. They passed resolutions not only removing the old leadership, but also calling for democratic control of the unions from the factory floor, independence of the unions from the state and from management, the right to independent parliamentary representation, and the abolition of privileges for those in the top positions in management and government.[41]

Once again, however, these gains were shortlived. By careful manipulation and infiltration of party members, the bureaucracy reestablished control over the unions, so that by the beginning of 1957 a party journal was able to complain that 'the trade unions, preoccupied only with the fulfilment of production plans, have progressively ceased to represent the working class and to defend its interests'.[42]

Workers' Councils

The most important struggle, however, concerned the workers' councils. These had been formed in October, partly spontaneously and partly as a weapon for the reforming wing of the bureaucracy to use against its opponents.

At first, Gomulka seemed to support the workers' councils, mouthing phrases about 'workers' self-management'. But as time went on he made it more and more clear that their role should be very restricted. From the beginning, he saw the councils as subordinate to the party apparatus. Even at the height of the agitation, on 20 October, he argued: 'For the moment we cannot touch on the question of the organs of workers' self-management. For we cannot organize anything concretely while our Party apparatus remains in the state it is in in many localities . . .'[43]

As the months passed, his opposition to the notion of the councils having any real power became much more explicit. He still paid lip-service to the idea of councils as a 'form of participation of workers in the administration of the enterprises', but he went on to argue that they were only one form among others. He emphasized that 'it would be an error to think that in the socialist countries without Workers' Councils the working class is deprived of all means of controlling the factories and the national economy'. Finally he warned against any call for a 'system of workers' councils from low to high in all branches of the economy'. For this 'needs to be capped by a central power . . .' And this would make the government 'superfluous'. 'In brief the whole conception is an anarchist utopia.'[44] Gomulka did not add, of course, that it was also the 'utopia' outlined in Lenin's *State and Revolution*.

The bureaucracy did not just argue against the councils, they also acted. It was impossible, immediately after October, for them to take direct, administrative action, but they could weaken the councils in other ways. They tried firstly to infiltrate them with party trusties, with the aim of turning them from independent workers' bodies to 'transmission belts', to keep the workers under bureaucratic influence. Secondly, by confining the councils to questions of administrative detail in isolated factories and workshops, they aimed to make their activities of little interest to the mass of workers, and to stop them questioning what really mattered – the overall running of the economy in the interests of the bureaucracy. Success on the second front tended to make workers more apathetic and thus increased the effectiveness of the first tactic.

The great merit of the writers around *Po Prostu* was that they recognized these manoeuvres and fought them.

It was argued that:

> In so far as we wish to remove the source of the deviations referred to as 'Stalinism' and to give to the dictatorship of the proletariat its real content, we have to see that the movement of councils of workers' self-management must entail a series of transformations in the political and economic structure of the state . . .
>
> Under the influence of the attitude of the workers the Eighth Plenum adopted an orientation towards democratization. One of the essential foundations of this orientation was to support the organs of workers' self-management. In relation to this began the second phase of the struggle for control, over the following point: should the council be the supreme power in the factory or merely a consultative organism?
>
> However, if it ought really to become the supreme power, then it is absolutely necessary to pass now or in the very near future from the existence of the councils in isolated factories to a system of councils. If these councils ought to become organs of effective power, they cannot be in a situation of subordination or dependence in relation to the old bureaucratic apparatus of administration, an apparatus adapted to the needs of the preceding socio-economic model . . .
>
> Bureaucratic centralism consists in the fact that even with the creation of a workers' council in a given factory, this latter remains subordinated to a central apparatus over which the working class does not exercise the least control. In a democratic centralization what is today called the central administrative apparatus would have to be subordinated to the various rungs of the workers' council system. Thus, for the series of central directorships that exist today would be substituted the representative of the working class, made up of the representatives of the workers' councils of the different enterprises, who, in their turn, would designate representatives at a higher level, a sort of general workers' parliament.
>
> A system of workers' councils constitutes an important step forward towards restoring its true content to the dictatorship of the working class. This will only, however, be tem-

porary if one does not remove the obstacles that exist at the other levels of the power system. Otherwise the rebirth and reinforcement of the bureaucratic apparatus will be inevitable.[45]

But *Po Prostu* soon had to recognize that things were not working out as it would wish. S. Chelstowski and W. Godek warned in January: 'Workers' Self-Management in Danger'.[46]

The workers are not being allowed to take control of the enterprise . . . They elect the council in which sit workers who enjoy the confidence of the other workers; the council chooses its Praesidium and starts work . . . But it is at this point that the real difficulties begin . . . The Workers' Council of the Metallurgical Enterprise of Bielsko had not yet done a single thing so far as administering the enterprise goes, although it had existed for a month. It had not been able to do anything because it had spent all its time so far in the struggle against the management clique . . . In the Enterprise for Railway Repairs at Nowy-Sacz the railwaymen rejoiced at having elected their councils at last. And the council? It dealt with a few matters concerning personnel. It is a general phenomenon: the majority of workers' councils are in general passive, do not engage in significant activity.

And yet the workers have put many hopes in the councils they have elected. In our discussions with workers we sensed a certain assurance, the assurance of men who know that they possess an organ of power which supports their interests. The workers see the councils as the top organs of power in the factory. The council is for them the symbol of the October changes, the concrete proof that they are finally the true co-owners of the means of production, the utilizers with full rights of goods which belong to the whole people, the wealth of the whole of society.

Why then does there exist a contradiction that leaps into view in almost every enterprise between the correct conceptions of the workers on the decisive role of the workers' council and its disturbing passivity?

The conditions in which the newly elected councils have to work are decisive . . . As the secretary of the party organization at Zeran said during a meeting: 'Bureaucracy and workers' councils cannot be continued together.' So it is not surprising if the bureaucracy defends itself and tries to torpedo existing councils with all possible means .

The old group of administrators, profiting from the fact that they still remain – above all in the provinces – in power, redouble their attacks against the workers' councils day by day. This struggle takes various forms. Sometimes, as at Bielsko, they falsify elections; sometimes they refuse to ratify the statutes of the councils; or sometimes they reduce their role to carrying out directions or at least advising the management . . .

In the actual conditions of centralized management, the role of the councils (we do not want to be the prophets of misfortune) is restricted in advance. If in the near future the system of management over industry is not radically modified, the councils can become a new Stalinist fiction, creating the illusion that it is the masses who govern . . .

For the moment the central question seems to us to be for the workers' councils to unify their efforts. It has been known since the publication of the *Communist Manifesto* that the basis for the victory of the revolutionary movement is the solidarity of the working class.

Today the expression of this solidarity in the struggle against bureaucracy must be an extension of the workers' councils. One could take for example Warsaw where the conditions for the realization of such an extension are without doubt the ripest. In this case, while the isolated councils break their heads against the bureaucratic wall, a common effort would enable a breach to be opened. Zeran and the Enterprise of Industrial Installations at Nowa Huta have already opened such a breach: when the extension and co-ordination of the efforts of the councils take place the number of such breaches will increase.

As it happened, the most pessimistic prophecies were to prove correct. In mid-1957 one observer noted:

There are about 20 workers' councils in which power is lodged in the workers who elect the workers' councils and control the director of the factory . . . All but the 20 real workers' councils are phoney insofar as their power is only advisory.[47]

Finally, in April 1958 the workers' councils were formally subordinated to the control of the party and the trade unions, but they had already been killed from within long before.

Strike and Repression

The bureaucracy's strategy was to use its ideological hold in order to fragment opposition, and then gradually to reassert direct physical control. But resistance continued, even though the opposition forces lacked central organization or any coherent strategy of their own.

At first Gomulka treated this opposition with caution. In no way did he want to inflame feelings or produce a mass reaction. So, up to May 1957, while the workers' memory of the October events was still fresh, he assured them that, although the party opposed strikes,

> We do not want to resort to administrative means when the workers stop work. Without depriving workers of the right to strike we have to say to them: the strike will not lead to wellbeing, it will reduce rather than increase the amount of bread in the country. So it is better not to have one.[48]

By the summer of 1957, however, Gomulka felt more secure. The structure of authority in the state had been rebuilt, while working-class self-confidence had been undermined. When tramworkers went on strike in Lodz, and clashed with the police, Gomulka's tactics changed. He complained that the police had not been vicious enough: 'The security forces have shown in relation to the strikers a tolerance that is beyond normal limits.' In February 1958 strikes were again officially prohibited.

Police action against strikers was soon followed by action against the 'October Left'. On 2 October 1957, the publication of *Po Prostu* was forbidden. When students organized a meeting to protest, the police broke it up. A further meeting the next day elected a delegation to deliver a protest, but the delegation was arrested.

Once again it was the official 'opponent' of Gomulka who gave him ideological support. Cardinal Wyszynski appealed for calm and condemned demonstrations, while the western press spoke of 'mob' action. Two days later *Trybuna Ludu* condemned *Po Prostu* for having raised the slogan 'All power to the Councils'.

Thus the 'Polish October' came to an effective end. The Polish state preserved the veneer of liberalism in a few areas of life for a few more years. Some of its leftist opponents could still express themselves through purely literary work or in academic publications. But effective power was back safely where it had been before, to be used when the occasion demanded just as crudely as before. Ten years after 'October', people were receiving prison sentences for such heinous offences as tape recording satirical plays and reading forbidden books. Those who dared to express public sympathy with them were expelled from the party and later deprived of their jobs. When students and young workers demonstrated for free speech they were denounced as 'hooligans' and beaten up by the police, their leaders arrested and imprisoned. The sordid sequel to these incidents was a wave of officially-inspired anti-semitism, in which Jews were blamed for the country's problems and forced out of their jobs, some into exile abroad. Such were the long-term fruits of the restriction of the Polish October within the peaceful channels preached by Gomulka.

It was to be more than a decade before the true spirit of 'October' again moved the Polish working class, in the northern ports. This time it was to bring down Gomulka.

7.

1956: The Hungarian Revolution

While in Poland popular discontent simmered on throughout the second half of 1956 and into 1957, in Hungary it boiled over. All the classic features of revolution took shape on the streets of Budapest: an armed and insurgent population, mass strikes, new forms of popular self-organizations, the barricades of the revolution against the terror of naked counter-revolution.

Yet the early days of 1956 gave few hints of what was to come. While Poland's 'democratization' was gathering momentum, Hungary's 'New Course' seemed to have been abandoned for good. Rakosi was back in full control of both party and government. Nagy and his followers had been ousted from positions of power. Vengeful reprisals against those writers and journalists still publicly calling for change were being prepared.

Urgent measures were required, it is true, in the economic sphere. As a western commentator described the situation:

> Hungary begins her five-year plan with industrial production stagnant and with agricultural production barely enough to meet the basic needs of the population. If Hungary's furnaces and larders are empty, it is not only the result of bad planning, but also of growing discontent among the workers both in industry and agriculture.[1]

Much of the recently-built plant could not be utilized because of electricity and coal shortages (coal production had fallen about 7 per cent since 1952); bread production was about 15 per cent less than was needed to feed the population. And, while the Russians might give Rakosi political support, he could whistle for economic assistance. 'Although Russia's aid to Bulgaria and Rumania is increasing, she is refusing to foot the bill of the overdevelopment of heavy industry and the underdevelopment of agriculture in Hungary . . .'[2]

Such difficulties were bound eventually to be of some political consequence. Virtually the whole of the population including significant parts of the bureaucratic apparatus, felt the economic draught. For the time being, however, those who held the monopoly of physical force were determined to resist pressures for change from any quarter.

But the Hungarian bureaucracy was not master of its own fate. Its future was tied inextricably to developments in Russia, which was experiencing economic and political contradictions of the same order as those in Hungary, although at a much slower pace.

The Twentieth Party Congress in Moscow wrecked Rakosi's comeback, and gave new hope to those forces pressing for 'liberalization' in Hungary. The dissidents within the bureaucracy and within the party at large began to organize immediately. Followers of Nagy holding positions in various parts of the apparatus used them to expand their influence. Rakosi's supporters, compelled to make ritual obeisance to the spirit of Khrushchev's 'secret speech', were in no state to take counter-measures. Even their most trusted followers were turning against them. When Rakosi addressed the annual meeting of the top echelons of the political police (the AVH) he was booed.

Over the next months, the focus for dissidence was provided by a party institution, the so-called 'Petofi' circle of the Hungarian Young Communists (the DISZ). This organized a series of debates at which the whole range of problems confronting party members, intellectuals, and students were discussed: the history of the workers' movement and Stalinism ; marxist economics ; philosophy and dogmatism ; freedom of the press ; the position of agriculture in Hungary.

Attendance at these meetings rapidly grew from a few dozen to hundreds or even thousands, when Rajk's widow spoke to demand the rehabilitation of her husband or when writers spoke out against censorship.

The party leadership could hardly ignore such public defiance, and passed a resolution on the Petofi circle: 'In the beginning these debates had a positive sense, but lately certain elements opposed to the policies of our party have tried to utilize them so as to put across their own anti-party ideas.'[3] Yet the party leaders' authority was no longer sufficient to enable them to stop the meetings. A month later all they could do was complain of the Petofi circle as a 'little Poznan', around which a 'second political centre began to form, which challenged the country's only real political centre, the central committee of the Hungarian Workers' Party'.[4] From their complaints it was clear that the trouble was spreading beyond the Petofi circle. 'The direction of *Szabad Nep* (the party daily) and of the press in general' had 'slipped out of our hands'.[5]

The character of the growing opposition is important. Rakosi and his supporters did not yet have to face the mass of the people. A few workers or ordinary peasants might have attended the Petofi circle meetings – but most of the participants were from the more privileged sections of the population. One American observer claimed that when Julia Rajk spoke one third of the 2000-strong audience were army officers.[6] Others were writers and professors, managerial and technical personnel, government and party functionaries of various sorts. In short, the opposition consisted chiefly of those who were relatively privileged, but were denied any real control over political life. Such people would respond readily to calls for freedom, for an end to terror and arbitrary power, but would be far less ready to respond if such demands were taken up in popular form, along with calls for the end of their own privileges and their own localized exercise of arbitrary power.

For the present, however, this was an opposition the ruling clique could not ignore, although it would not countenance surrendering power to it either.

There was a prolonged deadlock between the contending groups. Economic necessity demanded a change; the hierarchical form of the political apparatus forbade it.

In mid-July, after the Poznan rising, the Russian leadership intervened to try and end the conflict. Reconciliation, however, seemed impossible. Too much was at stake. The ruling group clung to power; their opponents bitterly remembered the 'mountain of corpses'[7] that lay between the factions. Rakosi was removed from office, but his henchman Gero took over.

The massive and complex machinery of direct and indirect repression that had held the rest of Hungarian society in check for years became more and more paralyzed. Those who questioned and criticized might be admonished, but punitive sanctions against them were no longer applied. The voices of writers and intellectuals discussing 'truth' and 'freedom' grew louder. And, among the 'silent masses' the factory workers who had previously held back from agitation, were also beginning to ask questions, although of a different sort.

Early in August the newspaper *Nepszava* reported that workers at the Matyas Rakosi works questioned 'their' shop committee chairman about the wage computation system (something not officially on the agenda of the meeting).

> 'Never before has anyone so harshly attacked the wage computation system,' roared Horvath (the Chairman).
> 'But are we right? Answer this question,' a voice interrupted.
> 'I am speaking now,' shouted Horvath. 'When I finish you, comrade, may ask for the floor.'
> 'We cannot be forbidden . . . to ask questions . . . we have the right . . .' declared foreman Lengyel.[8]

Among the workers of Budapest such small incidents multiplied. The factory floor began to articulate its own demands for the first time for ten years. As yet, there was no national movement, no fusion of workers' demands with the political questioning of the intellectuals. But everywhere the ferment was growing.

A worker in the telephone factory, where 3000 were employed, has described the atmosphere there:

> The trial of participants in the Poznan riots of which the Hungarian press had given considerable accounts, caused quite a stir – in particular the conclusion of the trial placing the principal blame on the Polish AVH for having fired on the masses . . . Also newspaper articles, in particular the declarations of the writers. These articles were posted up and workers would immediately discuss them. Contrary to the apolitical years following 1948, the workers were politically very active. They began to discuss politically, in an especially active manner, although such discussions did not come to any precise conclusions . . . Many workers who attended evening classes at the technical university were put into contact with the debates (of the Petofi circle). Through them other workers were informed of the debates and animated discussions followed. There was a tense political atmosphere, for a fresh breeze had entered the factory against the suffocating pressure of the party.[9]

As summer turned to autumn, the tension increased still further. A concession made by the government – permission for a ceremonial reburial of the remains of Laszlo Rajk – provided the occasion for the opposition's first massive demonstration. 200,000 or more turned out to participate in a passive and silent gesture of defiance.

The government made more concessions. The old chief of the political police, General Mihaly Farkas was arrested. On 14 October Nagy was readmitted to the party, although reference was still made to his 'mistakes'.

But partial concession can be worse than no concessions at all. People began to hope that their expectations would be realized, but also became increasingly aware that they would have to push harder first.

Institutions and newspapers nominally under government control now paid scarce attention to official directives, while the oppositional movement spread out from Budapest to the provinces, and from the writers and intellectuals to less privileged groups. The official radio gave news of new developments: in Szeged students were demonstrating for the reinstatement of sacked professors and were establishing an independent students' union ; local Petofi circles were being set up in Keszthely and Zalaegerszg . . . students at the Lorand Eotvos University in Budapest were setting up a '15 March Circle' and sending delegations to Budapest factories . . . The Petofi circle in Budapest was demanding Nagy's integration into the government.

At this point it might still have been possible for the apparatus to 'do a Gomulka' – to draw Nagy into the government, and hope thereby to control the situation by re-establishing the party's ideological hegemony. Gero, however, refused to consider such a concession. Instead he tried desperately to maintain sole control for himself and his supporters. And since the government would not budge an inch, the opposition was forced, often despite itself, on to the streets.

The Revolution Breaks

On 22 October various student meetings called for a mass demonstration the next day 'in solidarity with our Polish brothers'. The students sent delegates to the Petofi circle to seek support. At first, the government gave permission for the march, and allowed details to be broadcast over the official radio. Such a demonstration was unheard of, and the whole of Budapest was buzzing at the news. 'A certain restlessness reigned throughout the capital, whose walls, trees and hoardings were covered with the students' placards – which passers-by discussed passionately.'[10] Then came the announcement, as groups of students and others were preparing for the demonstration, that permission had been withdrawn.

This official change of heart did not, however, prove the government's strength: it merely showed that the government had not changed its ways. The students' determination to march increased, for they knew the government could not enforce its will.

As people assembled at a number of points throughout Budapest to begin marching, the government admitted its impotence. It could not stop the demonstration. One of Gero's henchmen, 'lifting his arms to the sky and almost crying, begged Gabor Tanczos (an oppositionist) to put himself at the head of the march . . . to save the situation'.[11]

The protest began in a mood of quiet exaltation, with people feeling that the regime could not now stop them. Here they were in the streets, 100,000 strong, and Gero could do nothing. Indeed his supporters had officially backed down. Oppositional activity could, it was proved, be effective.

At this stage the demonstrators did not want to make a revolution. No one carried guns nor even stones. At the head of the march were representatives of official bodies, and massive portraits of Lenin and Nagy. The most common political demand expressed on the march was for Imre Nagy, a leading Communist, a man whom the Russians had made premier only three years before, to take over the government.

At three o'clock the crowd, which swelled continuously as further groups arrived, gathered before the statue of a Polish hero of the Hungarian uprising of 1848, Josef Bem. Here speeches were delivered in solidarity with the Polish struggle.

The demands of the writers' union were read out:

> We have arrived at a historic turning point. We shall not be able to acquit ourselves well in this revolutionary situation unless the entire Hungarian working people rallies round us in discipline. The leaders of the party and state

have so far failed to present a workable programme. The people responsible for this are those who, instead of expanding socialist democracy, are obstinately organizing themselves with the aim of restoring the Stalin and Rakosi regime of terror in Hungary. We, Hungarian writers, have formulated these demands of the Hungarian nation in the following seven points:

(1) We want an independent national policy based on the principles of Socialism. Our relations with all countries, and with the USSR and the People's Democracies in the first place, should be regulated on the basis of the principle of equality. We want a review of inter-State treaties and economic agreements in the spirit of the equality of national rights.

(2) An end must be put to the national minority policies which disturb friendship between the people. We want true and sincere friendship with our allies – the USSR and the People's Democracies. This can be realized only on the basis of Leninist principles.

(3) The country's economic position must be clearly stated. We shall not be able to emerge from this crisis unless all workers, peasants and intellectuals can play their proper part in the political, social and economic administration of the country.

(4) Factories must be run by workers and specialists. The present humiliating system of wages, norms, social security conditions, etc. must be reformed. The trade unions must be the true representatives of the interest of the Hungarian working class.

(5) Our peasant policy must be put on a new basis. Peasants must be given the right to decide their own fate, freely. The political and economic conditions for free membership in the co-operatives must be created. The present system of deliveries to the state and of tax payment must be gradually replaced by a system ensuring free socialist production and exchange of goods.

(6) If these points are to materialize, there must be changes of structure and of personnel in the leadership of the party and the state. The Rakosi clique, which is seeking restoration, must be removed from our political life. Imre Nagy, a pure and brave communist, who enjoys the confidence of the Hungarian people, and all those who have systematically fought for socialist democracy in recent years, must be given the posts they deserve. At the same time, a resolute stand must be made against all counter-revolutionary attempts and aspirations.

(7) The evolution of the situation demands that the People's Patriotic Front should assume the political representation of the working strata of Hungarian society. Our electoral system must correspond to the demands of socialist democracy. The people must elect their representatives in parliament, in the council, and in all autonomous organs of administration, freely and by secret ballot.[12]

The protest had been made, the speeches delivered, the demands publicly articulated. But the demonstrators were not satisfied. They had no guarantee that their demands would be met. The authorities, after all, were still there, and they might easily go back to the old Rakosi-style methods. Yet here on the streets, were sufficient people to force concessions. The crowd, not with any clear-cut aim, but continuing to make their presence felt peacefully, began to move away from the Bem statue towards Parliament Square. Some of them were addressed by Imre Nagy, who had arrived in Budapest from the countryside. The majority did not hear him, and those who did found that his cautious phrases did not match their radical demands for a complete recasting of the system.

By this time the demonstration was broadening its spread, drawing in whole new sections of the Budapest population who wanted more than just a few reforms. Already the slogans were 'Out with the Russians', 'Death to Rakosi', 'Free and secret elections' as well as 'Nagy to power'.

In any case the crowd was angered by reports of a radio speech by Gero, who had just broadcast a diatribe against 'nationalistic demonstrations . . . (people who) slander the Soviet Union . . . assert that we trade with the Soviet Union on an unequal footing . . . attempt to create disorder, nationalistic well-poisoning and disorder . . .'[13] His speech made it clear that the group around him did not intend to give any real ground.

Into the already powerful brew of feelings of solidarity and collective power that swayed the crowd, a new element of bitterness was introduced. Despite everything they had done, Gero still held power and still dared to slander them in this manner. A large part of the crowd moved off from Parliament Square towards the radio station, demanding in increasingly insistent tones the right to broadcast a reply to Gero on the radio. At the same time another group of two or three thousand went off to the huge statue of Stalin in the

City park. If the powers that be would not get rid of the heritage of the past, the people themselves would at least remove the symbols. With hammers and ropes they tore at the monstrous figure, until it toppled and crashed to the ground, only Stalin's boots remaining as an inglorious testament to the past.

The demonstrators who went to the radio station found themselves confronted by another symbol of everything they hated. In front of the building stood lines of political police – the AVH – barring access. Gero was still using the old weapons to defend his lies. Nevertheless, the crowd agreed to send a small delegation to put their case. The delegation disappeared into the building. Time passed. There was no sign of the delegates, no sign of any concessions by the authorities. The demonstrators grew angry as it seemed that all their efforts had been wasted. The tens of thousands at the back began to force their way forward, thrusting those at the front, willingly or unwillingly, up against the AVH lines.

It was still a peaceful, if noisy, demonstration, not a revolution. The people of Budapest were trying to make the authorities move, not to overturn them.

The 500 AVH defending the radio station felt isolated. Everything *they* had stood for was being threatened. But their orders were clear: keep the crowd out. They remembered how they had dealt with previous protests, how easy it was. They tried tear gas bombs first. The crowd backed away a little, but the wind blew the tear gas back onto the AVH lines. The crowd surged forward again. A police machine-gun fired.

That single act began the revolution. A few demonstrators fell to the ground. But for the others, the thousands, the whole character and purpose of their demonstration changed: if they did not destroy the beast it would clearly destroy them. They began to fight back, with stones, with petrol bombs, and with the occasional gun. Within hours the fighting had spread throughout Budapest.

From the beginning, the insurgents had firearms. According to a supporter of the Russians (in a book misleadingly entitled *Fighting the Counter-Revolution*):

> among the throng were to be found a number of officers of the Home Defence Forces and many from the (civilian) police. Before the radio building one noticed above all a number of officers from the Petofi (military) Academy.

Part of these turned in words and deeds against the AVH defenders of the radio building.[14]

Another pro-Russian source states: 'A truck loaded with soldiers entered the crowd; men clambered aboard and demanded or were given the weapons of the occupants.'[15]

The demonstration did not involve only a few individuals, but rather represented a massive slice of Budapest's population. The rank and file, and even many officers, of the ordinary forces of the state were there with their families and friends. They responded like everyone else to the actions of the AVH.

After that first machine-gun burst at the radio station, the issues at stake were clear to everyone. People who only moments before had been spectators, listening to talk about 'freedom' and 'truth', and wondering what such abstractions really signified, now suddenly understood. Workers, who had stood back as the relatively privileged students and intellectuals demonstrated, were now drawn into action. The AVH, by their own action, had given the revolution a symbol of oppression that everyone could grasp.

The news radiated out from the demonstration to the rest of Budapest. Workers raced to their factories to tell their mates, and to fetch weapons from sports clubs. Others went to the soldiers in the barracks. Everywhere were knots of people discussing what was happening. The energies of a whole population were turned within minutes from the normal round of daily life, with its essentially private concerns, to intense discussions and arguments about what had just happened and how they should respond. Practical politics became a public, popular affair. A mass a-million-and-a-half strong was beginning to think how it should take control of its own society and to act accordingly.

As night wore on fighting broke out in a score of places in Budapest. Barricades were thrown up. A Russian bookshop was burnt down; the offices of the party daily were attacked; insurgents began to locate AVH headquarters.

From the time of the first shooting Russian tanks rolled into the city to restore 'order'. Youths fought them back with petrol bombs and light firearms. Meanwhile the Hungarian state apparatus, all-powerful days before, collapsed completely. Civilian police and soldiers handed over their weapons to the insurgents. Army tanks carried Hungarian flags. Those sections of the Hungarian armed forces who did not go over to the insurrection at least remained neutral.

An officer in the vital Killian barracks describes what happened there:

> In the course of the battle around Broadcasting House in Sandor Street, the crowd, infuriated by the slaughter started by the AVH, made for the nearest barracks, the Killian barracks, to get guns and ammunition. Lieutenant Voros, who had come on duty after me, was helpless. In vain did he assure them that there were no armed units in the barracks and that they would find no guns there. The crowd broke in the main gate, fished out the old guns we had collected in the basement the day before and for which there was no ammunition, and carried them away. The guard could not or did not want to prevent them from doing so. But the men in the barracks did not remain idle either. Some two hundred soldiers left the building and went along with the insurgents. In the barracks there was complete chaos. A short while after – on Maleter's orders – a company of cadets arrived from the Kossuth Military Academy, with guns but without ammunition, to remove the civilians from the barracks. After endless arguments and persuasion, but without violence, they completed their task by morning.[16]

The New Government

With the outbreak of the revolution the conflict between the contending groups within the Communist leadership seemed to be resolved. Early the next morning Gero began to announce concessions to the reformers' demands. A new government and party leadership, with Imre Nagy as prime minister, was declared. Two pronouncements were made in its name, one calling Russian troops to 'restore order', the other proclaiming martial law.

But the fighting did not stop. The insurgents knew that if they laid down their arms while the Russian army remained, they would be handing over control to it. Gero and his friends, they noted, remained in positions of influence. Workers from the suburban factories marched to the centre of the town to give support to those fighting. Those who were too old or too timid to march went on strike. The revolution began to spread from Budapest to the provinces.

The government issued repeated calls for 'order'. An amnesty was offered to those who stopped fighting by 2 p.m., along with threats to those who did not. But all to no effect. Despite governmental assurances that order was being 'restored' the revolution continued to spread. If nothing else the behaviour of the governmental forces ensured this. On Wednesday evening (24th October) in a confused incident, an unarmed demonstration of two or three thousand men and women was beginning to fraternize with Russian tank crews in Parliament Square. It was fired upon[17] by unknown snipers, probably AVH men. As dozens died the fate of the government's radio appeals was sealed. Everywhere ordinary people took up the fight against the Russian tanks, laid seige to AVH buildings, began to take power into their own hands.

Again the government tried to ameliorate the situation by making concessions. Gero himself was replaced the next day by the 'reformer' Kadar. Nagy broadcast an appeal in which he promised to 'submit an all-embracing and well-founded programme of reforms' and to engage in 'negotiations on relations between the Hungarian People's Republic and the Soviet Union, concerning among other things, the withdrawal of Soviet forces stationed in Hungary . . .'[18]

But to those on the streets and in the strikebound factories these promises sounded hollow. The implication of Nagy's words was that the Russian intervention had been justified. Leaflets appeared on the streets, not particularly hostile to the new government, but very clear in the demands they expressed.

'We summon all Hungarians to a general strike', read one signed by 'Hungarian Workers and University Students'. 'As long as the government fails to grant our demands and until the murderers are called to account, we shall answer the government with a general strike. Long live the new government under the leadership of Imre Nagy.' Note the ambiguity, which must have been deliberate: 'We shall answer the government' but also 'long live the government'.[19]

A Yugoslav Communist reporter described the military situation:

> Thousands of people have obtained arms by disarming soldiers and militia men. Some of these soldiers and militia men have been fraternizing with the embittered and dissatisfied masses. They are said to have broken into barracks; the Budapest arms factory was taken; machineguns and even light infantry appeared in the streets. According to eye-witness reports the authorities are paralyzed, unable to stop the bloody events.[20]

The Russian tanks replied to the insurgents with all the blind ferocity that has characterized counter-revolution throughout the ages. A Hungarian officer describes how their actions swung the commanding officer of the Killian barracks who had previously been neutral, to side with the revolution:

> The Soviet tanks have been attacking in groups of three and four since early morning – without infantry. They shell the barracks, and the buildings opposite, the houses and the boulevard. Indiscriminately, without any definite purpose it seems. But they are helpless against the insurgents hiding behind windows and behind the chimneys on the rooftops; wherever they turn they are met with a shower of Molotov-cocktails and gunfire. They rumble up and down the streets firing machine-gun volleys into the windows and bringing down the walls with demolition bombs. The fire of the insurgents increases in strength and more and more Soviet tanks turn to meet it. Their guns boom away constantly and after each shot thick walls, pillars crumble and collapse.
>
> The medical unit works untiringly. By noon we have quite a number of wounded among our own but more and more soldiers take their places in the line of fire. They have no commander, no-one gives them orders, they go into battle voluntarily with their rifles and submachine-guns. Excitement and indignation blaze high among our men:
>
> 'Is this what they call friendship? Smashing everything to bits? Was it for their guns that we rebuilt Budapest?'
>
> Colonel Maleter is deeply worried. When the Soviet tanks attack with renewed vigour he telephones the Ministry of War. He asks to speak with the Minister. I am standing close to him, and distinctly hear the answers rising thinly from the receiver. Maleter is deeply agitated but the tone of his voice remains determined and moderate:
>
> 'Is this how the government wishes to restore order in Budapest?' he shouts in the deafening noise of battle which must have been heard also at the other end of the wire. He demands that the Minister intervene with the Soviet High Command to recall the tanks operating in the neighbourhood.
>
> The reply of the Minister is far from encouraging: 'I am sorry, Comrade Colonel. I am in no position to interfere with the Soviet military operations.'
>
> Maleter's expression hardens, he takes a grip on himself and his voice is even more determined. He articulates every word solidly and clearly:

'In that case, sir, I report that I shall open fire on the first Soviet tank that comes within range of the Killian barracks.'

That is all. The die is cast.

We take stock of our arms and ammunition; there isn't much of either. We have a few rifles and a few tommy-guns. No machine-guns, no hand-grenades, and we don't even have petrol bottles. Maleter orders those who have firearms to take up positions on various points of the building. Those with rifles are to shoot at the periscopes of the Soviet tanks, those with tommy-guns are to take care of any infantry that might be accompanying the tanks.[21]

The Emergence of Workers' Councils

The struggle against the old dictatorship was not confined to street fighting. By the third day of the revolution, 26 October, people everywhere were establishing institutions to give expression to their new power. They formed 'Revolutionary Councils' in the towns, the villages and the quarters of the cities, in newspaper offices and governmental ministries, in colleges, on collective farms, and above all in the factories. As the Hungarian people ripped into the fabric of the old order, they used these new organs of power, which were directly under their own control, to begin to build an alternative order. Such tasks as the running of factories, the distribution of food, the publication of newspapers all passed from the disintegrating apparatus of the old state to the new organs of popular power.

In the provinces the successful revolution put local radio stations at Gyor and Miskolc into insurgent hands. These stations began broadcasting on behalf of the local revolutionary committees and issued statements from the various workers' councils.

Radio Free Gyor reported:

Delegates from the workers' councils of the petroleum industries of Szony this afternoon visited the workers' council of the railway carriage factory of Gyor to find out about events in Gyor and about the activities of the workers' councils. The Szony workers told them that national committees and workers' councils were being formed everywhere between Gyor and Tatabanya. The factory workers of Komarom and Szony were in solidarity with the workers of Budapest . . .[22]

By the next day the official radio in Budapest was reporting similar developments there.

'Workers' councils have been formed in numerous factories . . . Workers' councils have been formed in the Duna shoe factory, in the cotton spinning mill, in the Goldberger textile factory, in the Tancsics leather factory.[23]

A workers' council has been formed in the bus factory in Budapest . . . it procured food for the workers and has given or will give important supplies of provisions at its disposal to clinics and hospitals . . . Workers' councils have been constituted in Csongrad, in most of the factories of Szeged and Hodmezovasarhely and in the department of Heves . . . Similar reports came from the clothing factory and the machine tools factory of Bekescsaba, from the station and the tobacco factory of Nyiregyhaza and from the various factories of Dunapentele.[24]

In Budapest the continued fighting on the streets made it impossible for any central authority whatever to operate. The workers' councils were of necessity confined in their practical activities to particular localities. Outside Budapest, however, whole areas of the country were falling under their command.

For two days the town of Miskolc has been under the leadership of the Workers' Council and the Student Parliament. The Workers' Council has taken over control of the garrison and the police . . . As you know the County Strike Committee has called on all the plants in the county to strike, with the exception of the post, transport, communications, food supplies and health services, and the power plants . . .[25]

In Gyor too the Revolutionary Council had assumed control over the whole area. Peter Fryer, at that time *Daily Worker* correspondent in Hungary, describes his impressions:

The Town Hall (was) the seat of the Gyor national committee. The word 'national' was not intended to imply that this body arrogated to itself authority outside its own region; such committees called themselves indifferently 'national' or 'revolutionary'. In their spontaneous origin, in their composition, in their sense of responsibility, in their efficient organization of food supplies and civil order, in the restraint they exercised on the wild elements among the youth, in the wisdom with which so many of them handled the problem of Soviet troops, and, not least, in their striking resemblance to the workers, peasants, and soldiers councils which sprang up in Russia in the 1905 revolution and in February 1917, these committees, a network of which now extended over the whole of Hungary, were remarkably uniform. They were at once organs of insurrection – the coming together of delegates elected by factories and universities, mines and army units – and organs of popular self-government which the armed people trusted.

Of course, as in every real revolution 'from below' there was 'too much' talking, arguing, bickering, coming and going, froth, excitement, agitation, ferment. That is one side of the picture. The other is the emergence to leading positions of ordinary men, women and youths, whom the AVH domination had submerged. The revolution thrust them forward, aroused their civic pride and latent genius for organization, set them to work to build democracy out of the ruins of bureaucracy.[26]

As such developments proliferated throughout the country, the government again announced concessions aimed at re-establishing its authority. On Saturday, 27 October, there was a re-shuffling of ministries. New members were brought in, a few of them from non-Communist parties. At the same time the government recognized the existence of workers' councils. The radio began to mention them favourably, and the remnants of the party machine tried to seize the leadership of the council movement by encouraging the formation of councils in those factories where they did not exist. The official trade-union executive issued a call for the creation of councils and listed their demands. For example, in the telephone factory, a worker relates:

> On 25 October, after participating in the revolutionary fighting, I went to the factory. Of the three thousand workers some eight hundred had assembled in the cultural hall. The director, the party secretary, the head of the factory committee and some of their subordinates were standing on the platform, facing the workers. These officials were telling the workers that the SZOT (National Trade Union Council) had issued an appeal, approved also by party headquarters, that workers' councils be constituted in the factories so that in the future the workers should have a say in the affairs of the factory and manage it themselves.

The workers interpreted the appeal not quite in the way the SZOT and party headquarters expected. They took it seriously. They proceeded to elect workers, their own representatives, to the council and not the men suggested by the leadership. In our factory nobody was asked, although, sensing the mood of the workers, the above-mentioned officials thought it advisable to resign. The director asked the assembled workers to allow him to remain in the factory and work as a toolmaker, as he had done before being appointed director. The workers agreed. We elected a workers' council consisting of approximately twenty-five members and immediately resolved to strike because, owing to the confused decrees it issued, we refused to acknowledge the Imre Nagy government. It was proposed that the workers' council should elaborate a Memorandum of Protest to be forwarded to the government after the workers of the factory had approved it. Our first demand was that the Soviet troops be withdrawn from Hungary, that is, the country's independence, and the second, that after the Soviet withdrawal a government headed by Imre Nagy but consisting of members enjoying the confidence of the people should manage the affairs of the nation.

Each shop delegated two or three members into the council and so did the administrative departments. As a consequence, nineteen or twenty of the twenty-five council members were workers.

Approximately half the council members were young, between the ages of 23 and 28. They were, in our factory, representative of Hungarian youth. They had participated in the actions preceding the revolution, the demonstrations, the pulling down of the Stalin statue, in the fight in front of Broadcasting House; some of them attended the university and with their youthful, revolutionary spirit could carry away the older workers who felt like them but left the initiative to the young. The older workers, among whom, particularly in the telephone factory, there were many old trade-union members, and many who had been in prison during the former regime or even in the Communist regime, considered that the young should take the lead. They said that, if the young had been good enough to start such a glorious fight, they were good enough to be our representatives. It didn't count whether or not one had been a Communist Party member. Approximately 90 per cent of the workers' council members in the telephone factory belonged to the party, some had even been active Communists, but the workers trusted them because they had always stood up for them. We were very careful that only men whose hands were clean should be elected into the workers' council.[27]

The various radio stations made it clear that although the governmental changes were welcome, they did not go nearly far enough. The workers' council of Borsod County declared 'that they greet the new government but will continue the strike until our demands, and above all the one concerning the withdrawal of Soviet troops, are met . . .'[28]

> The miners of Balinka sent a delegation of seven to Radio Free Gyor. They have also formed their own workers' council, and the miners are keeping order and discipline. However, they are watching events in Budapest with concern . . . Their first demand is that Imre Nagy calls on the Russian troops in Hungary to begin their withdrawal.[29]

From Pecs came a slightly different note:

> In these critical days the Pecs May (railway) headquarters stands as one behind the reorganized central leadership and behind Comrade Nagy . . . But we were greatly shocked by news . . . that the government has appointed Lajos Bebrics as Minister of Communications and Postal Services – the same Bebrics who introduced an arbitrary, terroristic system on the railways.

The better organized and more resolute councils sent delegations to see the ministers and press their demands. Already on the fourth night of the revolution delegates from Gyor had been in Budapest putting their case to Nagy. Over the next three days various representatives from factories and groups of resistance fighters in Budapest, as well as from the provincial national councils, presented their demands to him. Always the tone was the same: 'We will give our full support to the new government . . . when the new government accepts our programme, particularly the withdrawal of Russian troops.'

It was clear that the central government had a straightforward alternative. Either it could crush the revolution mercilessly, using enormous numbers of Russian troops and tanks. Or it could make huge concessions to the insurgents, accepting – or at least seeming to accept – their demands.

The government and party leaders chose the second alternative. The official radio and press began to speak on behalf of the revolution, not against it. Nagy for the first time admitted in a broadcast that most of the insurgents were not 'counter-revolutionaries'. He promised immediate withdrawal of Russian troops from Budapest.

Spasmodic fighting continued, however, for a further two days. Soviet withdrawal was promised, then the Russians said they would wait until the insurgents had laid down their arms. Rumours circulated of new troop movements into Hungary, while other rumours spoke of definite withdrawals. By the night of Tuesday, 31 October, however, Russian units were no longer seen in any of the major cities.

That day also, with the revolution now a week old, a new government was formed. Nagy announced, without ambiguity: 'The cabinet abolishes the one-party system and places the government on the basis of democratic co-operation between coalition parties as they existed in 1945.'[30] The new government contained a majority of members nominated by the old non-Communist parties. Nor was this reform restricted to the top of society. Steps were immediately taken to set the old party machines in motion again after an eight-year lapse. Old premises were reopened and old newspapers republished.

The new government also appeared to accept most of the revolution's demands. Russian troops would be asked to leave Hungary completely ; the workers' councils and the revolutionary local authorities were to be officially recognized ; the crop delivery system, 'which has borne so heavily on the peasantry'[31] was to be abolished.

The revolution, it seemed, had been successful. Yet many of the issues at stake were still far from resolved. And five days later the victory was to be brought to an abrupt stop.

Revolution or Counter-Revolution?

This is an appropriate point to interrupt our narrative to discuss some of the issues involved in the revolution.

The crudest explanation of what took place – and the explanation that dominated the left in the West at the time – was that the Hungarian events were a 'counter-revolution' fermented by 'Horthyite reactionaries' and 'western agents'.

Such an interpretation was accepted by all western Communist Parties in 1956, by most of the East European Communist regimes (including the Rumanians, who later rebelled against Russian dominance) and by the Chinese.

However, as we have attempted to show, those who challenged the party leadership throughout the spring and summer of 1956, and who laid the ground for the 23 October demonstration, were not 'Horthyites' nor 'western agents', but rather were dedicated members of the Communist Party. Many of them, men like Jozsef Szilagyi and Geza Lasonczy, had been imprisoned and even tortured during the Horthy period, or, like Nagy, had been forced into exile.

As for the events that followed, there are numerous eye-witness accounts from leftists, and even western Communists, indicating that although individual 'fascists' might have tried to take a hand, and although western propagandists tried to interpret events to their own advantage, these were far from being the dominating elements in the revolution. We have quoted the testimony of Peter Fryer, the *Daily Worker* correspondent above. Here we may also note the comments of the *official* Communist newspapers of Yugoslavia and Poland.

Thus *Trybuna Ludu* (Warsaw) of 28 October:

> We repeat . . . although, as usually happens in mass movements, irresponsible, and in some cases reactionary elements joined in action, they do not constitute the backbone of such long-lasting and intensive struggles.[32]

Borba (Belgrade) of 1 November:

> From everyone with whom we talked we have received the reply that there is no danger of abolishing revolutionary achievements, such as returning property and land to former owners.[33]

An observer of the Polish 'left' was even closer in his assessment:

> The division is clear: the nation on one side, on the other the Stalinist faction of the government and the AVH. There are thousands of Communists among the insurgents . . . The whole working class youth and the students are on the barricades.[34]

But probably the most telling witness is the man who put down the revolution and became Hungary's new ruler – Janos Kadar. In a radio broadcast on 1 November he declared:

In a glorious leap our people fought the Rakosist regime. They conquered freedom and independence for our country, without which we could not have socialism. We can say with assurance that those who prepared this rising were from our ranks. It was communists, writers, journalists, students, the youth of the Petofi circle and, by the thousands, workers, peasants, old militants unjustly imprisoned, who fought in the front line against the despotism of Rakosi and against political banditry. We are proud of you, who took your proper place in the armed rising.[35]

But, some commentators argue, though the motives of those who did the fighting were not 'fascist', the real danger was that by weakening the state they might be preparing the ground for counter-revolution, for a 'restoration of capital'.

Such a view is wrong on at least three separate counts. Firstly, it implies that workers who have taken control of their own factories through workers' councils will for some curious reason passively hand them over to private capitalists ; and that peasants having thrown off the burden of compulsory deliveries to the state, divided amongst themselves land previously controlled by collectives and by the state, will agree peacefully to hand the land over to the pre-war landowners and to pay rent voluntarily. The whole history of the last two hundred years testifies to the tenacity with which peasants will resist all attempts, from whatever quarter, to take away their land. The Hungarian peasants were no different. The left social democrat, Anna Kethly, a member of Nagy's last government, in fact describes how :

> After his leaving prison, Prince Eszterhazy (head of the greatest of the old landowning families) sent to peasants on his own land some parcels of food. Despite hunger and real poverty, the peasants returned all of these packages and protested against this interference in their affairs. They did not want to accept anything from him.[36]

And as for the workers : people who seriously believe that workers at the height of a revolution need a police guard to stop them handing their factories over to capitalists certainly have no real faith in the possibilities of a socialist future.

Secondly, those who argue in these terms seem never to consider what any private capitalists would do if by some miracle they did take control of a country like Hungary. Would they, for example, divide the factories among themselves, creating an economy in which one car factory competed with another, one steel plant with another?

Only if they were mad. Modern capitalism is characterized by continual growth in the size of industrial firms, as economic power is concentrated into fewer and fewer hands. Thus the largest US car firm, General Motors, produces, in terms of value, more than most countries of the world. Small old-style companies can hardly compete against such modern economic giants. The small firms are relegated more and more to unimportant areas of production. But in the major industries, the price of survival is a concentration of firms, through mergers and cartels, until in most sections of industry there is effectively only one major concern in each country. The exceptions – for example, the American oil companies – prove the rule by the way they work together rather than competing.

When small countries, newcomers to international competition, try to develop industries in such a highly monopolized situation, they cannot afford the luxury of having more than one home-based company competing on the domestic market. Often – even with rabidly anti-Communist governments such as those in pre-war Eastern Europe – the only way to organize and finance such new industry is through nationalization.

In the Second World War, the occupation of countries by German forces accelerated concentration of capital, not vice versa. The result was that even in a country like Lithuania, where industry had been nationalized for a few months only, it was not handed back to the old bourgeoisie. It is hardly likely, therefore, that old-style, private capital would even consider breaking up Hungarian industry into small competing units. After all, no one expects the break-up of General Motors into small competing units of the size typical under nineteenth-century capitalism. In all likelihood such private capitalists would act together, co-ordinate their efforts, in order to have some chance of surviving where it really matters – in competition with the giants on the world markets.

But, thirdly, it might be argued, these private capitalists would be interested in profits. That would be a step backwards. There is no denying, of course, that they would be interested in profits. The only way private capitalists can survive is by continually pumping as large a profit as possible out of their workers, so as to finance the investment they need to compete successfully on international markets. If they can, private capitalists force wages down, cut living standards, and build bigger and bigger machines so as to be able to survive in competition.

But, under Rakosi in Hungary wages were forced down, living standards were cut, in order to increase production so as to build bigger and better machines, and so on. And why did Rakosi's government do this? Quite simply, so they could sell enough goods abroad to prevent a deficit in their balance of payments and so that their master, Stalin, could build armaments and machinery on the same sort of scale as his rivals in the West. In other words, the controllers of Hungarian industry behaved as they did so as to compete, economically and militarily, with western capitalists. Rakosi, in short, behaved very much as a group of private capitalists controlling Hungary would have done.

For the Hungarian workers, there might have been some changes of a minor sort if private capitalists had replaced the 'Communist' government. But in essence their situation would have remained the same. In either case, blind competition would have dominated their lives.

However, this was not the issue at stake. By taking control of their factories and by destroying the power of the old regime, the Hungarian workers had laid the basis for a form of organization of society superior to either the bureaucratic state capitalism of Rakosi or the monopoly state capitalism of the West, a form of organization based on workers' control from below, and on production for human need not for competition.

That is why so many of the same manifestos that demanded free elections and the withdrawal of Russian troops, also declared roundly:

> We repeat, we will not return the land to great landowners, the factories to the capitalists, the mines to the barons and the direction of our army to the Horthyite enemies of the people.[37]

Class Forces in the Hungarian Revolution

However, to identify and understand the forces at work in the revolution, we must do more than simply refute the charge of 'counter-revolution'. We need to analyze the different currents in the revolution, comparing their programmes and locating their social roots. Unfortunately, such an analysis of the Hungarian events has rarely been developed. Most commentators have been satisfied to describe the 'people' who rose up as if they were a homogenous mass, all devoted to the same goal. But the Hungarian events merit a rather more discriminating examination.

Prior to the 1956 revolution, there were three major classes in Hungary: the mass of workers, the mass of peasants and the *central political bureaucracy*, which exercized complete control over the means of production (including the state and 'collective' farms) and which forced workers to sell their labour power to it, and peasants their produce. Between these three major classes were various inter-mediary strata, who received privileges in return for the services they performed for the central bureaucracy, but who did not share its control over the means of production. The intermediary strata contained tens of thousands of supervisors, managers, ideologues, army and police officers, and so forth.

The bureaucracy is characterized, like the private capitalist class in the West, by its control over the means of production.[38] This control it exercizes collectively: here it differs from old-style private capitalism, where individuals own separate chunks of property. (In the West, of course, individual ownership is less and less the pattern, with the growth of massive companies, increasingly merging with state, and often depending on its resources for financing expansion.)

Not all the members of the central bureaucracy share equally in this control. Just as the capitalist class in the West includes those who employ hundreds of thousands of workers, and also those employing a few hundred or a few dozen, so the bureaucracy includes both those whose share in the collective control is meagre and those with enormous power.

At the apex of the bureaucratic pyramid sits the inner group that makes overall decisions on behalf of the bureaucracy as a whole. This group is comparable, perhaps, to the board of directors of a capitalist company – except that they have concentrated in their hands not merely economic decisions, but also control over the police, the enforcement of law, the use of military power.

This group, however, is as constrained in its actions as are the directors of any capitalist company. In order to survive, the cen-tral bureaucracy must take account of its external environment. Imports and exports must be made to balance ; its military power must be built up to prevent some foreign ruling class from taking over. Above all it must expand the means of production at its disposal, since these provide the measure of its power, its prestige and therefore its independence internationally.

In Hungary this central political direction had built up a whole apparatus of domination aimed at imposing its central goal – the development of heavy industry – upon the rest of society. And it had used this apparatus to provide a framework of discipline for the bureaucracy as a whole, in order to keep every bureaucrat's attention firmly on its imposed target. Finally, this same apparatus of domination was used to ensure that its Russian protectors' demands were met.

Essentially our argument is that Nagy's opposition (like Gomulka's in Poland) was motivated in the main not by any questioning of bureaucratic control as such, nor by any rejection of the bureaucracy's goal of accumulation, but by strong dissatisfaction with the *particular means* used by the political direction under Rakosi, Gero, and so forth in attempting to reach these goals.

Nagy himself never intended to question the overall structure. All his arguments and appeals during his second period of opposition (1955-56) were directed to those who controlled the bureaucratic apparatus in Hungary, or to one of its Russian masters, Khrushchev. His 'agitation' was restricted to a narrow circle of party and governmental functionaries. It was anathema to Nagy to go outside the ranks of the bureaucracy. For him the proper place for discussion was within the ranks of the party's leading members – and even here the norms of bureaucratic control had to be preserved. 'Imre Nagy believed in complete respect for legality within the party' and rejected any idea of forming an intra-party faction.[39] The various memoranda that he sent to the party's leading bodies[40] continually stressed his loyalty to the central goals of the bureaucracy as a whole. His charge against Rakosi and his followers was that *they* had endangered these.

Nagy did address himself to wider concerns. He talked of the degeneracy and immorality of the Stalinist set-up, the need to raise living standards, the necessity for 'workers' democracy'. And there is no reason to doubt his sincerity. What is significant, however, is the means by which he expected to obtain reform. The majority of the bureaucracy (and the Russians) must be persuaded that his proposed reforms were in *their* interests. Motivations of this kind characterized

Nagy and his immediate associates and, at least in the early days, Janos Kadar.

The grouping that formed round Nagy in the summer of 1956 was, however, far from homogenous. Two of Nagy's biographers have pointed to five distinct sources for its members: [41]

1. Nagy's immediate entourage
2. a group of writers and artists
3. a layer of party functionaries, consisting of economists, agronomists, historians and young marxist theoreticians
4. 'Rajkists', ex-collaborators of Rajk who had been imprisoned or purged
5. groups of ex-social democrats and 'peasant socialists'.

Such a conglomeration of different elements extended across the whole range of levels within the bureaucratic hierarchy. It also included groups and individuals who had no share at all in bureaucratic power, such as writers and intellectuals who, although relatively privileged, exercized no real control over society. In addition, Nagy's supporters included men who, although among the most powerful members of the bureaucracy, had come to support the Stalinist system out of a misguided idealism, and whose marxism often pre-dated 'Communist' rule in Hungary. A few, like Miklos Gimes, argued for the formation of a serious oppositional faction, and saw the insurrection as a 'positive factor'.

The most important organizational nucleus of the oppositional movement had been the Petofi circle. This provided a physical link between the few people who were close to Imre Nagy and the many other groups and individuals – the writers and journalists, the agronomists and army officers, the university professors and government functionaries – who had heard of his programme and saw it as a means of improving their own situation without at the same time shaking up society too much.

The Petofi circle was not, however, a *revolutionary* organization. One of its three secretaries has described its deliberation prior to the demonstration of 23 October:

> The leaders of the Petofi circle and the representatives of the students met at the headquarters of the DISZ (official youth organization) to decide what route the demonstration would take and to ensure its peaceful character . . . (They) thought that only the nomination of

Imre Nagy to the premiership could reduce tension (in the capital) . . . (As the demonstration gathered on the streets) the Petofi circle restrained the movement more than it drove it forward.[42]

The aim was to 'reduce tension', 'restrain the movement', 'ensure its peaceful character' – *not* to make a social revolution.

Interestingly enough, the same party leaders who had condemned the Circle began to feel they had at least enough in common with its organizers to request them to play this restraining role. The leaders of DISZ 'implored the members of the Bureau of the Petofi circle to put an end to the movement' of students forming independent unions ; Apro, a Rakosi supporter, begged them to 'control the situation' by taking the lead on the demonstration.[43]

In a pamphlet which circulated in Budapest after the revolution was crushed, an anonymous member of the opposition gave a description of its vacillations :

> History proved the opposition right, but at the same time condemned it for not having been loyal to itself and for not having organized itself as an independent force. While the denunciatory party resolutions spoke about an organized anti-party grouping – and are again speaking about it – the opposition was still debating whether to organize or not; they were not trying to establish contact with the people, in the first place the working class, or with the various bourgeois democratic parties. In the first days preceding the revolution they were still at the petition-composing stage, and pronounced brave but futile prophecies of doom. This is why the outbreak of the revolution found them not on the barricades but in the corridors of the petrified party headquarters. It was the opposition who 'prepared' the revolution and yet no one was so dumbfounded by its outbreak than they – with the exception of a very few among them. On 23 October they marched happy and triumphant in the procession, but in the evening they watched helpless and uncomprehending now history, taking a sudden leap forward, advanced along its incalculable road. The people had made itself independent of the opposition because, essentially, the opposition had made itself independent of the people.
> Among the members of the Imre Nagy group, the writer-journalist movement, the Petofi circle, few were present when the weapon of criticism was replaced by the criticism of weapons, and even the large mass base of the move-

ment, university youth, gave fewer armed fighters than was believed during the first few days. According to the few hospital statistics 80-90 per cent of the wounded were working class youths, only 3-5 per cent university students. These figures show more convincingly than any argument the opposition's responsibility in failing to organize independently and with determination.[44]

The opposition's hesitations were not accidental. Their ambivalence was rooted in the very character of their inner-party organization. The majority were still enmeshed in an ideology that held that Hungary was somehow on the road towards socialism. The ruling group used marxist language – or rather marxist language reduced to the level of scholastic gibberish – to define itself, and the opposition accepted this definition, even if 'critically'. They still saw the institutions of the bureaucratic apparatus as offering the means to achieve social reforms. They relied on 'socialism from above', and therefore looked to the mechanism 'above', namely the levers of party power. They pleaded with Gero, they pressurized him, they even organized to replace him, but they never thought of totally recasting the society that had produced him.

At the same time, many of them had a direct material interest in the maintenance of the official interpretation of society. Subordinate participants they may have been, but still they were participants in the bureaucratic exercise of power. A defeat for the apparatus as a whole would be a defeat for themselves. The mechanisms through which *they* could get things done – for the benefit of the passive mass or for their own benefit – would be smashed. Even those who were not concerned with their material privileges still clung to the official ideology, fearing anything arising from below that might not be run by the self-proclaimed 'Marxist-Leninists' of the apparatus. Their ideas continually drove them to attempt to lead protests from below along 'safe' and 'orderly' bureaucratic channels. Just as many of the 'left' in Poland argued, in support of Gomulka, for 'discipline' in the crucial October days, so in Budapest the opposition attempted to limit the scope of the insurgency, to harness it behind the Nagy government.

> After the first shots had been fired the most determined among the members of the opposition established contact between Imre Nagy and the revolutionaries . . . but very

large steps had to be taken to unite the Imre Nagy group with the popular movement.[45]

The characteristic feature of the Nagy group during the early days of the revolution was its anxious passivity. Nagy himself was, according to some rumours, a virtual prisoner in the party office, forced to put out proclamations with which he disagreed – like the call for martial law – and unable to repudiate (even if he wanted to) the calling in of Russian troops. His 'captivity' typified the ideological imprisonment of the social layer he represented during these early days. Nagy and his supporters feared the mass insurgency, and yet saw Gero still blocking their path to controlled reform from above.

Only the surrender of the official power after the fifth day ended this paralysis. Now the Nagy group devoted most of its energies to trying to regain popularity and to reasserting its hegemony over the movement below. Yet, paradoxically, some at least of the reformers would have been horrified had they been able to see the eventual destination to which the 'Polish Road' they hoped to follow would bring them.

Mass Insurgency

The character of the popular uprising is best considered in three parts: the workers' councils, the fighting groups and the political parties.

The workers' councils were spontaneously created bodies, whose composition and whose programmes reflected the manner of their formation. Their spokesmen came from a variety of political backgrounds or, because of their youth, from none. Many were old social-democratic and trade-union militants, some of whom had been in prison under Horthy or under Rakosi. Some had been Communists. A few prominent individuals – in particular Attila Szigeti who led the powerful Gyor National Council – had been political functionaries under the Communist government.[46]

Within the workers' councils there developed an intense and continuous debate about the direction of the revolution and its goals, the appropriate methods of action, and so on. On immediate issues the views of the councils were unambiguous: no Russian troops, workers' control of the factories, no return to Stalinism, no return of the pre-war factory owners. But the same ideological inversion that afflicted the inner-party opposition was also felt in the councils. Those who spoke in marxist language could be the most conservative, not the most militant and self-conscious of the workforce. Active membership of the Communist Party might have taught this or that worker a few marxist phrases, but often it had entailed privileges in return for co-operating with the management under the old regime. Many of the best and most militant workers completely rejected the normal terminology of socialist revolution. For them that terminology had associations with Rakosi, or even with an Imre Nagy they did not fully trust. After all, why should they wave high a red flag they had seen flying over concentration camps?

And yet their slogan – the factories are *ours* – summed up the essence of marxism. Hence the peculiar linguistic distortions given to the councils' debates. Those who spoke most of socialism often meant the 'socialism' of Gomulka's Poland. Others used the term less, but were trying – out of their new experiences or out of the rudiments of an old education in the pre-1945 socialist and trade-union movement – to figure their way through to a new conception of society, a conception quite alien to all the old Hungarian parties, and prefigured only in the Russian experience of 1917 and in Lenin's *The State and Revolution*.

Formally, at least, politics 'on the streets' were more 'right wing' than in the factories. The terminology and traditions of the old trade-union movement had less influence here. What mattered was the ability to fight the Russians and flush out the AVH; courage and determination were the qualities that commanded respect. Men from a variety of political backgrounds could display such attributes. So the 'leaders' of the fighting were a very varied bunch: Pal Maleter, an army officer who had been in the Communist Party from 1943; Janos Szabo, an elderly and unpretentious figure who led a motley group of young fighters; Jozsef Dudas, a former member of the Communist and the Smallholders' Parties, imprisoned for eight years, and variously described as a 'progressive nationalist, a mystical demagogue',[47] and 'a labourer, but a natural leader, combining personal magnetism, visionary characteristics and a penchant for demagoguery'.[48]

The same ideological contradictions found in the factories and amongst the intellectuals also existed on the streets. The most militant fighters rejected out of hand the old system and everything associated with it. For them, the pseudo-marxist jargon in which the regime had cloaked itself was a symbol of their own oppression. Yet at the same time they were absolutely clear that they were *not* fighting to hand the factories over to a new set of capitalist oppressors or to give the land back to the old landowners. Hence an apparently contradictory phenomenon, noted by some observers: 'From everyone with whom we have talked we have received the reply that there is no danger of . . . returning factories or land to former owners . . . However, everyone is predicting a right-wing course in Hungary.'[49]

In Hungary the traditional meaning of 'left' and 'right' had been turned completely upside down. In official terminology Nagy was on the 'right', Rakosi on the 'left' (note the contrast with Poland, where *Po Prostu* was on the 'left'). This led many people who, in terms of their own *practice,* rejected the western type of organization of society quite as much as Stalinism not to understand this themselves. The dominance of Stalinism, and its inversion of marxist terminology, made this inevitable. Few Hungarians had visited the West and seen the harsh side of life there (in the slums of Derry, say, or the ghettoes of the US cities, let alone in the poverty-stricken areas of the third world). All they had was a vague idea of the West's superior standard of living, an idea conveyed by the only source of information other than the official media – the western propaganda stations. Many of them identified with a mythical West that symbolized an alternative they wanted – freedom of speech, production for human need not for accumulation.

Yet this pro-western tinge could not aid the fighters in their struggle against the Hungarian ruling class. It could not help in the fighting (since the West repeatedly made it clear it would not intervene militarily); it could not assist them in developing any concrete solutions to Hungary's economic problems – since a capitalist Hungary would have tried to force down wages in order to accumulate, just as Rakosi had done; above all western ideology had nothing whatsoever to say about the immediate tasks confronting the revolutionaries – how to construct a new form of popular power. The idea of workers' councils was as diametrically opposed to the political forms of the West as to those of the East. Indeed, one suspects that the only practical effect the 'rightist', pro-western mood could have had, as with the Catholic influence in Poland, would have been in helping the re-establishment of monolithic state capitalism under a Hungarian Gomulka.

When after seven days the old political parties began re-organizing, this same contradiction expressed itself again. After eight years of political repression, people rushed to join the old parties as a way of exercizing their new-found freedom to discuss issues, to articulate their standpoint, to intervene in political life for themselves. Yet the old parties had nothing at all to say about the immediate problems facing the country.

All of them accepted the minimum programme that the revolution itself had spontaneously produced – land to the peasants, factories to the workers' councils, withdrawal of Russian troops. But beyond this they could not go, for their ideas had been frozen in 1945. No one thought it possible to return to the old, backward Hungarian society, with its large feudal remnants, which had preceded the war. Indeed the parties took it for granted that they must consider how to run a country most of whose industry was controlled by the state, and with an independent private sector which, of necessity, would be marginal (as in Poland today).

The largest of the old parties, with 60 per cent of the votes in the last free elections, had been the Smallholders' Party. Its leader Bela Kovacs stated its position: 'No one must dream of going back to the world of counts, banks and capitalists . . . A true member of the Smallholders' Party cannot think along the lines of 1939 or 1945.' But Kovacs did not go on to indicate what new lines of thinking differentiated his party from the broad movement.

So, while people rushed to join the old parties they were largely irrelevant to the real debates taking place, above all in the workers' councils. Instead, they concentrated on recruiting members. The chief concern of their old leaders often seemed to be not so much with discussing how to change the organization of Hungarian society as with finding important roles for themselves in a reformed version of the existing structure. They were eager to join the government, but once there they did little to challenge the policies propounded by the 'reformist Communists'.

The one party that might have played a different role was the Social Democratic Party, which laid claim to the marxist tradition. But its leaders displayed, after an eight year lapse, the same vacillation and equivocation, the same inability to take a determined stand

and press for it, that had characterized their behaviour previously under the domination of private capitalism.

Not surprisingly, many of the young revolutionaries who had fought on the barricades and who dominated many of the workers' councils felt nothing but contempt for the parties. A delegation from the workers' councils of Borsod County demanded that 'attention should not be concentrated on a reformation of parties and the return to party bickering . . .'[50]

Dual Power

In every great social revolution the state apparatus representing and maintaining the old ruling class collapses. It is torn apart as opposed social forces contend for mastery over the control and co-ordination of social life. Each revolutionary class is compelled to throw up its own organs of power as it remoulds society in its own interests.

In the Russian revolution of 1917, the collapse of the Czarist regime produced precisely such a splitting up of the state power. On the one hand stood the bourgeois provisional government; on the other stood democratically elected workers' councils (soviets) which had sprung up spontaneously in each locality to represent the direct interests of the workers and to organize the revolution. The provisional government controlled all the official symbols of state power, the ministries, the official seals, the police chiefs and army generals. But the means to carry out their old functions had been torn away from them. The generals were without an army, as the rank and file looked elsewhere for their commands.

The Soviets in the Russia of 1917 had the means to power in society, and in abundance. They were made up of the direct delegates of society at its local levels; they came directly from the workers, soldiers and peasants. In the localities only the Soviets or councils had power, only they could get even the most elementary things done. But, until October, they were not prepared to exercize centralized power over society as a whole. From February to October, society was run on the basis of a series of uneasy and unstable compromises between the provisional government and the Soviets.

Precisely this *dual power* situation occurred also in the Hungarian revolution.

Officially the government ruled. It controlled the ministry buildings, it was recognized by other states, its predecessor had handed it all the paraphernalia of authority.

Yet in reality the whole state machine had collapsed. The army had disintegrated. Where the government retained some authority, that was because of rank-and-file loyalty to the occasional popular officer. The civil police had merged with the groups of freedom fighters or were waiting for quieter times. The Political Police had fled like rats to their holes, where they hid or fought desperate and brutal rearguard actions, hoping that the upsurge of hatred and vengeance would pass. The propaganda organs of the state had by and large been taken over by their production staffs, who owed allegiance to themselves alone, or had been seized by the new-born revolutionary councils.

Everywhere in the localities, on the streets, in the factories, it was not the old state apparatus but the new revolutionary councils that could get things done. A factory that must work? Ask the council. Food to be obtained? See the council. The danger of disorder? The council will prevent trouble.

Without a stable or meaningful apparatus, the government had only one weapon: the personal prestige of Imre Nagy. There was, of course, one other power in the land – the Russian army. But for the government to have called on the Russians to smash popular resistance would have been to set back the economy, to contradict the very motives behind the reform programme and finally to destroy whatever hope Nagy's supporters had of lessening Hungarian dependence on the Russians.

The government preferred – at least from the third day of the insurrection – to try to bring the movement under its control by peaceful means. If Nagy's physical weapons were few, his ideological armoury was quite well stocked.

Every revolution is characterized by a second peculiar contradiction that complements that of dual power. The same people who engage in the most revolutionary acts on the streets or in the factories also continue to bend the knee to old ideas. At first only a few daring individuals conceive of overthrowing the old order completely. Most still look upwards, even when they are creating a new power of their own below. Habits of deference, inculcated since birth, are not removed overnight. Many of the insurrectionaries try to create a revolution that still bows before established authority.

In Hungary a transitory accord between the two sources of power was possible. On the one side the government, which had only just emerged victorious from a bitter oppositional struggle and wanting to carry through some reforms; it was willing to promise more in order to placate popular insurgency. On the other, the masses, only just beginning to move after years of dormancy, had not yet shaken past habits from their minds. For a time each side's image of the future seemed to coincide with the other's.

This harmonious appearance of unity was seen first on 23 October. For a time Nagy served to represent everything the mobilizing masses stood for. Yet once Nagy was in the government the illusion of harmony faded away. As the Hungarian student paper *Egyetemi Ifjusag* put it on 29 October:

> On Tuesday evening . . . the entire country demanded Imre
> Nagy . . . the entire Hungarian people trusted Imre Nagy
> . . . Since then this confidence has weakened day by day.
> Today the entire population is by no means behind Imre
> Nagy; people feel disappointed in him.[51]

Concessions . . .

To re-establish this superficial spirit of harmony the government had to somehow satisfy insurgent demands. Hence the beginning of Soviet troop withdrawals, the establishment of a coalition government, the promises of free elections. Further similar measures were taken in the days following the cessation of fighting. Pal Maleter, the most popular of the army officers to join the insurrection, was made Minister of Defence. Representatives of the old parties were given additional portfolios. The government itself approved the orderly arrest of former AVH men.

These measures, however, were not sufficient. The various councils continued to enunciate their objections to government policy. And they began to co-ordinate their efforts in order to increase their effectiveness.

Already the Revolutionary Council in Gyor had been under pressure from demonstrators to establish a counter-government. Only the announcement of the governmental changes on 30 October reduced this pressure. Nevertheless later that day, when 400 delegates from right across western Hungary met in Gyor to form the 'Transdanubian Revolutionary Committee', 'the majority decided to continue the strike until the government had satisfied the revolutionary demands ... The Transdanubian National Council will not recognize the government unless these demands are satisfied'.[52] The major unsatisfied demand was for the proclamation of Hungarian neutrality. But, significantly, there was reference to the setting up of a 'Central National Council, to approve the appointment of army officers pending general elections'. In Budapest, on the other hand, 'prior to 4 November (i.e. prior to the second Russian intervention) the idea of a Central Workers' Committee never arose'.[53]

But the individual workers' councils did have to debate whether or not to end the strike. Many continued to insist that they would not start work until there was a complete withdrawal of Soviet troops. Although the fighting had ended, the government's authority was not restored.

One incident illustrates this. The insurgent group led by Dudas was far from satisfied with the new government. Dudas's chief demand was for representation for the revolutionary forces in the government. Cynical commentators have suggested he meant representation for himself, but whatever the case, when negotiations with Nagy failed, his group, which had already seized control of the *Szabad Nep* offices and obstructed its publication, attempted to seize the Foreign Ministry building on 2 November. This putsch ended with Dudas being taken into custody for a couple of hours. The incident reveals the extent to which the government still did not govern but was at the mercy of the unco-ordinated efforts of different insurgent groups.

On 1 November, Nagy made the final concession. He proclaimed Hungarian neutrality, and announced his government's intention of leaving the Warsaw Pact. He commenced the formation of a unified National Guard, based upon various army units, insurgent groups and sections of the civil police. This took over the maintenance of order in Budapest, arrested AVH men, prevented looting, but also 'cleaned up' and disarmed the remaining hostile insurgents.

The government radio in Budapest and the insurgent radio at Gyor announced that they had now agreed to transmit identical programmes. They stated:

The fact that the two radio stations, which were developing in opposite direction for some time, have found each other is an expression of national unity. Today Budapest and the provinces, the people and the government, want the same thing.

The government and the councils between them were running the country. That was the secret behind the restoration of 'order'. The 'legitimate' national power and the effective local power were once again complementing one another. The issues dividing them seemed to vanish. Ministers, including hardened Communists like Kadar, praised the councils and the insurrection on the radio, while the councils expressed full approval for the government.

Yet, as in the early hours of the insurgent movement, the appearance of harmony was illusory. The long term political and social questions had not been settled. It was not yet decided who would control the factories: the workers through a national system of delegated councils making the major economic decisions and seeing to their implementation; or a central bureaucracy, allowing workers' councils to 'participate' in the execution of its plans at the local level. It was still undecided, too, what the content of political life would be. Was it to be a choice every so many years between a variety of the old parties with similar programmes, or was it to be a real debate over the direction of society involving the mass of the working population?

The essential question was hardly even mentioned yet: would the councils control the government, or would the government control the councils?

Such questions were hardly likely to be asked, let alone answered, in the space of a few days. The mass of workers were still unsure of themselves, grappling with ideas, trying to figure out what they wanted and how to get it. In the Russia of 1917 it had taken eight months for the workers' and soldiers' councils to resolve to concentrate power into their own hands. In Spain in 1936 it had taken a similar time for the Republican government and its allies to remove power from the armed masses.[54] The Hungarians were not to have two weeks, let alone eight months, in which to resolve the issue.

Yet some people, even if they were not yet fully conscious of the problem, were aware of some of its aspects. Many of the young workers and students were acutely suspicious of the activities of the old parties, and the sort of state they wanted. They felt that the councils that had been created in the insurrection represented a new type of self-government, which the emergence of the parties could only disrupt. Such feelings were, as yet, far from generalized. Other workers felt that the councils should only run the factories, with a freely elected national assembly dominating political life.

At this time the most advanced demands as regards the functions of the councils were coming not from Budapest but from Miskolc. The president of the National Council there outlined demands put to Nagy, and alongside calls for the withdrawal of Russian troops and for an economic programme to satisfy the demands of workers, students, miners and soldiers, was the proposal that:

> The government must propose the formation of a Revolutionary National Council, based upon the workers' councils of the various departments and Budapest, and composed of democratically elected delegates from them. At the same time the old parliament must be dissolved.[55]

Betrayal

Order was emerging from the insurrection. But it was an order in which many questions were still undecided, and it was an order, too, that was far from satisfactory to those who had ruled Hungary for the previous eight years. The concessions made by the government seemed to make safe bureaucratic rule, even in the 'reformed' manner, a more-and-more distant prospect. The reformers, the former inner-party opposition, no longer possessed a unified and clear perspective on the future. Some were willing to rely on their own prestige as a guarantee that they would be able to copy Gomulka in re-establishing control, as well as achieving a degree of national independence from the Russians. To others, however, this seemed an increasingly unlikely prospect. They wondered whether perhaps they should not risk ending their bid for national autonomy and put their faith in Russian troops.

On Thursday 1 November Kadar declared, on Radio Kossuth, 'In their glorious uprising our people have shaken off the Rakosi regime.' That evening, however, Kadar and his associate Munnich disappeared from Budapest. When he returned, three days later, it was with talk of the 'terrible situation our fatherland has been driven to by those counter-revolutionary elements'.[56]

Russian troops had been withdrawn from Budapest on the Wednesday evening. But the propaganda war against the 'counter-revolution' continued in the official Communist press of Russia and Eastern Europe, apart from Poland and Yugoslavia. And suspicious troop movements also continued. Some battle-scarred and demoralized Russian units were leaving the country; others were moving in to replace them. Although the Russian leaders gave assurances that they were merely in transit, the new detachments were conveniently placed at key points, cutting Budapest off from the provincial centres. The Nagy government began to complain, through official communiqués and at the United Nations, of violations of Hungary's new-found neutrality.

On the Saturday, 3 November, the Russians invited the government to send a delegation to negotiate the terms for a full withdrawal. Maleter led the Hungarian military delegation in the talks, which seemed to be proceeding satisfactorily through the afternoon and evening. Then, late at night, while Budapest slept, Russian secret police officers interrupted the discussions, arrested the Hungarian delegation and hauled them away to prison.

The Counter-Revolution

The next day, Sunday, the whole of Budapest was awakened by the sound of artillery fire on the outskirts of the city. Russian tanks were pouring in, concentrating around insurgent strongpoints like the Killian barracks and the Corvin theatre. These they shelled mercilessly. Government offices, communication points like the radio station and the Hungarian News Agency office, the parliament buildings where Nagy was situated were all surrounded.

At 5.30 Nagy spoke on the radio:

Today at daybreak Soviet forces started an attack against our capital, obviously with the intention of overthrowing the legal Hungarian democratic government. Our troops are fighting. The government is in its place.

Thirty minutes later he appealed to the members of the military delegation negotiating with the Russians to return to organize resistance. No one yet knew of their arrest and imprisonment.

The Russians moved with speed and efficiency. Within hours the strategic points in the capital were in their hands. In the provinces they were also moving in for the kill. Nagy and other ministers fled to the Yugoslav embassy for sanctuary.* But if the 'reform' government had collapsed, popular resistance certainly had not.

The Hungarian people fought back with rifles and pistols, with the occasional light machine-gun, and above all with petrol bombs. The workers of the great industrial complexes were at the centre of the resistance. Kadar had called his quisling regime a 'Revolutionary Workers' and Peasants' Government' but the revolutionary workers proved his lie. In Csepel, in Ujpest, in Pecs, in Miskolc, and above all in Dunapentele they took to the streets to defend their gains. Those who could not fight physically waged battle with a general strike.

In Csepel posters poured scorn on Moscow's lies: 'The forty thousand aristocrats and fascists of the Csepel works strike on.'

The Russian troops met the armed resistance with barbarous fury. The same inhuman savagery that put down the Paris Commune in 1871, that crushed Bela Kun's regime in 1919, and that laid Warsaw waste in 1944 was now seen on the streets of Budapest.

The Kremlin did not dare let its troops take on the combatants, rifle against rifle. Their infantrymen might be contaminated by strange ideas, might see that those opposing them were workers like themselves, not fascists and western spies. Instead any building that might harbour resistance was systematically bombarded from sealed tanks. In the process whole areas of the working-class districts were reduced to rubble. Twenty thousand or more people died.

But still armed resistance was not crushed. Although the Russians had secured most of Budapest by the evening, in the centre of the city small groups of national guards, army personnel and freedom fighters held out for three days. In the working-class eighth district of Budapest, in the industrial belt on the outskirts of the city, and in the industrial centres of the provinces fighting was still going on a

*Nineteen days later Kadar gave the Yugoslav ambassador a guarantee of safe conduct for Nagy and his co-ministers whenever they wanted to leave the embassy. They got into a bus to leave. A few hundred yards from the embassy members of the political police took over the buses. The government issued an announcement that Nagy had 'requested to be taken to Rumania'. Eighteen months later the Kadar government announced that Imre Nagy, Pal Maleter, Jozsef Szilagyi and Miklos Gimes had been executed.

week later. At Dunapentele shelling by tanks had to be supplemented by aerial bombardment.

When the continuous onslaught of fire and destruction forced the towns into military submission, groups of workers, occasionally supplemented by Russian deserters, took to the hills. In the Mecsel mountains near Pecs and Komlo miners were still fighting back in the first week of December.

One by one the radio stations fell to the Russian invaders, making last desperate calls for help before closing down. Appeals went out to the United Nations, which did nothing but pass fine resolutions and later produce an interesting report, and to the western powers, who also did nothing but make propaganda speeches. The Hungarians called for assistance in vain: the western leaders had an agreement with the Russians that went back to 1945. Already, in the early days of the revolution 'the state department sent messages of reassurance to the Kremlin through Marshall Tito denying any intention of exploiting the conflict against Soviet interests . . .'[57] Eisenhower made his position clear in a speech a week later: 'We have never urged or argued for any kind of armed revolt . . . the US does not now and never has advocated open rebellion by an undefended people . . .'[58]

If the freedom fighters had some illusions in the western powers, the western powers had no illusions in them. They knew that the idea of a society ruled neither by capitalists nor by bureaucrats, a society democratically run from below by workers' councils – the idea for which the freedom fighters were dying – was as dangerous to monopoly capitalist rule as to its state capitalist rival.

The Second Period of Dual Power

The Russians' military power gave them territorial control over Hungary. But they still did not control the Hungarians. The workers could no longer fight back on the streets, so they fought back with the strike weapon. Everywhere work stopped from the first day of the fighting; nowhere did it show any signs of restarting. There followed one of the most prolonged and most solid general strikes in working-class history.

Kadar's government controlled the government buildings, but that was all. Its functionaries hardly dared walk in the streets without

Russian escorts. They certainly did not run the country. Industrial production had stopped, there was no electricity, food was in short supply, the telephone networks and the post office could only function when their workers wanted them to.

Yet everyday social life had to continue. To some degree, at least, society must be co-ordinated. The official government could not do it, and the task of necessity devolved to a large extent upon the workers' councils.

One of the leading workers' council delegates describes the situation:

> The workers saw that there was complete confusion, production had completely stopped and even maintenance work was forgotten and, therefore, the workers of the large industrial plants attempted to work out regional co-operation. When we heard that the workers' councils of the neighbouring district had met, we too organized a meeting and this is how the district workers' councils were formed. Co-operation made things easier, we could exchange information and harmonize our resolutions. We all wanted the same thing so why should we have passed conflicting resolutions? And because we all opposed the new government we felt that a large organization would wield greater power.
> The workers felt that something had to be done; the country had no responsible leaders. True, there were about 200,000 Russian troops in the country and there was also the Kadar government, but Kadar was master only in the parliament building . . . Owing to the senseless actions of the Russians many people had become homeless. These had to be helped. Social assistance also required co-operation. True, the district workers' councils discussed their resolutions but, as the tasks accumulated, it became from hour to hour more urgent that the representatives of all Budapest industrial plants should get together.[59]

On 12 November, the workers' council at Ujpest put out a call to the factory and district councils for an all-Budapest meeting the next day. As delegates converged on the advertized meeting place, they were met by Ujpest workers and led elsewhere. The members of the Ujpest council had been arrested the night before.

> We held our first meeting with the representatives of the most important industrial plants. It was a common aspira-

tion that there should be a central workers' council to organize the work of the district and factory councils, but we came to no agreement how this was to be achieved. This occurred on 14 November at four o'clock in the afternoon. Sandor Bali, representative of the Belojannis Works, rose and told the meeting that he and representatives of the Hungarian Steel Works, the Csepel Vegetable Oil factory and the Csepel Iron Works had just come from Parliament, where they had talked to Kadar and had handed over their demands. It has to be pointed out here that all the resolutions from the factory and district councils were almost identical. They all demanded the withdrawal of Soviet troops from Budapest and the entire country, free elections, a multi-party system, socialist ownership of the industries, the maintenance of workers' councils, the restoration of democratic trade unions – and, naturally, all the demands of the revolution: the right to strike and to assemble, freedom of the press and religion, etc. It was interesting that, though the participants of this meeting all came from different places, their demands were as much alike as if they had previously discussed them. True, they were all sent by workers, and workers everywhere demanded the same things. There were delegates also from the countryside who said that workers' councils had been formed everywhere as soon as they learned about the Budapest initiative.

When Bali told the meeting that they had informed Kadar of their demands everyone was glad that the government was now familiar with the resolutions of the workers, but they agreed it was a pity that the initiative had not come from a representative central body, because it would have carried greater weight. The meeting decided that the central body to be created would begin its work on the basis of the above-mentioned demands.[60]

The delegates confronted one major problem. Despite the general strike, the workers did not have the power to enforce the demands they had stood for before 4 November. Any hope of a complete victory was gone, and all they could do now was to aim at squeezing concessions. Kadar made this very clear by refusing even to receive memoranda from workers' councils with the invariable beginning, 'We refuse to recognize the Kadar government'. So, after much discussion, it was agreed to support the position of Belojannis works:

We do not officially recognize the Kadar government but we are ready to negotiate with them because, whether we recognize them or not, they are the de facto masters of the country. They give the orders, at least on paper. However, we refuse to recognize it as a government elected by the people. The strike cannot be kept up because the workers have no reserves. Therefore we propose to the Kadar government that we resume work on Monday 19 November, if the government guarantees that it will begin prompt negotiations with the Russians concerning the withdrawal of the Russian troops and if it guarantees that Imre Nagy will be brought back into the government.[61]

The newly constituted Greater Budapest Central Workers' Council began work from the Transport Union Headquarters. Immediately it became the central focus for all the workers in the capital.

It immediately became evident (a delegate wrote), that the population had great confidence in us. They sought our help in the solution of all their problems and worries. The government was simply ignored; everyone who had a problem to settle came to us. Therefore dealing with people's more or less serious problems became one of our important daily tasks. We helped in the distribution of food, clothing and medical consignments arriving from abroad, exposed and put an end to abuses etc.[62]

In order to try and stop the deportation of thousands of former insurgents to Russia, the Council began direct negotiations with the occupying authorities.

The Council's most important decisions had to be ratified at mass meetings in the factories. Often those decisions – particularly those involving the 'de facto' recognition of Kadar and ending the strike – were sharply questioned. Because the council was made up of direct representatives of the workers in the factories in the various districts, disagreements in the factories were reflected in the council's meetings. A small minority of its members were expelled for not representing their constituents' views and for arguing for an unconditional end to the strike.

Delegates from the council tried to negotiate with Kadar and press their views on him. He gave the impression of being prepared to give ground, and often of agreeing with them. He said that he too would like to speak to Nagy, only Nagy was in the Yugoslav embassy – 'persuade him to come out'. He said he had invited other, non-Communist politicians to join the government. Generally, Kadar tried to give the impression that he was not really responsible for the repression. 'You must help me. Understand that I stand alone among all these Stalinists.'[63] Yet he made no concessions to the real demands of the Council. Although his government said it was in favour of councils in the factories, it made it clear that their functions should be severely restricted. He strenuously opposed the continuance of the power of the councils in the railways, the post office and ministries. He objected to the workers democratically replacing certain former Council delegates, and he rejected outright the Council's request for its own daily press organ.[64]

In reality, Kadar felt that despite the overwhelming Russian presence, he would do best to avoid taking on the Budapest working class in a frontal battle in the factories. He tried to placate their leaders, to find ways to influence their position, so as to restore normal economic life, in the hope that he could then gradually subordinate the councils to bureaucratic control.

The Council, however, was a kind of institution Kadar had never before encountered – one genuinely subject to democracy from below. It could not easily be contained or corrupted.

Kadar's approach did, however, have certain advantages for the Council. For a time it was able to function almost legally. Its members received passes from the Russians enabling them to move about Budapest. It could negotiate over particular issues with either the Russians or Kadar.

Above all it could begin to prepare the ground for the creation of a national organ to represent the working class. A conference of delegates from workers' councils throughout the country was called for 21 November. At first Kadar and the Soviet authorities seemed prepared to tolerate this. A guard of unarmed Csepel workers was organized by the Central Council to keep order. But:

> At eight o'clock the Soviet troops arrived . . . There was heavy artillery, tanks, automobiles, all in all, approximately four hundred units. Machine-gunners armed to the teeth, tanks ready to fire. They surrounded the stadium and blocked the streets leading to it. We set out towards the MEMOSZ headquarters but left a few men behind to watch out for the arrival of the provincial delegates. The Budapest delegates had not been invited because the factories were all represented by the district Councils. But we had invited the representatives of all the large mines and factories of Debrecen, Veszprem, Inota, Mohacs, Pecs,

Dunapentele, etc. etc. Hungarian industry was represented in full. The provincial delegates had also been elected democratically. They were all supplied with proper credentials. They were full of indignation when they arrived. They said that they were not at work but we were, that we had betrayed and cheated them. The industrial plants outside Budapest were still striking and they had even flooded the mines at Tatabanya.

We took them along to the MEMOSZ headquarters but couldn't get in because we were held up by the pupils of the Zrinyi Military Academy sitting behind machine-guns. There was nothing else to do but to go back to the Akacfa Street headquarters of the Central Workers' Council. But only the members of the Central Council, no-one else. However, as we approached the building, we were met by the miners who demanded admittance or else they would start trouble. They said the situation was untenable; we saw now that it was impossible to negotiate with men like Kadar: he sent tanks against us; there was nothing left for us but to continue the strike.

The Budapest workers' representatives tried to explain to those from the countryside why we had stopped the strikes. They wouldn't listen. At last the representative of Gyor came over to our side and told the others to try and understand our motives.

We argued that it was easy in a small town or village where everyone knew everyone else, to keep each other informed of what was going on. There, if something happens, everybody knows about it within half an hour. Budapest, on the other hand, has one and a half million inhabitants. If we continued to strike, we would lose all contact with the workers and, moreover, we had to maintain contact also with the countryside.

By nine o'clock in the evening they admitted that we were right. We were the best of friends. We came to the conclusion that if we were to create a National Workers' Council now, we would provoke fate, and not only fate but also the Soviet tanks. We decided to keep the Central Council because that was a legal organization accepted by the government and keep in touch – illegally – with the provincial councils through liaison men. We would always inform them of our resolutions and they could decide whether they approved or not. We would always consult them about everything.

Thus, an illegal National Council came into being, but, in name, it remained the Central Workers' Council of Budapest to the very end.[65]

Our contact with industrial centres throughout the country had become permanent and close. The delegates of Veszprem, Pecs, Tatabanya, Komlo, Salgotarjan, and Miskolc, and those of the region beyond the river Tisza and the region between the Tisza and the Danube, resided in Budapest. Every day the Central Workers' Council received the visit of 30-40 provincial delegates who were placed with the various factories for board and lodging, and who maintained contact with their organizations by telephone or by messages sent by railway workers.[66]

In Budapest the Council had proved that it led the working class: it alone had been able to persuade people to return to work on 19 November. Now, in protest at the prevention of the national meeting, it was able to call the whole of Budapest to a halt for forty-eight hours. Kadar's tanks could not keep the factories open.

The following statement gave an account of the Council's role after its first week of existence:

APPEAL OF THE CENTRAL WORKERS' COUNCIL
OF GREATER BUDAPEST TO ALL FACTORY,
DISTRICT AND COUNTY COUNCILS

FELLOW WORKERS!

The Central Workers' Council, democratically elected by the Budapest industries and districts, turns to you with information and an appeal in order that we might make our ranks stronger and more united.

As you know, the Central Workers' Council of Greater Budapest was created on 14 November on the initiative of the large industries in order to co-ordinate the work of the workers' councils in the factories and represent our common demands. Since that time the Central Workers' Council has put forward our demands uncompromisingly before various forums and, although the results achieved until now are far from satisfactory, we may say that we have never, in the course of our negotiations, deviated from the aims and basic demands of the glorious national revolution of 23 October.

As so often before, we again declare that we have our mandate from the working class and that, true to our trust, we shall defend our factories and our fatherland from capitalist and feudal restoration, if necessary at the cost of our lives. At the same time, however, we want to build our social and economic system independently, in the Hungarian way, and we shall not relinquish the aims of the revolution. We consider work to be the basis of society. We are workers; we want to work. It was this aim that guided us when, on 21 November, we summoned the representatives of the country and rural districts to the sports stadium at Budapest to discuss, in the frame of a national conference of workers' councils, our most important problems, the question of the resumption of work.

The government prevented us from holding this well-meaning conference, although we had previously informed the government of its purpose and had invited a representative of the government to the meeting. This unexpected measure embittered the situation. When the government intervention became known, the Budapest factories and public transportation immediately stopped work and started a protest strike.

However, in spite of the government's intervention, we arranged a meeting with the provincial delegates. We adopted a resolution saying that throughout the country *after* the 48 hour protest strike, we would be ready to resume work while reserving for ourselves the right to strike, if the government were willing to recognize the National Workers' Council as the only negotiating organ of the working class and were ready to continue negotiations immediately concerning the demands formulated on 14 November, containing the basic revolutionary aims. On this basis our committee, including a member of the miners' delegation from Pecskomlo, had a talk with the Prime Minister, Janos Kadar, during the night of 22 November.

On the morning of the 23rd, a member of our delegation, Jozsef Balazs, communicated the outcome of the talk. The essence of the communication was that the Prime Minister recognized the Central Workers' Council of Greater Budapest as an authorized negotiating partner and promised to submit to the Council of Ministers the further demands of the Central Workers' Council of Greater Budapest relating to the jurisdiction of the workers' councils, at the same time making it possible for us to inform the workers of the results of further talks with the government. We have to admit that this is very little. Nevertheless, we resolved to resume work because in making this decision we considered *solely and exclusively* the interests of the people. We shall not permit ourselves to be deceived. We are convinced that we shall win, and therefore, we are careful not to pass resolutions detrimental to ourselves.

On 23 November the news was broadcast to the world that, after reaching an agreement with the Hungarian government and receiving satisfactory guarantees, Imre Nagy and other public personalities left the premises of the Yugoslav Embassy in Budapest. On the same day, moreover, Radio Budapest reported that Imre Nagy and the persons who had been with him at the Yugoslav Embassy had asked the Rumanian People's Republic for asylum. As the news created extraordinary uncertainty among the workers, the Central Workers' Council of Greater Budapest dispatched a committee to contact the Hungarian government, the Soviet military command and the Rumanian Embassy to obtain information concerning Imre Nagy's whereabouts, and in possession of that information, to demand that they should be given an opportunity to speak to him personally.

Although it is indubitable that this important development had increased our lack of confidence in the government, we decided, exclusively in the interest of the people, as we said before, to resume work. At the same time, we asked all industrial plants in the country to weigh the happenings thoroughly and join us in our appeal.

The factories are in our hands, the hands of the workers' councils, but to increase our strength further and to make possible a common stand on behalf of common measures, we hold the following tasks to be the most important:

1. In every district and county where district or county workers' councils have not yet been created such organs should immediately be elected democratically from below. To this end, large industries – particularly those in county seats – should initiate the creation of central councils.

2. Each district and county central council should immediately establish contact with the Central Workers' Council of Greater Budapest (Budapest, Akacfa utca 15-17. Tel. 422-130). The chairman of the Central Council is Sandor Racz, chairman of the workers' council in the Standard (Belojannis) Works; his deputy is Gyorgy Kalocsai, delegate of the workers' council of the Csepel Vegetable Oil Factory, and his secretary is Istvan Babai, chairman of the workers' council of the Budapest Tramways.

An authorized delegate of the county workers' council should come personally to Budapest and contact the Secretariat of the Central Workers' Council of Greater Budapest to establish relations and discuss the pressing problems.

3. One of the most important tasks of the factory workers' councils, apart from the organization of work, is the urgent election of permanent workers' councils. At these elections we must fight as vigorously against Rakosi tyranny as against any attempt at a capitalistic restoration.

We want honest, clean-living Hungarian workers with clean hands in the councils! The workers must be guaranteed at least a two-thirds majority in the councils. As far as the jurisdiction of the councils is concerned we cannot agree with the decree issued by the Praesidium bearing on this subject. We insist that there should be workers' councils for the public transport workers, railways, tramways, bus depots and everywhere where workers desire it. In the course of negotiations on 26 November, the Prime Minister promised to submit our views to the Council of Ministers. Until then we request the workers' councils already constituted in these places to carry on their activities. We also disagree with the resolutions of the Praesidium concerning the jurisdiction of the revolutionary committees in the ministries and in other high places of authority. We consider necessary a much wider jurisdiction for the revolutionary councils than at present. With regard to managers, our position is that managers should be chosen by the workers' councils on the basis of competition and the filling of these positions must not be made contingent upon approval by a minister or a ministry. We call on the workers' councils to fight with all their energy for the realization of their position, but not to accept discredited, arrogant men who have lost touch with the people and were appointed from above and to beware of unreliable, careerist elements.

4. Furthermore, it is very important that the elections of the new factory committees should be taken in hand by the representatives of the genuine will of the working class, the workers' councils. The new 'free trade unions' springing up like mushrooms are trying to gain popularity by demanding maximum wage increases. However, in these 'free trade unions', discredited persons of the Rakosi era and not elected representatives of the working people play a leading role. The trade unions are now trying to pretend that the creation of the workers' councils was a result of their struggles. Needless to say, this, to speak freely, does not correspond with the truth; it was the workers alone who fought for the workers' councils and the trade unions often hindered, instead of helping, the workers' councils in their struggles.

Our opinion is that there is a real need for agencies representing interests, for trade unions, and for factory committees, but only such as have been democratically elected from below and in which honest representatives of the working class are the leaders. This is why it is so important that, after the definitive constitution of the workers' councils, factory committee elections should take place under completely democratic conditions so that their composition should be a guarantee for the realization of the aims of the revolution.

We are against retaining the institution of exempted trade union functionaries. We consider the work of the factory committee as well as that of the workers' council social work.

We do not wish to become exploiters of the revolution and we shall not suffer others to become such.

We want trade union membership to be voluntary, all the more so as this will prevent the trade unions from becoming bureaucratic and losing touch with the people.

We protest against the attitude of the newly formed 'free trade unions' which are ready to accept the workers' councils merely as economic organs. We declare that in Hungary today the workers' councils represent the real interests of the working class, that there is no stronger political power in the country today than the power of the workers' councils and that we must concentrate all our forces on strengthening the power of the workers.

5. The district and county workers' councils should at once establish contact with the distribution centre of the Red Cross and should send their representatives to headquarters in order to ensure just distribution on a social basis. It is important to have an expert among those delegated.

6. The district and county workers' councils should appoint social control organs to keep an eye on prices in the markets and shops. Social inspectors should regularly visit sales premises and report possible abuses to the proper authorities, after exposing the perpetrator to public contempt.

7. The district and county councils should make every effort to keep public opinion informed; if there is an opportunity, they should demand space in the local press and constantly inform the workers of the factories and other industrial enterprises of the true situation. To this end, the central councils in large plants should also make certain that our appeal reaches every workshop. At our repeated request the Prime Minister has promised to submit our demand for a daily press organ to the meeting of the Council of Ministers on the 27th inst. If this request is approved, the problem of information will also be solved.

In conclusion, it is necessary today that the workers' councils should serve the cause of the national revolution of

23 October in complete unity even in the resumption of work. We took the first step; now it is up to the government, but it will take several months. During that time we must remain vigilant because many discredited members of the Rakosi-Gero clique are trying to fish in troubled waters and bring about a restoration of their rule. We are increasing in strength every day. Our honest writers, who did such excellent work in the preparation of the revolution, have joined with us and are with us; we are supported by the actors, artists, musicians, and the Revolutionary Council of the Hungarian Intellectuals embracing every organization of the intellectuals. As a result of our struggles we are achieving a hitherto unknown national unity in which every honest Hungarian is with us. Let us come even closer together, let us keep in close contact with one another, we workers' councils, and fight unitedly with true revolutionary vigilance for our aims, an independent, democratic, socialist Hungary built according to our national character.

Budapest, 21 November 1956

> The Central Workers' Council
> of Greater Budapest.[67]

The co-existence of the Council and the Kadar government could not last, for they represented diametrically opposed forces. With every new day, Kadar took a further step towards creating a new state apparatus ; every day the working class felt more acutely the consequences of its military defeat. However long the workers struck, they did not seem able to shake the Russians. The shortages of food, of power and basic materials were increasingly hurting the workers themselves.

The Central Council was forced from the beginning to recognize the shifting balance of power. All the heroism in the world would not drive out 3000 Russian tanks and 200,000 troops. It was forced to try bargaining with Kadar's government, which was still willing to say flattering things about the Council ('I must say that the comrades who work in the Council have given us valuable support in the task of restoring order and discipline and of resuming productive . . .'[68]). Although Kadar was destroying the revolution, he also had somehow to get production going – and productive life was under the control of the councils. Not only the factories, but the normal telephone and postal services, the power stations and railways, could only be run with the consent of the workers themselves.

A reporter for *The Observer* recognized this:

> A fantastic aspect of the situation is that although the general strike is in being and there is no centrally-organized industry, the workers are nevertheless taking it upon themselves to keep essential services going, for purposes which they themselves determine and support. Workers' councils in industrial districts have undertaken the distribution of essential goods and food to the population, in order to keep them alive. The coal miners are making daily allocations of just sufficient coal to keep the power stations going and supply the hospitals in Budapest and other large towns. Railwaymen organize trains to go to approved destinations for approved purposes . . .[69]

It is no wonder that the Council had little difficulty in organizing national communications.

The first order of the Soviet Command issued on 6 November had insisted that 'Any person attempting to prevent them (workers) from going back to work will be arrested'. So far the only effect of the order was to produce further periodic skirmishes between troops and workers in the industrial areas. But while guns could drive the workers to the factories they could not make them work.

Kadar was willing to satisfy certain workers' grievances. Massive wage increases were granted – despite the deplorable state production was in. Many workers were even paid for the period of the general strike. By January 1957 overall wages were 22 per cent higher than a year before.[70] But on one thing Kadar was adamant: there could be no concessions that weakened the newly created apparatus's monopoly of power.

However, even in this area, Kadar had to give the impression of considering concessions. His government's programme (broadcast on 4 November) declared that:

> on the basis of the broadcast, workers' democracy, workers' management should be realized in all factories and enterprises . . . Democratic elections will be guaranteed in all existing administrative bodies and revolutionary councils.[71]

As long as the strike remained a real weapon in the Central Council's hands (until the last week in November) Kadar thought it worth while to carry on the pretence of negotiations. There was even a broadcast discussion between Council members and government ministers. For the government, Apro insisted that there must be a return to work of white and blue collar workers 'in the ministries, national offices and national concerns . . .'

The workers replied through a delegate from the Ganz factory in Csepel: 'A fortnight ago we conducted fairly thorough discussions with the government on this matter . . . We were given the assurance that the demands of the workers would be met. Up to the present, no steps have been taken in this matter . . .' Another delegate added his voice: 'The ministers now seem to spend their time receiving delegations, and the delegations leave these meetings without having achieved any results.'[72]

Perhaps at this point Kadar still hoped to be able to inveigle the workers' councils into accepting a bureaucratic framework for their activities, within which their power would be destroyed only gradually, over a period of months – as was to happen in Poland. Certainly some statements from workers' council leaders suggested that they thought the councils could survive if their powers were limited to the economic sphere. Thus, in the radio broadcast referred to above, Sandor Bali declared:

> The Hungarian working class developed these workers'
> councils quite spontaneously . . . We are well aware that
> they cannot be political organizations. We are fully aware
> of the need for a political party and trade unions . . . We
> know the workers' councils will become organs directing
> the country's economy. That is exactly what we want them
> to be. We do not want to commit the same mistake as the
> party did in the past, when it was at the same time master
> of both the country and of the factories and also the
> organization which represented the interests of the work-
> ers . . . If we commit this mistake we shall be where we
> were in the past.[73]

Bali's speech is witness to a confusion of ideas here. The Central Workers' Council, whether it liked it or not, was a political body. It was speaking for society generally, and specifically for the working class, against its official rulers. By trying to organize a de facto national council it was constituting itself as an alternative government. Nor could it consider its long term economic concerns as 'non-political'. Any government's political decisions are intimately connected with the economic questions that affect workers on the factory floor. For example, it was Rakosi's *political* decision to speed up heavy industrial construction that forced down wages, led to speed-up in the factories, and necessitated an intensification of bureaucratic terror. If the workers' councils did not control such 'political' decisions, they would thereby be refusing to concern themselves with matters of crucial importance to their constituents and would as a result necessarily degenerate as their support declined.

The words of the delegates are reminiscent of the attitudes of many of the representatives in the Russian Soviets of February 1917 or in the German workers' councils of 1918-19. They were acting to organize the working-class, and behind it all the oppressed sections of society, against the old order, yet often they wanted to deny in words what they were doing in practice. There was, however, one difference. In both Russia and Germany there had been, from the start, organized minorities – albeit at first small minorities – possessed of a political analysis that led them to demand 'All Power to the Workers' Councils'. In Hungary, however, one result of eight years of Stalinism was the practical non-existence of any such organized minority prior to the revolution.

The workers' councils continued to behave, in practice, as political bodies. They constituted the principal opposition to Kadar's drive to monopolize all power in his own hands. Thus the Central Council organized a protest demonstration of several thousand women on 5 December. Nor did the duplicated bulletins written by the Central Council and reproduced in every factory confine themselves to purely economic issues. One issue, for instance, contained declarations from peasant councils in the Borsod area and from the Alliance of Hungarian Writers. It also complained that old trade-union leaders were being reappointed by the government, while the 'people only recognize as truly free trade unions those with leaders freely elected from below'.[74]

Some of the Council's leaders may possibly have thought they could coexist, under protest, with Kadar, but Kadar knew he could not coexist with them. On 6 December an attempt was made to arrest two of the Council's leaders, Sandor Racz and Sandor Bali, while they were at work. Only the physical resistance of their fellow workers in the Belojannis factory kept them at liberty.

The Central Council responded with a statement which is worth reproducing here:

The Central Workers' Council of Greater Budapest is deeply aware of the heavy responsibility it bears in the grave circumstances our country is going through.

The workers of Budapest democratically elected us. The delegates from the departments as well as from the industrial centres have joined with us.

Our desire is that of the Hungarian workers and of the entire people: well-being, life without fear, and independence, with power firmly in the hands of the Hungarian workers and peasants.

We know that the working class is the strongest force capable of ensuring the creation and maintenance of such a power.

To this end we wished from the beginning for a peaceful outcome and took the initiative in negotiating with Janos Kadar, the Chairman of the Council of Ministers. At the same time we have kept away from all those who have incited the Hungarian people to armed or terrorist actions so as to disturb order.

We have to state that the negotiations have not produced the desired results. While workers in factories throughout the country, putting their faith in us, by and large restarted work, provocations have continually occurred in various places that have entailed the cessation of work.

We believed that following the return to work legal order would be established more and more, that the workers' councils in the factories, the mines, and the public utilities would have sufficient strength to put a stop to all attempts at provocation, from whichever source they came.

It is with profound regret that we state that in fact this did not happen.

In our opinion, Janos Kadar, the Chairman of the Council of Ministers, did make efforts to put the life of the country along a normal course. However, it seems to us that he does not have the power necessary to remove people who gravitate around him and are so detested by the working people. These men deliberately mislead him as to the desires and feeling of the people. The same men have reintegrated into the security service individuals compromised in the past. From above, they prevent the purging of the state apparatus. Finally, they put obstacles in front of those men of goodwill in the government and millions of the Hungarian masses finding a common road towards a favourable outcome.

We know wery well that in the case of free elections all such compromised persons would be compelled to give up their leading positions. However, so far the course of events has led people to lose their confidence and hope in such an outcome.

We see that Janos Kadar, Chairman of the Council of Ministers, in opposition to his declarations, is not basing his power on the workers' councils, which in their full development would represent four and a half million Hungarian workers, but that nowadays precisely the compromised elements of the criminal Rakosi-Gero regime are coming more and more to the fore.

The Central Workers' Council of Greater Budapest has always assumed responsibility for its acts and for the publications that have gone into factories under its imprint. Yet we find that the presidents and members of the workers' councils who reproduce and distribute our news bulletins are often arrested. In many places the meeting of the area and departmental workers' councils is forbidden.

It has even been known for peaceful meetings, discussing the resumption of work, the solution of economic tasks and the struggle against provocations, to be broken up with armed force.

And now we have the security service, upon the basis of denunciations and for no adequate reason, taking the presidents and members of workers' councils from their homes at night without warning. There have been cases where the whole workers' council of a factory has been arrested.

It has happened that the workers' council having taken the lawful decision to suspend the factory manager of his functions and notifying the government of this, in response had the council president summoned by the local police.

We protest forcefully against such acts and such outrageous measures and we demand that the authors of all such acts be effectively dealt with.

It seems that throughout the country an attack that seems to be organized is being directed against the workers' councils. If such acts continue we will lose the only real possibility of restoring order and assuring a normal life. If these acts do not cease to occur the confidence of the workers will be lost for once and for all and the ringleaders of provocation will have attained their aim of turning the working class completely and definitely against the government. The conclusion will be grave: a general strike spreading right across the country, the spilling of blood and a new national tragedy.

Those in the country today who do not want to base themselves on the working class and on the elected workers' councils, those who engage in and collaborate with an organized onslaught against the workers' councils or who even tacitly tolerate them are committing a crime against the Hungarian working class and against the entire Hungarian people.

We have had enough of carnage and devastation. We have not time to wait for the judgement of history on these events. At the moment no-one can doubt that the workers' councils, the hastily formed peasants' councils and the revolutionary councils of Hungarian intellectuals represent the overwhelming majority of our country.

We call upon all honest Hungarians, but in the first place on Janos Kadar, Chairman of the Council of Ministers of the Hungarian People's Republic, to put an end immediately to the attacks. It is high time this was done.

Everyone must understand that the Hungarian people want to live in peace with their neighbours, in the first place with the Soviet Union, and with the peoples of the whole world. Everyone must also understand equally that anyone who does not see the problems of ten million Hungarians wishing to build socialism, peace, anyone who does not take account of the just and real economic and political aspirations of the people, anyone who permits the new Socialist Workers' Party to be organized in many places by the hated lackeys of the old Rakosi-Gero regime and thus opposes from the beginning the new party to the people, any such person is merely a political adventurer.

Today the Central Workers' Council of Greater Budapest is making its last efforts to bring the attention of the government to all these dangers so as to avoid imminent catastrophe.

Our warnings have not had success. For this reason the Workers' Council of Greater Budapest took the following decisions at its plenary meeting this evening:

1. This memorandum is to be communicated to all the workers of every factory tomorrow, 7 December.

2. The government must enter into negotiations with the Central Workers' Council of Greater Budapest tomorrow, 7 December.

3. The government must let its position regarding all the questions dealt with here be known over the radio by 8 p.m. tomorrow, 7 December.

Budapest, 6 December

> The Central Workers' Council
> of Greater Budapest.[75]

The government responded with more and more arrests of workers' council members in Budapest and in the provinces. At a clandestine meeting the Central Council prepared a forty-eight hour national general strike for 11 and 12 December. The government tried to forestall this. On 9 December – exactly four weeks after the Russian intervention – it seized various leaders of the Central Council and ordered the dissolution of all councils above the level of the industrial factory.

The members of the Central Council, it was alleged, 'preferred to occupy themselves exclusively with political questions so as to build a new power opposed to that of the executive organs of the state'.[76] Sandor Racz, the president of the council, and its general secretary, Sandor Bali, again escaped arrest and sought protection among their work-mates. Two days later they came out of hiding, on Kadar's invitation, in order to 'negotiate'. As they presented themselves at the parliament building, they were grabbed by Kadar's police and carried off. A police statement later alleged that:

> They have played a primary part in turning the workers' councils into an instrument of counter-revolution and have striven with all their might to obstruct the restoration of order, calm and peaceful work. They organized provocations and used misled youths for leaflets against the government.[77]

The Destruction of the Workers' Councils

On 3 December 1905, fifty days after its birth, the first central workers' council in world history, the Petrograd Soviet, was arrested in its entirety. Its members were in no state to resist. They were not sufficiently prepared in military terms. The arrests, however, were by no means the end of the Russian workers' movement. A wave of strikes swept Petrograd, while a general strike in Moscow gave way to a ten-day insurrection. Through the following two months revolts flared up in Siberia, in the Baltic provinces, in the Caucasus. And, most important of all, twelve years later, after a long period in which the revolutionary movement often seemed quite dead, the workers' councils were to re-emerge on a massively expanded scale, to spread from backward Russia to half of Europe.

Now, on 11 December 1956, thirty days after its birth, the first real Soviet to be seen in Europe for nearly forty years, the Central Workers' Council of Greater Budapest was arrested in its entirety. As in Petrograd in 1905, its members were in no state to resist, for they had already been defeated militarily. But, like their Russian fore-runners, their leaders' arrest did not mean the end of the Hungarian workers' movement.

The general strike took place as arranged. The Yugoslav Communist daily, *Borba*, reported:

> Anyone who went out into the streets of Budapest could see that the underground was not running and that there were no buses. In the afternoon only one trolley bus of the 75 line passed . . . Later that trolley bus too disappeared from the streets . . . On the line to Kispest a street car was running under the protection of a military escort.[78]

In the capital there was no electricity. At the Salgotarian mine, demonstrators fired at Kadar's police in order to secure the release of arrested strike leaders. The official radio explained the complete closure of industry: 'The workers are being terrorized by counter-revolutionary strikers.'

Hardly had the general strike ended when a dozen Budapest factories were shut by further strikes in protest against the arrests. At the Csepel steel mills a sit-down strike was proclaimed.

The power of the workers' councils in the factories had by no means been destroyed. A fortnight later the official party daily complained of the Budapest Electrical and Cable Factory that: 'The workers' council . . . dismisses and persecutes Communists and practically forces the local organization of the Hungarian Social Workers' Party into illegality.'

On 15 December the death penalty was introduced for 'inciting strikes'. Janoz Soltesz in Miskolc and Jozsef Dudas in Budapest were executed for their part in the fighting five weeks before. But strikes continued through December and into January. On 10 January fighting broke out in the Csepel works and lasted for three hours. The next day the government announced that one man had been killed and eleven injured.

Yet the government did not dare rely on repression alone. It had to extend its policy of economic improvements. It suspended production norms, raised wages, promised freedom to travel abroad for technicians, and ten thousand new houses for miners. It still made formal declarations about the need for workers' councils, but now hastened to add 'but they must be directed by the Communists'.

The workers of Hungary had fought hard and long. They had fought on 23 October and for a week after, both on the streets and through the strike. They had fought on 4 November and for a week afterwards against overwhelming military force. They had struck from 4 to 19 November. They had struck from 21 to 23 November. They had struck from 11 to 13 December. Now they continued to try to protect themselves through localized strikes.

Yet a strike is not a weapon of total victory. It may force an opponent to make concessions, but when his vital interests are really threatened he can outlast the strikers. It does not destroy him. While strikers starve he retains control over an army and a police force that can still intervene long after the strikers have been forced back to the factories. In the history of the workers' movement a general strike has only had ultimate success when it has culminated in an insurrection. But 200,000 Russian troops, 3000 Russian tanks, the Soviet airforce and countless Hungarian dead stood between the Hungarian workers and another successful uprising. The Central Council had recognized this when it declared as 'a criminal provocation against the Hungarian people, posters calling for an armed insurrection on 6 December . . .'[79]

So, eventually, the Hungarian workers were forced back to work. They had been defeated not, as so often in working-class history, by their own lack of organization nor by their internal divisions, but by massive military forces.

On 6 January the Csepel Workers' Council unanimously dissolved itself.

> Events have prevented us from fulfilling our mandate. We have no other role than to carry out government orders. We cannot carry out orders that oppose our mandate . . . It is our opinion that our continued existence would help to deceive our members. We therefore return our mandate to the workers.

Many other councils followed this lead, refusing to become subordinate committees which could merely implement government orders.

However, others continued to survive. As late as 14 March the Communist daily was complaining that in places 'there are still alien infiltrated elements in the workers' councils . . . We do not conceal our wish that the workers begin, as soon as possible, to distrust such elements . . .

Unfortunately for the party authorities the workers seem to have had more sense. The attitudes of the party to the councils became more severe. By 20 April the same newspaper was complaining: 'The workers' councils were formed during the counter-revolution and for a long time they bore its traces in their aims and activities.'

The deputy premier, Apro, stated: 'The overwhelming majority of the workers' councils were dissolved because in many places their activities were both economically and politically harmful and their composition was wholly unsuitable.'

On 25 November 1957 the government finally issued a decree dissolving all remaining workers' councils. The secretary of the government-run trade unions wrote of 'so-called workers' councils brought into being by the counter-revolution as a weapon in the fight against working class power'. He went on to claim:

> The workers' councils misled the working masses by their social demagogy. They introduced a series of measures that seemed to serve the interests of the workers but, in reality, acted against the interests of the workers . . . The workers' councils were not formed with the purpose of becoming organs of the broadening of factory democracy . . . The workers' councils have lost the confidence of the masses.[80]

In the minds of the party bureaucrats the workers' councils were a nightmare that reminded them of everything they feared most. In the minds of many Hungarian workers, even today, the memory of the councils must remain as a powerful image of what they really desire.

Conclusion

The Hungarian revolutionaries were defeated. But even in defeat they did not lose everything. Despite the murder of Nagy and other ministers, despite the imprisonment of writers and intellectuals, leaders of the workers' councils and those who ran the strikes, despite the thousands forced into exile in the west or deported to the east – despite all this, Hungary never reverted to the level of terror and privation typical of the Rakosi regime. Indeed, the regime in Hungary today compares favourably with the one that the 'reformer' Gomulka established without Russian intervention in Poland. By taking to the streets on 23 October the workers of Hungary gave Kadar a fright he never dared to forget.

But the real significance of the Hungarian revolution does not rest in any attempt at a crude balance sheet, with workers' deaths on one side and economic gains on the other. It is to be found elsewhere. The myth that 'totalitarian', state capitalist societies are immutable, with their populations brainwashed into acquiescence, was smashed once and for all. Hungary proved that the Stalinist monolith itself bred forces that could tear it asunder.

The course of events in Hungary also pointed to the underlying forces determining the future of modern society. The industrial centres the regime had created in its blind drive to accumulate proved to be the centres of resistance to that regime. Out of the conflict of forces within the old order came a harbinger of a completely new form of society. The workers' councils were one product of the uprising. They rapidly became the voice with which the insurrection dictated the programme of the Nagy government, and when the insurrection was smashed, they became the self-organization of society against the Kadar government. For four weeks and more the workers' councils represented, organized, regulated and maintained ; their infra-structure expressed the will of the whole country.

Many people have been so impressed by the activities of the workers' councils of Budapest that they have concluded that the working class can take control of modern society without the intervention of any political party. If by 'political party' is meant a party of the usual sort, in which a few leaders give orders and the masses merely obey, or in which a few politicians put their name on ballot papers and their followers merely draw crosses, then certainly such organizations added nothing to the Hungarian revolution. But we have tried to indicate that the workers' councils who led the revolution were not made up of men with identical and clearly defined standpoints. There were those with various degrees of trust in Nagy. There were others who believed some degree of compromise with Kadar was possible. The majority were still prepared to conceive of handing political life over to parties of the old type, while others saw further. The short life-span of the Nagy government prevented these differences from coming to the fore during the first phase of the revolution, while the liquidation of the councils under Kadar ended debate when it had hardly begun. Yet it is clear that the councils were far from achieving any kind of spontaneous agreement to substitute themselves for the old political system. Such agreement could only have come about as a result of systematic, organized and co-ordinated intervention over a period of time, initially from the minority. Such an intervention would have had to be made not only in the councils, but among the working class at large. In other words, not just the workers' councils were needed, but also an organization, a 'party', that stood for the councils taking power. Like the old parties, such an organization would have had to propagate its ideas, contrasting its position with the others ; unlike them it would, of necessity, have had to have been a genuinely democratic organization.

8.
1968: Czechoslovakia - Arrested Reform

In the years after 1956 the Eastern European regimes acquired a temporary stability. In Poland, the apparatus, under Gomulka, reasserted its hold. And in Hungary, a combination of Russian troops and concession based upon aid from Russia[1] enabled the regime to reestablish control in the factories and to rebuild the state apparatus.

There were still disagreements between the Eastern states, and a recurrence of bitter polemicising between the Russians and the Yugoslavs. Moscow and Peking fell out. Albania and then, more quietly, Rumania asserted their independence from the Kremlin. But the Russian rulers restricted themselves to verbal tirades, without the threat of major military intervention.

Inside Russia itself, Khrushchev made another onslaught on the Stalin cult, and on Stalin's successors, in 1961 and 1962. But the results were not as cataclysmic as they had been in 1956. Khrushchev's own removal from office in 1964 led to limited policy changes only.

Many observers now saw the events of 1953 and 1956 as mere teething pains, a consequence of mistaken policies in two or three countries. Typical of this attitude was the assertion (by Perry Anderson in *New Left Review*) that: 'The Soviet intervention in Hungary was the unwilling reenactment of Stalinism by a regime proceeding towards de-Stalinization'.[2] But a rude shock awaited the supporters of this view. The film of 1956 was to be re-run, although at a different speed.

Czechoslovakia had been among the most monolithic of the Communist regimes in the 1950s. The Slansky trial of 1952 had provided the grisly climax to the whole anti-Titoist wave of purges in Eastern Europe. A veritable bloodbath followed as ten government ministers were hanged, 60,000 Communist Party members imprisoned and 130,000 people from all layers of society were carted off to labour camps.

The revulsion against the effects of Stalinism that shook other regimes had very little impact in Czechoslovakia in the mid-1950s. There were a few speeches at congresses of intellectuals in 1956, a few of the more vicious secret police investigators were arrested, a few token denunciations of the 'cult of the personality', and then control from the top was reimposed as before. The mass of the population seemed resigned to permanent acceptance of this state of affairs. Cynics in Warsaw remarked that in 1956 'the Hungarians behaved like Poles, the Poles like Czechs and the Czechs like pigs'.

In the early 1960s things began, slowly, to change, and there was a limited liberalization. Nevertheless, the small group at the top of the party retained its monopoly of effective power. The party secretary, Novotny, demonstrated this in 1962 when he had the Minister of the Interior, Rudolf Barak, sentenced to fifteen years in prison, and again as late as the summer of 1967, when three leading writers, Vaculik, Liehm and Klima were expelled from the party for making critical speeches at a writers' congress and when the writers' union paper, *Literarni Noviny,* was closed down. When, shortly afterwards, Prague students demonstrated against inadequate facilities and bad conditions in their hostel at Strahov, they were attacked by police and beaten up, and their leaders conscripted into the army.

Then suddenly, in the early months of 1968, the apparatus of repression ceased to function. At the top, Novotny lost first his position as party secretary to a little known Slovak, Dubcek, and then, in March, lost the presidency to a veteran Second World War general, Svoboda.

The new communist leaders began to denounce their predecessors, often in bitter tones. The Slovak Communist Husak (imprisoned for 'bourgeois nationalism' in the 1950s) admitted that:

> The question of redress of the wrongs which have happened during the past 20 years is being felt acutely by the general public ... Wherever we turn we come across a sea of demands and complaints, many grievances which have built up through the years.[3]

The Action Programme produced by the party leaders in

April spoke of a society in which repression would play only a minor role:

> The Communist Party . . . does not realize its leading role by ruling over society but by serving its free, progressive socialist development in a devoted way. The party cannot impose its authority: this has to be won again and again by party activity. It cannot enforce its line by means of directives but by the work of its members, by the truthfulness of its ideals.[4]

These words were more than matched by a growing ferment in society generally. Journalists began to write in the papers about the world as they actually saw it. Ministers and ex-ministers were grilled on television as to their activities. Leading functionaries were forced to resign their positions; a few even committed suicide. Weekly journals contained debates between writers with quite different points of view. The censors requested the government to do away with their job. Meetings were held outside the control of the Communist Party, where people argued, debated and signed petitions. New political organizations not controlled by the party leadership's 'National Front' sprang up.

But Czechoslovakia was no more allowed to go its own way than Hungary. The Russian leaders began to view the situation with alarm. Using the excuse of 'Warsaw Pact exercises' they moved troops into Czechoslovakia in June. These were eventually withdrawn, but not before Dubcek had promised that he would 'normalize' the situation in the country. In July, Moscow's *Pravda* began to express fears about the re-establishment of a 'bourgeois' regime in Czechoslovakia. Once again Dubcek had to make pledges to the Russian leaders, at talks in Bratislava and Cierna.

Finally, losing patience with the Czechoslovak leaders, the Kremlin sent troops from Russia and her four reliable Warsaw Pact allies to invade Czechoslovakia at 11 p.m. on the night of 20 August. Within three or four hours all the main airports, frontier posts, cities and towns were dominated by thousands of Russian tanks and hundreds of thousands of Warsaw Pact troops. The Czechoslovak leaders, Dubcek, Cernick (the prime minister), Smrkovsky and Kriegel were flown to Moscow under arrest. As in 1956 the Communist rulers of Russia used their military strength to deal with another Communist government.

However, this time there was little armed resistance to the Russian troops. Total Czechoslovak casualties did not exceed fifty or a hundred.[5] Instead, the Russians were met with mass non-cooperation. Whole sections of the state machine continued to function as before, in defiance of the Russians: the parliament and party congress met to condemn the invasion; radio and television stations broadcast the condemnations and news of resistance; printing presses churned out denunciations.

Svoboda was summoned to Moscow, not as a prisoner, but as an honoured guest, and six days after the invasion, Dubcek returned to Prague, a free man and still party secretary, to tell the population that an agreement had been reached with the Russians on the basis of 'free comradely discussions'.[6] The Russian troops would remain temporarily in the country, while the situation was 'normalized', but the main changes implemented in the spring would continue.[7]

For a few months longer, the effects of the reforms did persist, more and more *despite* the government. The papers remained relatively free for another seven months, finding ways of evading a growing censorship, though even then, particular issues were banned. The party leaders insisted ever more vehemently that there must be 'law and order' and an 'end to anarchy'.

The government and party leadership were reorganized to please the Russians. First Kriegel (who opposed the agreement with the Russians) was squeezed out. Then the chairman of the national assembly, Smrkovsky, was manoeuvred from office. In April 1969 he was followed by Dubcek and later by the premier, Cernik. A purge of the lower ranks of the party gathered momentum through the summer of 1969, as anyone who had given positive support to the official government measures of a year before was threatened. The dissident journalists and broadcasters were sacked, the dissident journals closed down, dissident trade unionists forced to resign, dissident teachers evicted from their jobs. By the autumn of 1969 the ferment had been suppressed and a regime close to Novotny's in its harshness had been re-imposed. Today, some of the dissidents of 1968 are still rotting in prison.

Yet the re-establishment of complete bureaucratic control was a much more difficult task in Czechoslovakia than it had been in Poland twelve years before. Popular involvement in the democratization movement grew to a vast extent in the months immediately after the invasion, so that it was eight months before the authorities were able to impose anything like an effective press censorship. Indeed, they faced difficulties finding printers prepared to produce material justifying the Russian occupation.

Massive spontaneous demonstrations directed against the occupation occurred in Prague at the end of October and the beginning of November. Students who organized a protest sit-in in their colleges received the backing of factory meetings in the main industrial areas. The ousting of the most outspoken reform-oriented party leader, Smrkovsky, led to threats of a general strike from the Metal Workers Union. When a young student, Jan Palach, burnt himself to death in January, 1969, in protest at the abandonment of reforms by the party leaders, crowds of up to 800,000 people expressed their backing for his protest. There were similar mass demonstrations throughout the Czech lands at the end of March, ostensibly in celebration of the victory of Czechoslovakia over Russia in an ice hockey match. On these occasions the Czechoslovak army and police seemed almost powerless to intervene. Five months later, on the anniversary of the invasion, they did act, beating up demonstrators and using tear gas. But even that did not prevent a hundred thousand people expressing their open opposition to the occupation.

Most of the accounts of the 'Czech spring' of 1968 that have been published in the west have identified the anti-Stalinist movement that developed with the Dubcek group in the Communist Party leadership. According to these accounts, it was the dedication of these men to a new, humanistic version of socialism that explained the overnight transformation of Czech political life. The same explanation in inverted form, is preferred by apologists for the Russian invasion: a group of men had gained power in Prague who were putting in danger the socialist organization of society.

In fact, however, it was not Dubcek and his supporters that produced the crisis in Czechoslovak society; it was the crisis that produced both the Dubcek group and the ferment among the mass of the population that the group did its utmost to contain.

The aim of this chapter is to point out the main features of that crisis and to show how the different sections of the population responded to it.

Origins of the Crisis

The political stability of Czechoslovakia in the mid- and late-fifties rested upon the successes of its economy which grew without faltering at the time that the Hungarian and Polish economies were running into grave difficulties. The average estimated rate of growth in the period 1953-63 of about eight per cent a year was based overwhelmingly on industries producing heavy industrial goods. The labour force to man enlarged industry came from an influx of former peasants driven off the land by 'collectivization'. But the disadvantages of collectivization were felt less in Czechoslovakia than elsewhere in Eastern Europe. Peasant resistance still led to a fall in food production (so that in 1962 it was still only 92.7 per cent of the 1936 level).[8] But this fall was compensated for by imports, which Czechoslovakia was able to pay for because it had emerged from the war as the most advanced industrial country in Eastern Europe. Other Communist bloc countries intent on industrialization were only too eager to buy its output. They themselves were barely developed enough to produce comparable goods, and the cold war made it impossible for them to gain access to alternative suppliers in the West.

As a result, for fifteen years the Stalinist repression in Czechoslovakia paid visible material dividends. Individual members of the apparatus suffered in the most horrible ways, and others lived in permanent fear, but every year the mass of bureaucrats saw the industry they controlled growing in size, and the basis of their own privileges and international prestige expanding. Steady growth also provided opportunities for many individuals from other social classes to improve their conditions. Many people not actually participating in the exercise of bureaucratic power could nonetheless identify themselves with it. Real wages rose by about 60 per cent over the ten-year period (Polish figures are given for comparison):[9]

	Pre-war	1950	1953	1955	1961
Czechoslovakia	100	96	84	108	154
Poland	100	85	72	80	112

The various sources of conflict and antagonism inside Czechoslovakia did not disappear. But they were held in check. The bureaucracy did not lose faith in its own leaders. The writers and intellectuals did not lose faith in the bureaucrats. The latent discontent among workers did not explode on the streets. Internationally, too, antagonisms were held in check. The Russian ruling class dominated Czechoslovakia much as they dominated the other regimes, subordinating the Czechoslovak economy to its own ends. But, with Russia and her allies providing a seemingly limitless market for Czech goods, the subordination was tolerable.

All this changed suddenly in the early 1960s. The old markets for the products of Czech industry were no longer secure. Industry now existed in East Germany, in Poland, in Russia and elsewhere that could produce capital goods previously bought from Czechoslovakia. Moreover, the decline of cold war tension had eased the difficulties of buying western goods. Czechoslovakia's rulers faced the dilemma of any successful capitalist entrepreneur. After a period, success inevitably breeds competitors who encroach on originally safe markets.

The whole basis of industrial expansion was undermined. Goods which could not be sold abroad were stockpiled. Reduction in foreign currency earnings reduced the government's ability to import essential raw materials or sufficient food. New investment projects could not be completed on time. In the streets workers had to queue for bread.

By 1963 no one in the ruling bureaucracy could ignore the economic difficulties. That year Czechoslovakia experienced not just slow growth, or even stagnation, but an actual fall in the national income by an estimated 2-3 per cent, with industrial production down 0.7 per cent.[10]

The economist Dr Ota Sik was given the task of drawing up a 'New Economic Model' for running the Czech economy, which was put into effect at the beginning of 1967. The aim of Sik's reforms was to make the Czech economy 'competitive'. This did not mean, as some apologists for the Novotny regime have held, making some new principle of competition the motive behind the economy. In the fifties Czechoslovakia had competed internationally in two ways: firstly as part of a Soviet bloc in competition, particularly in military competition, with the west; and, secondly, as a country more dependent than most on its ability to sell its products abroad. Czech dependence on external trade is illustrated by a comparison of per capita foreign trade for different countries (in 1965, in Czech crowns):[11]

World average	842
Comecon countries	878
Advanced capitalist countries	2750
Underdeveloped countries	353
Czechoslovakia	2758

But the crisis of the early sixties had revealed that the old methods of running the economy were no longer adequate for survival in the new circumstances of heightened competition. Changes were introduced with the aim of driving the more backward, inefficient sections of the economy out of business, and concentrating new investment in the areas of high productivity whose products corresponded to the needs of Czechoslovakia's external trade.

Such an approach had an important side effect. Whereas the economic reforms suggested in Poland and Hungary in the mid-fifties clearly meant rising living standards for the mass of workers, the impact in Czechoslovakia was likely to be the exact opposite. Although there was talk of increased 'incentives', these were restricted to a minority of skilled workers and managers. For the majority, wages were to be kept static or even cut 'temporarily'. It was claimed that there were between 300,000 and 500,000 'hidden unemployed' – that is, workers who were in excess of the real needs of industry – and that these had to be 'redeployed'.[12] For many workers, therefore, the reforms were likely to mean the 'stick' rather than the 'carrot'.

The whole leadership of the Communist Party had avowed support to the New Economic Model, but the reforms did not have the desired effect. Wholesale prices rose by 29 per cent instead of the desired 19 per cent.[13] Inefficient plants were protected by such price rises from the blast of competition. Investment was encouraged in fields where it was not really needed. Workers were not squeezed out of their jobs. The economy remained as distorted as before.

The 'reformers' increasingly blamed these failures on what they saw as political obstacles to complete implementation of the reform programme. At every level of Czech society, they felt, there were inefficient bureaucrats who had too much to lose if the new policies succeeded: local party bosses who stood to lose power to managers and economic experts; managers whose power and prestige flowed from control over inefficient plant; all those, in short, whose very lifestyles were dependent on the old system. And as the 'reformers' saw it, tacit support for this inert opposition came from those at the very top of the party – above all, from the old Stalinist president and party secretary, Novotny.

As before in Hungary and Poland, the demand for economic reform developed into the demand for political change. And, also as before, those most opposed to reform were those politically best placed to resist its implementation.

The events of the summer and early autumn of 1967 provided the last stand. Dissent at the writers' congress and demonstrations by students showed that the party's inability to solve the main problems of society at large was narrowing its basis of support. Novotny's response to dissent showed his readiness to use the crudest forms of repression against any who threatened his power. There was no guarantee that the reformers in the party would not be next in the firing line.

An analysis of the period written for the new party leadership six months later describes how:

> The old guard continued in power inside the party and any criticism of them was limited to the mildest of hints . . . In 1967 . . . this struggle . . . became so acute as to produce a decisive showdown. The Writers Congress and the Strahov incident (the student demonstrations) not only highlighted the antagonism between the Novotny group and the younger generation and Communist intellectuals; it also reflected the tension between the party leaders and the broad masses of the people . . . The country stood at the crossroads. Either the party leaders would have to change policy or the gulf between them and the public would grow still deeper. This was the situation when Novotny introduced his 'hardline course', relying on coercion and authoritarian measures against all members and officials of the party who disagreed with him.[14]

Novotny's Fall

The economic reformers were not strong enough to confront Novotny's power by themselves. In the last two months of 1967 they managed to patch up an alliance with other sections of the party leadership to divest Novotny of his most powerful position, that of party secretary. Some of their allies were individuals with personal grudges against Novotny, but who otherwise shared his old-style Stalinist approach. Others recognized that some sort of crisis was developing, saw Novotny as responsible, but had no clear conception themselves of what needed to be done. The biggest single anti-Novotny grouping came from the section of the bureaucracy based on Bratislava that ran the Slovak speaking part of Czechoslovakia – men whose general attitudes were very conservative indeed.

These allies were able to ensure that when Novotny presented his customary report to the party's central committee he was suddenly in a minority.[15] In the past his own power to promote or demote the individuals who ran the different sections of the bureaucracy had ensured near-unanimity for whatever proposals he put forward. Now, however, such was the feeling of crisis that the majority of the key functionaries of party and state were willing to risk standing up to him.

Novotny did not give up without a fight. His task was made easier by the fact that his opponents had no clear alternative – either in terms of policy or in terms of a candidate to replace him. He succeeded in postponing the final decision until the beginning of January.

In the past, the leaders of the Czechoslovak Party had met threats to their power from within the party with physical force. Novotny saw no reason for not resorting to the same means now. When an appeal to Moscow for support failed – the Russians seem at this point to have recognized that Novotny could offer no way out of the crisis facing Czechoslovakia – he turned to the army.

Leading generals organized a series of meetings where a coup against the opposition in the central committee was discussed. Most of them signed a statement opposing any changes and began a mobilization of reservists for 'exercises' in the Prague area. According to some reports, Novotny's minister of the interior, Kudrna and the state prosecutor, Bartuska, drew up a list of 1032 oppositionists who were to be arrested – including such names as Dubcek, Cernik, Smrkovsky, Sik, Vodslon, Spacek and generals Dzur and Prchlik.[16]

The projected coup never materialized, because of prompt counter-action by General Prchlik. But these moves were a warning to the opposition: this was not an academic discussion to be settled through reasoned argument. Real social forces would decide the outcome, and the losers could expect loss of power, imprisonment or even worse.

Moreover, Novotny himself was trying to draw in on his side forces beyond the ranks of the top of the bureaucracy. His associates toured the country, trying to whip up opposition to the reformers' plans. Their chief appeal was, quite naturally, to tens of thousands of old bureaucrats whose jobs might be threatened if the reformers took over. But they also tried to appeal to rank-and-file workers, demagogically playing on fears of the economic changes. Novotny forgot, or ignored, the fact that workers had suffered more than any other section of the population from years of police rule. In his desperation, he set the dangerous precedent of drawing the masses in to arbitrate in a quarrel between their masters.

The opposition had little choice but to look for extra-bureaucratic allies of their own. They turned initially to the two groups that had already incurred Novotny's wrath, the intellectuals and the students. They indicated that they would protect writers and journalists who campaigned openly in the press for policy changes and who produced material aimed at discrediting Novotny supporters. The repression against the students was lifted and their victimized leaders were released from the army.[17] Dubcek supporters toured the factories countering Novotny's threats with promises of their own.

The reformers were able to oust Novotny by allying themselves first with the Slovak section of the bureaucracy and then with the intellectuals and students. But in the process they created immense problems not only for themselves, but for the bureaucracy as a whole.

The New Leadership

In itself the advent of the new leadership was not a shattering break with the past. Dubcek had for most of his life been a typical, undeviating member of the apparatus. In the early fifties he had been quite willing to repeat the most ridiculous lies about those whom the party leaders chose to sacrifice. Without a qualm he had joined in the general chorus of abuse against Slansky and the other ministers who were executed, calling them 'traitors' and 'emissaries of imperialism'.[18] He had spent three years at a party training centre in Moscow, learning Russian methods at first hand. Further, he was a close friend of Kadar, the butcher of the Hungarian revolt of 1956.[19] In the past his moments of dissent from the party line had been few indeed. He had suddenly taken up the cause of Slovak nationalism in 1967[20] – but this was clearly related to the building of a base to fulfil his own ambitions.

The Russian leaders certainly expected Dubcek to maintain Czechoslovakia as a stable, bureaucratically organized society. Hence their willingness to countenance the removal of Novotny.

Yet things did not work out as they wished. The demand for 'democratization', the movement from below against bureaucratic control and in favour of freedom of expression, continued to grow throughout the spring and summer of 1968.

Most liberal commentators in the Western press at the time attributed this to Dubcek's commitment to 'socialism with a human face'. But an examination of Dubcek's statements and behaviour in 1968 indicates that the collapse of state control over the media took him as much by surprise as it did anyone else.

He exerted much of his energy in the months from January to August in pleading with editors and journalists to display 'responsibility'. He spoke of 'the need to restrict various manifestations of anarchy or some tendencies testifying to anarchistic inclinations chiefly where the elementary principles of internal party life . . . are not respected'.[21] 'Anarchy' he virtually defined as any expression of opinion going beyond the limits set by his own leadership:

> It is anarchy (he said) to understand democracy as a situation in which everyone interferes with everything and does what he wants. That has nothing to do with real democracy . . . I understand democracy to be a system which . . . includes discipline.[22]

In June, after a group of intellectuals had suggested (in the manifesto *2000 Words*) that mass pressure should be used to displace officials and functionaries who were unresponsive to popular demands, Dubcek attacked them in no uncertain terms. 'Democracy for Czechoslovakia means realizing that some words and appeals for strikes or strikes themselves could lead to anarchy and disruption.'[23]

In line with this approach the party praesidium (on 21-22 May 1968) condemned attempts to revive the Social Democratic Party and to set up independent youth groups. He instructed newspapers not to publicize any of the activities of the Social Democrats (and only three disobeyed this censorship – *Literarny Listy*, *Student* and *Svobodne Slovo*).[24] The Ministry of the Interior announced that 'organized activity purporting to be that of a political party is illegal'. Of 70 petitions to set up new organizations, only one (from the League for Human Rights) was granted. Dubcek himself claimed, after his downfall, that prior to the Russian invasion 'we had prepared the liquidation of K231 (the club of former political prisoners) and decided that KAN (the club of committed non-party members) should not be permitted to become legal'.[25]

Although the Action Programme of the Communist Party declared that the party 'does not realize its leading role by ruling over society', the new leaders of the party were no more prepared than their predecessors had been to permit any group not controlled by the party to put forward alternative political programmes. They wanted the 'voluntary support of the people' but were not prepared to let the people consider alternatives before giving this 'voluntary support'.

The Action Programme itself made it clear that 'debate' must be contained within the framework of the party-controlled National Front. Organization of political opinion outside the National Front would be, it said, 'obviously unacceptable'.[26]

Dubcek reiterated the point: 'We resolutely reject the establishment of any opposition party which would stand outside the policy of the National Front.' [27]

The line of the other leaders of the reform wing of the party leadership was no different. Goldstucker spoke of 'guarantees of socialist democracy, while having only one leading party.' Spacek said, 'We must accept the existence of a single leading party as a fact.'[28] When a group of old social democrats wanted to revive their party, Kriegel and Smrkovsky were among those who were insistent that they should not do so.[29]

Thus it was not such a breach of the new party leadership's principles as it seemed when, in the negotiations after the Russian invasion, they agreed 'to control the communications media', that 'party and state organs will watch over the cleansing process of the press, radio and television by means of new laws and ordinances' and that 'an overhaul of the senior personnel in press, radio and television will be inevitable'.[30]

In fact, Dubcek's pronouncements in the first half of 1968 hardly flowed from principles at all. Rather they represented pragmatic responses to a difficult situation.

In January the reformist section of the bureaucracy had needed a counter to Novotny's attempts to appeal to workers on a demagogic basis and to mobilize the generals against the opposition. It achieved its end by giving journalists the green light to expose the faults of the old regime as ruthlessly as they could. Novotny's final defeat in March, when he was forced to relinquish the presidency, did not free them from the need to ward off conservative bureaucratic forces. Former Novotny supporters continued to hold positions of influence at crucial points in the party apparatus.

The problem of imposing a new monolithic line was made worse by the fact that Novotny had been overthrown by a coalition of groups in the party, each with a different approach when it came to making positive proposals. The coalition partners had united together against Novotny because there was no other way for any of them, individually, to obtain what they wanted. But now they were confused and divided as to what to do.

Dubcek and a number of other leaders – including Cernik and Smrkovsky – believed that the base of the party leadership had to be widened and that it had to encourage other sections of the population to support its rule through 'participation'. At the same time the pressure of accumulated problems required the removal of dead wood that was impeding our development'.[31] Tens of thousands of local bureaucrats who were incapable of adjusting to the new circumstances, and in particular to the new forms of economic management, had to be weeded out.

The problem was that the group of party leaders supporting this approach remained a minority within the leadership – both within the central committee and also, at first, within the praesidium. That made impossible the 'removal of the deadwood' through a conventionally directed purge from the top. Any precipitate attempts to carry such a purge through would, at best, split the party from top to bottom and, at worst, unite the rest of the leadership around a policy of purging the reformers.

Dubcek himself pointed out 'the fact that we do not yet have a positive programme . . . creates . . . a vacuum and difficulties for political work at this time'.[32] In order to deal with this 'vacuum' he tried to follow a strategy very similar to Gomulka's in 1956. His aim was to take advantage of the 'democratization' to force his opponents inside the party to relinquish their ground. Then, he believed, he would be able to persuade those who controlled the media gradually to end the 'democratization'. He later explained:

> I acted on the belief that by the summer the overwhelming majority of our population was in favour of the official party policy and that the most active elements in the party had found their bearings and were strengthening their political influence.[33]

The key event, in terms of such a strategy, would be a party conference in the autumn, where the power of the reforming wing of the bureaucracy would be consolidated. With his men in full command of the central committee and the praesidium, Dubcek would then be able to enforce his will on the rest of society – by 'non-violent' ideological means if possible, by other means if necessary. 'New important laws will be discussed . . . (which) will give (the government) the opportunity to face effectively the attempts of anti-Communist forces to gain an organizational basis for public activities.'[34]

In comparing Dubcek and the other reformers with Gomulka, we are not questioning their personal sincerity. They may or may not have meant what they said when they spoke of building a higher, more humane sort of society. What matters is that their starting point was the consolidation and strengthening of a political system in which those who controlled the bureaucracies of the Communist Party, the state and industry would continue to run things. That is why they continually stressed that 'there is no way ahead for a really socialist development without unleashing a struggle for power other than the road along which the Communist Party . . . will lead the future process of development'.[35]

But the Communist Party was in no sense a party of the majority of society. Despite its pretence to be a 'workers' party' half its members were not workers and the proportion of workers declined steadily the further one went up its hierarchy.

As Dubcek inadvertently admitted: 'The party's cadres form the predominant part of the administrative and managerial structure of society.'[36] In other words, the party was the political expression of the bureaucracy and those whose privileged position in society was based on bureaucratic power. It was a structure for imposing their common class interests on the rest of society.

The reforms weakened the hold of those who manned the higher apparatus of the party. But that was not the same thing as changing the party itself into something other than a party of the bureaucracy. Those who increased their power at local and regional level were the ones who ran the state machine and the industrial enterprises, as opposed to those who ran the central party apparatus itself. They were still a hundred times removed from workers on the factory floor.

Reports indicated, for instance, that the Czech district party conference of 28-30 June 1968, although free from Novotnyite influences, tended to be dominated by local party secretaries with titles like 'doctor' and 'engineer'.[37] At the extraordinary congress of the party in August 1968, only 18 per cent of the delegates were 'working men' (although workers made up 58 per cent of the population) as compared with 23 per cent 'political workers' and 32 per cent 'technical and economic workers'. At the previous congresses the proportion of workers had been lower.[38]

The Dubcek group hoped that the party would need to resort less to crude physical repression than in the past. But they continued to insist on 'the dominant political influence of the party under the new system', as was made clear in the document on 'The Party's Political Tasks' prepared for the party congress.[39]

> The party's leading role must be secured institutionally . . .
> It will be necessary to ensure by a complex of well-thought-out measures that relations within the National Front and the system of elections continue to guarantee the hegemony and privileges of the Communist Party so that the party shall not find itself in a minority position in the National Front or the representative assemblies.[40]

At one point the congress document discussed how to design a system of parliamentary elections which would guarantee the party a majority of seats even if it got only a third of the vote!

The expansion of the National Front's role was meant to turn it into a 'forum where policy is agreed by agreement between the various interests, which are able through the Front to express themselves in institutional forms'. But not all interests would be equal – the Communist Party leadership would have control over the structures of the 'forum' and a veto over its deliberations. It would be able to silence any real opposition easily. 'The Front must be able to exclude from its ranks an organization if it . . . acted against the political purpose of the institution.'[41]

Social groups other than the bureaucracy would be permitted a limited expression of their interests – provided they accepted the overall domination of the bureaucracy: a situation compared explicitly to that in a bourgeois democracy, where different social classes appear to struggle for power but where state, industry and media are so organized as to accord a permanent predominance to one class.

However, because the starting point of the reformers' analysis was the need to increase the efficiency of bureaucratic rule and to improve the international competitiveness of Czechoslovak industry, the aim of liberalizing that rule was bound, in the long run, to fail. A political structure capable of co-opting genuine representatives of the different social groups demanded, as a minimal condition, sufficient economic reserves to buy off at least some of the working class's resentments, as had happened in Poland in 1956-57.

But the economic reforms planned for Czechoslovakia implied attacks on the conditions and wages of many of the workers. Certainly the reformers could not at the same time increase investment in modern technology and concede the sort of wage demands workers were likely to make in any system open to the expression of independent ideas.

Once the mass of the population outside the bureaucracy became involved in the 'democratization' movement, the economic reforms themselves would be put in danger, and with them the continued stability of bureaucratic rule itself. Under such conditions those whose starting point was the consolidation of the power of the Communist Party were bound to accept a reversion to forms of censorship and police control.

The Dubcekites believed, prior to the Russian invasion, that they could manage for the time being without such measures. Dubcek himself was apparently convinced that his own popularity would enable the new system to be implemented peacefully. He boasted that the party had won the support of the people.

However, he continued to provide many of the former Novotnyites with key jobs: for instance, making the conservative Svestka

editor of the party daily *Rude Pravo* and putting another conservative, Salgovic, in a key position in the ministry of the interior, from
which he could organize secret police backing for the Russian invasion.[42] Dubcek saw his differences with them as disagreements over
tactics, over the methods by which to strengthen party control, not
as differences of principle.

His reaction to the threats made by the Russians was similarly
conditioned. In his view, there was little more involved than a failure
of communication. The Russian leaders just did not appreciate how
much he had things under control.

It was entirely consistent with this approach that he should
reject all attempts to prepare to defend Czechoslovakia against an invasion attempt. One of his supporters, General Prchlik, argued that

> it would be impossible to defend the country against an
> army which could if necessary muster a million men . . .
> Troops could nevertheless be used to hold the largest
> towns and civilian guerilla forces should be encouraged
> to take to the hills and prevent the 'enemy' from gaining
> control of the countryside.[43]

Such a strategy certainly made sense. Behind the Warsaw Pact
armies were civilian populations – in Poland, Hungary, the Ukraine,
in Russia itself – whose disaffection with bureaucratic rule could have
received a massive impetus from a long drawn-out revolutionary war
in Czechoslovakia. The events in Poland two years later showed how
combustible the tinder was. But Dubcek rejected Prchlik's advice, and
instead removed him from his military post.

The Reformers and the Invasion

Even the invasion did not shake Dubcek's views. The praesidium meeting that received news of the attack gave explicit orders
to the population that there should be no armed resistance. 'The
declaration of the praesidium included an appeal to party members
and to members of the armed forces to keep calm and not to offer any
resistance to the invading army.'[44] Dubcek later boasted that he
'made every effort with president Svoboda, by telephone and by other
means, to ensure that this part of the declaration in particular was
effected'.[45]

After Dubcek's own arrest, his supporters continued to pursue this same policy. The secret party congress that met in Prague agreed to

> do everything we can not to exacerbate the situation here any further . . . That is the reason for appeals for calm, for work, for the resumption of normal everyday life, for the avoidance of any provocation that might lead to reprisals or be used as a pretext for the introduction of an occupation regime.[46]

> The members and candidates of the Central Committee and Central Control and Audit Commission appeal urgently to all to co-operate with state bodies and National Committees in preventing panic and provocation, in averting the disorganization of industry and transport . . . We appeal to them . . . to preserve law and order in factories and offices, in towns and villages.[47]

Not only did the congress oppose armed resistance to the Russian forces ; it also opposed any idea of general strike action. An initial draft of a proclamation from the congress contained reference to a general strike, but was altered. It was explained that 'there is a typing error on page 2, where instead of saying that at 12 noon on Friday 23 August there will be a one hour strike protest, it says there is to be a general strike in protest'.[49]

Prague Radio, on government instructions, broadcast appeals for people 'not to take part in any demonstrations'.[49]

The Dubcekite party leadership did not want the mass movement to oppose the Russian occupation, but rather saw it as a bargaining counter for use by the Czechoslovak ruling group in its negotiation with the Russians.

When he heard of the invasion, Dubcek's immediate reaction was that he expected 'someone would come to me on behalf of the allied troops and we should convene a praesidium meeting to decide on further action'.[50]

After Dubcek's arrest, his supporters on the central committee announced that they were aiming at 'establishing contact with the command of the armies of the five Warsaw Pact countries with a view to bringing about a speedy normalization'.[51] Jiri Pelikan, usually regarded as one of the more extreme liberals, asserted at the congress that 'the party's representatives must negotiate a solution to this extraordinary situation.'[52]

The Dubcekites did not object to the idea of collaboration with the occupying troops as such, but to the possibility that such a collaborationist government might be formed by their conservative opponents inside the party. That would have ended any chance of carrying through the economic reforms. It would also have meant that those party members who had backed reform would have lost their positions, and possibly faced physical reprisals, loss of jobs and imprisonment.

They therefore set about trying to channel popular hostility to the invasion into hostility against the minority of conservative party leaders who were intent on forming a *new* collaborationist government. In this they were overwhelmingly successful. The conservative minority on the praesidium and in the central committee were unable to get the support they needed from other sections of the party and the state machine. Utterly isolated, they could not provide the Russian troops with the leverage necessary to take over immediate control of every aspect of Czechoslovak society.

Instead, the main sections of the state bureaucracy – the industrial managers, the army, the police (including most of the secret police) and the media – continued to take their orders from the remaining members of the government and party leadership. The army and the police communications networks were used with effect to continue transmission of radio and television programmes denouncing both the invasion and those party leaders supporting it. Presses were found to print pro-government newspapers, despite the presence of the occupying forces.

The Russian troops were confronted with a continual barrage of hostile propaganda. Yet such was the degree of opposition among the Czechoslovak bureaucracy to any new collaborationist regime – and the support for this opposition among intellectuals and workers – that the Russians could not locate the sources of this propaganda and could not even find the secret location where more than a thousand party delegates convened for the congress.

Dubcek's supporters were successful in convincing the Russians that they alone had the ability to keep the state machine functioning, and if the Russians were to establish a new collaborationist government it would be completely isolated from the mass of the population.

Such a government would be able to function only on the basis of a systematic repression and economic dislocation as great as, if not greater than, that of Hungary in 1956. By isolating the conservative minority of party leaders on the one hand and by holding in check the mass of the population's active hostility to the invasion, Dubcek was able to ensure that *his* was the collaborationist government. He was taken from prison to the negotiating table. The discussion over 'normalization' wanted by his supporters in the party leadership took place, and he was permitted to return to Prague to implement the measures agreed upon.

'Normalization'

On his return from Moscow, Dubcek told the population in no uncertain terms, that 'normalization' had to be achieved.

> We have agreed that the (Warsaw Pact) troops will move immediately from the villages and towns to areas reserved for them. This is naturally connected with the ability of our own Czechoslovak organs to ensure order and normal life in the individual areas. (Steps were being taken) in order that our organs may . . . regulate our civil life.[53]

But Dubcek found that any overnight attempt to put the old apparatus into operation would meet massive opposition and would make it impossible for people to identify with the regime.

Already the apparent harmony between rulers and ruled that had characterized the preceding period was beginning to disappear. A resolution by 40,000 Skoda workers referred to the outcome of the negotiations as 'a shameful capitulation'.[54]

The magazine *Student*, in its last issue on 28 August 1968, argued forcefully:

> Comrades, the representatives of the Czechoslovak Socialist Republic have fully capitulated in the face of the brutal force of the invaders. Regardless of the pressure to which they were exposed, their action is equal to a betrayal of this republic and a betrayal of the people . . . This is a betrayal not only of ourselves, but also of the historical role assigned to this country: to shake the inhuman structure of Stalinism and to find a human form for a socialist order.

Dubcek later explained that he saw little alternative except 'to proceed step by step', to do the 'spade work' that was to enable 'normalization' to take place (under Husak).[55]

These 'steps' involved a gradual reassertion of party power –

ratifying the treaty legalizing the occupation, tightening up censorship, gradually bringing order into the chains of command in the police and the party bureaucracy, the squeezing out of the party leadership those who advocated limited resistance to the Russians and sacking those who ran the radio and television services. But at every stage Dubcek proceeded with caution, moving more slowly than he might otherwise have done so that he might avoid a mass popular movement of protest, which might be directed not only against the Russians, but against the Czechoslovak party leadership as well.

But Dubcek was not able to repeat Gomulka's success in Poland. Discontent continued to build up in the lower strata of society. Mass demonstrations of anger shook the country in November, January and at the end of March. Huge crowds demonstrated against the Russians on the streets and students and workers passed strike resolutions. The forces of the Czechoslovak state were powerless to intervene. 'Normalization' had gone so far, but would go no further.

The Russian leaders were furious. They had invaded the country in order to bring the ferment to an end, and now it was as great as ever. Further intervention was threatened if the Czechoslovak bureaucracy did not put its own house in order.

Whole sections of the reformist wing of the bureaucracy now saw that the alternative before them was either abandoning reform or being completely ousted from control by the Russians, who had used the months since the invasion to build up their own support inside the party (particularly in Slovakia) – support that had been lacking in August. Most preferred to abandon the reforms rather than to abandon power. They made 'concessions' to the conservative section of the party, enabling them to extend their control over parts of the state machine and to enhance their ability to demand further 'concessions'.

Virtually all the leading reformers chose to go part of the way with the 'concessions'. But they did not all go all the way. Some felt that reforms remained essential if bureaucratic rule was ever to be stabilized. Some resented the loss of independence for the Czechoslovak bureaucracy implied in the Russian demands. And some preferred to let others incur the popular odium of presiding over a regime based upon mass repression.

Dubcek himself began weeding out from the party leadership those most committed to reform, like Kriegel and, later, Smrkovsky. He put up no open resistance to the demand for further concessions, and helped the conservative elements strengthen their forces as the Russians insisted. He even accepted the need for greater repression after the ice hockey demonstrations. He later claimed 'I was one of the originators of the decisions of the April and May 1969 Plenary sessions'.[56] But he did not feel able to implement these measures himself. Instead, he voluntarily relinquished power to Husak, who did not have the same qualms. He backed Husak in public, 'making three speeches in which I declared my support for the decisions of the April plenum'[57] – i.e. for Husak's appointment as secretary of the party and for the strengthening of censorship.

This self-abnegation was not just an individual quirk of Dubcek's, but was shared by most of the other reform leaders. Smrkovsky had expressed public anger at the manoeuvre to get him out of office in December 1968. But he rapidly changed his tune, begging his supporters to drop their resistance, even though the million-strong metal workers' union was promising strike action to back him. He 'dissociated himself from the campaign by progressives to have him elected head of the new federal government' two days after the leader of the metal workers, Toman, had pressed that demand in *Prace*.[58] He admitted to his 'errors' publicly in the columns of *Rude Pravo*[59] after being reprimanded by the praesidium of the party at the beginning of April.

Only two of the party leaders, Kriegel and Vodslon, refused to acquiesce in the Russian occupation. They voted against the legalization of the Russian occupation in the national assembly (only two other representatives voted with them, with ten abstaining), and when they were expelled from the party's central committee in May, they defended themselves forcefully.[60] But their approach was completely atypical – and even they do not seem to have gone outside the ranks of the party hierarchy itself in their search for support.

In general, the Dubcekites were quite incapable of putting up any resistance to the Russian occupation and to the growing repression. They themselves had risen to prominence under Novotny precisely through the roles they played in the bureaucratic structure. They saw politics as essentially bureaucratic in-fighting. And because of that, they jettisoned the reform movement in the hopes that the Russians would then let them continue to play their role in the apparatus.

Slovakia

The role of Slovakia and Slovak nationalism was central to the crisis that developed in Czechoslovakia in 1967-69. It provided the crucial allies that enabled the economic reformers to break Novotny. And it provided the main basis for the reconsolidation of bureaucratic rule after the Russian invasion.

An understanding of the double-edged significance of Slovak nationalism is not only important for the particular developments in Czechoslovakia. It also throws light on what can be expected from movements of national minorities in other Communist countries – especially the USSR, where national minorities make up more than half the total population.

Slovak nationalism really dates back to the formation of Czechoslovakia as a unified state after the First World War. The Czech bourgeoisie sought to monopolize all the advantages of running the new state apparatus. Slovakia remained economically backward and its inhabitants found themselves at a permanent disadvantage compared to Czechs when they tried to advance themselves individually through the bureaucracies of state or industry. Their resentments were channelled into a growing separatist, nationalist movement.

Conditions under the Communist regime from 1948 onwards were such as to revive the nationalist sentiments. The new central bureaucracy based in Prague concentrated all economic and political decision-making in its own hands. Obsessed with the need to accumulate, it liquidated every element within itself that might conceivably obstruct the process. And it saw such an obstruction in the idea – promised in the early post-war period – of a separate government in Slovakia. In 1948 the Slovak Communist Party was merged into the Czechoslovak Party. Leading members were purged in the early 1950s for 'bourgeois nationalism'. Clementis was executed, Husak and Novomesky imprisoned. The government institutions were turned into rubber stamps for the Prague apparatus. Slovaks were, as before the war, at a disadvantage as far as rising in the state administration, in industry or in the party apparatus was concerned.

Once such a structure of centralized power had been created, it developed a logic of its own. Any assertion of the independence or importance of Slovak culture became a demand for change in the political structure and therefore suspect. The traditions of Slovakia were treated as nothing but a hangover from a reactionary past, obstacles to the unification of the Czechoslovak nation.

The majority of Slovak bureaucrats were prepared to accept this state of affairs in the 1950s. Slovak industry grew from 13 to 20 per cent of the national total, and with it grew their own relative importance, even if within a Czech-dominated structure.

The crisis of the 1950s, however, gave new life to Slovak nationalism. With the overall slowdown in economic growth, the backwardness of Slovakia was again emphasized.[61]

One of the first casualties of the de-Stalinization drive of 1961-62 was the secretary in charge of the Slovak section of the party, Bacilek. The leading figures in Slovakia saw every advantage for themselves in seizing the power and patronage that came from running the local party machine. They snubbed Novotny and appointed a local apparatchik, Alexander Dubcek, to the job. A few months later they further enhanced their autonomous power by forcing the Czechoslovak premier, Sirocky, from office.

At this time, the Slovak bureaucrats began to turn to the traditional symbolism of Slovak nationalism. This gave them a means to express their resentments against those who lorded it over them from offices in Prague. It enabled them to broaden their base of popular support by seeming to articulate the frustrations and resentments felt by Slovaks at all social levels. And it served to deflect anger among the population away from the local bureaucracy to Prague.

While they were strengthening their own positions in the early sixties, the Slovak leaders also allowed local intellectuals to launch attacks upon the Stalinist past of those in power in Prague. For a time the Slovak capital provided the focus for intellectual opposition within the country as a whole. But once the Slovak leaders had entrenched themselves in their positions of enhanced power, the emphasis tended to be the other way. A supporter of Dubcek observed early in 1967 that: 'In Slovakia the period between 1963 and 1965 was particularly complicated in the political and ideological field . . . Thanks to the leaders . . . its accompanying dissension is behind us.'[62]

The Slovak leaders threw in their lot with the economic reformers in the battle to overthrow Novotny because of their desire for an increased level of investment in Slovak industry and increased autonomy for themselves. In every sphere of social life Slovak institutions were created in place of the previous federal ones, and with them came increased opportunities for Slovaks to enjoy administrative office.

But over the wider issue of economic and political reform, the people who ran Slovakia had little in common with those who were pressing for reform in the Czech lands. Because Slovakia was more backward, its industry still had room for growth under the old system, once it was granted the resources. The manpower shortage was less acute and there was not the same urgency for technological sophistication.

As 1968 proceeded, the bureaucracy in Slovakia turned increasingly against its former allies in Prague. The local party conferences in the Slovak areas were dominated by conservative bureaucrats, who resisted the changes being imposed in the Czech areas. Significant sections of Slovak intellectuals aligned themselves with conservative party leaders and against the Czech intelligentsia. When separate trade unions were formed for Slovakia, they were almost immune to the ferment that gripped unions in the Czech lands.

The Slovak rulers were able to maintain their grip more tightly than their Prague counterparts precisely because they could use Slovak nationalism for their own ends. They could convince other sections of the population that the most important thing was that men of Slovak nationality were now in charge, not Czechs. They could make it appear that a very important change had taken place even though the bureaucratic structure remained as before. Indeed, they could go further and identify the 'democratization' movement as Czech and therefore an alien threat to Slovakia. That was one of the weapons used in ousting Smrkovsky from office – he was holding on to a job that should be in 'Slovak hands'.

The Slovak leaders were not wholly successful in their efforts. The agitation in the Czech factories did spread to some of those in Slovakia, and Bratislava students did support the Czech students' sit-in in November 1968. Had the threatened general strike of January 1969 materialized in the Czech lands, many more workers in Slovakia would have realized that speaking the same language as managers and policemen did not mean sharing common interests.

Nevertheless, the experience of Slovakia shows that in the Communist states nationalist ideologies which weaken the central bureaucratic structure at one point in time can help it re-establish its hold at a later point. Those who seek to overthrow bureaucratic rule for good have to oppose national oppression by the central bureaucracy. By the same token, they also have to argue against nationalist illusions among the working classes of the oppressed nations.

The Intellectuals

Shortly after he came to power, Gustav Husak revealed what had most perturbed him and other functionaries about the events of 1968:

> Many workers in the cultural field . . . began to create co-ordinating committees without consulting the Party or the National Front; they created a new political programme for students and workers, for the intelligentsia and workers. Against what? Against the policy of the Communist Party.[63]

The party leadership had intended the reforms to involve a change in personnel and policies limited to the top of society. The 'democratization' movement below gathered momentum despite them, because of the activities of writers, journalists and broadcasters. There had already been discontent, as we have seen, at the writers' congress the previous summer, and a group of radical students had been fighting with the bureaucracy for control of their own affairs for nearly three years, culminating in the Strahov incidents. The divisions within the party leadership now opened up new possibilities for such movements, which also began to develop among other sections of intellectuals, particularly those working within the mass media.

After 1948, the ruling group had built up a structure of control over the media, which ensured that journalists and broadcasters transmitted its ideas to the rest of society. This structure operated through its ability to grant privileges to some intellectuals and to victimize others. The precondition for advancing to key posts in the media was membership of the Communist Party and party membership meant obedience, without question, to the orders of the party leadership.

So even where a paper was nominally independent of the party, as in the case of the papers of the various unions of creative artists (writers, film and television artists, etc.) the party leadership could mobilize its membership to enforce its decisions. Non-party members were not permitted to organize to oppose this control. Anyone who was too outspoken in opposition to the line of the party leadership would be expelled from the union on the initiative of the party group and so deprived of the opportunity to earn a living.

Just in case this system was not fully effective, it was reinforced with formal censorship. A censor sat in each newspaper office. Editors had to obey. Disobedience could, in theory, lead to court action, but in practice the editors, who were party members, were forbidden by the party to contest the censors' decisions.

The split in the party leadership rapidly led to the breakdown of these control mechanisms. The reforming section of the leadership, looking for allies to counter Novotny's plottings, encouraged journalists to criticize aspects of the old leadership's policies and rescinded the draconian measures taken against the writers' union the previous summer.

The alliance between the intellectuals and the reform wing of the party leadership was cemented at a series of giant meetings in the period immediately before Novotny finally resigned the presidency.

Thousands of students and intellectuals packed the Slavonic House on 13 March. It was

> jammed with excited men and women, suffocation-tight all the way down the stairs and out to the pavement; questions on little screws of paper coming down like snowflakes from the galleries; speakers talking like free men. A woman, long imprisoned, denounces President Novotny for his part in the show trials. A playwright says the public prosecutor has eleven judicial murders on his conscience. A novelist says the Defence Minister has the mentality of a half-educated corporal.[64]

Among the speakers was Smrkovsky, who spoke in support of 'democratization', but stressed the need for continued close relations with the USSR.

The next day another meeting of 3,000, organized by students, received a message of support from Dubcek. Sik told the students to overcome the 'conservatives who for so long have used repression and suppression to silence new ideas'. But he also urged them to 'exercise caution' and avoid 'reckless steps'.[65] Finally on 20 March, more than 10,000 students gathered in the Congress Hall in Fucik Park to hear speeches from Smrkovsky, Husak, Sik, Goldstucker and various intellectuals.[66] Two days later Novotny resigned.

The journalists and broadcasters did not limit themselves to criticisms of particular aspects of Novotny's politics. A wholesale critique of conditions in Czechoslovak society began to emerge. The demand was raised for the censorship law to be abolished, rather than merely amended as the new party leadership proposed. The party members in the various unions of creative artists refused to take any further orders from the party and to impose them on the other members. The papers of the various unions began openly to express the views of their members. Editors who refused to do this were voted out of office. The ferment spread to other papers: the staff of the party daily, *Rude Pravo*, demanded that it be the paper 'of the whole party', not just of the leadership. The youth paper, *Mlada Fronta*, and the trade-union paper, *Prace*, dissociated themselves from the old bureaucratic leaderships of the youth and union organizations. By the summer there was not a single paper in the Czech lands putting forward the conservative line that had, until January, been orthodoxy.

There was near unanimity among the intellectuals as to the faults of the Novotny regime: its suppression of free debate, its use of terror, its economic inefficiency, its concentration of all power in the hands of a few top Communists. But there was by no means the same unanimity when it came to discussing alternatives. A polarization began between those who supported a reformed version of bureaucratic rule and those who demanded much more radical changes.

The party leadership itself was conscious of the disaffection of the intellectuals and developed a programme for bringing them closer to itself:

> The party must in the first place face the problem of integrating its own highly qualified minority, the party intelligentsia, into the whole party mechanism. There are two aspects here, bringing the minority into deciding the party line and employing them adequately in party offices.[67]

Appropriate rewards were to be offered to intellectuals – and other members of the middle class – who identified with the economic and political goals of the bureaucracy: 'The incomes policy we are pursuing will . . . proceed towards a genuine differentiation in favour of skilled and complicated work.'[68] In words almost identical to those used by Stalin in the 1930s, the party leadership called for 'the elimination of the principle of egalitarianism'.[69]

On the basis of such promises whole sections of the middle classes – managerial and supervisory personnel, professional workers and, among the intellectuals, economists – showed a willingness to back the party leadership. One of their chief complaints was that differentials as between the middle class and the working class were less than elsewhere in Eastern Europe or in the West – only a small minority of top party functionaries enjoyed really high living standards, while the mass of the middle class received only 25 to 30 per cent more than the average industrial wage.[70]

However, there were important and influential groups among the intelligentsia who did not identify in this crude way with the goals of managerial efficiency. The writers and their influential paper *Literarny Listy* (circulation 250,000) were moved by far more than dislike of 'inadequate differentials' or 'lack of labour discipline'. Their alienation from the Novotny regime had quite different roots. The writer Ludwik Vaculik tried to explain these at the writers' congress in the summer of 1967. He drew a contrast: on the one hand were the demands put by the government on writers:

> Power makes contact with art wherever there are no real answers to a problem but where, nevertheless, answers have to be found in one way or another . . . Power prefers people whose inner disposition is similar to its own. But because there is a shortage of them it must also use other people whom it adapts to its needs.

on the other hand was the reality of life:

> All that our cultural life has achieved, all the beautiful things that people have created . . . all these have been achieved in spite of how our ruling circles have behaved in recent years . . . in 20 years not one human problem has been solved in our society![71]

The problem for writers was that they were expected to provide glowing accounts of a society towards which both they and their readers felt distinctly cool. A similar contradiction faced philosophers, who were expected to justify the dehumanized reality of society by reference to the ideas of humanity's greatest thinkers.

Discussion on these issues necessarily led writers and philosophers to touch upon all the main problems facing the majority of the Czechoslovak population. At first they confronted these problems at one remove, through the medium of artistic or philosophical discussion, rather than directly and openly. In the early months of 1968, their debates remained at a very abstract level, especially when it came to the highly practical question of how society should proceed after the most apparent faults of the Novotny era had been eliminated.

Literarny Listy refused at first to publish articles containing wholesale criticism of bureaucratic rule.[72] 'The writers' union was incapable of formulating any politically relevant programme and left all decisive political initiative to the Communist Party.'[73]

As the months passed, a much more critical attitude came to predominate, culminating in the publication of the manifesto *2000 Words* in *Literarny Listy* and three daily papers. This called on people to intervene directly to purge society of those most associated with Novotnyite policies:

> We should demand the resignation of people who have misused their power . . . We should find ways and means of persuading them to resign, through resolutions, demonstrations, demonstrative work brigades, collections for retirement gifts for them, strikes and picketing their houses.[74]

The call received support from large sections of the population. Prague Radio reported that a decisive majority of 'letters, phone calls and resolutions' it received about *2000 Words* were strongly in favour;[75] according to *Prace*, the overwhelming majority of some 70,000 letters and resolutions it received supported the manifesto. By contrast, the party leadership, from the most extreme 'progressives' to the hardened conservatives, opposed and criticized *2000 Words* to a man.

Because the intellectuals took the slogans of 'democratization' seriously, they found themselves increasingly on the opposite side to the party leadership. Their practical, political demands, however, still remained fairly abstract. Articles in *Literarny Listy* criticized the Action Programme for insisting that all political parties had to work within the party-dominated National Front. 'It is an illusion that the internal democratization of the party would provide a sufficient guarantee of democracy . . .'[76]

But, *Literarny Listy* still assumed, if different parties developed 'they would not put forward various ideas about the country's economic and social organization dictated by class'[77] – in other words, that any new parties' aims would be the same as those of the bureaucratic ruling group. Only their methods would be different.

The main body of intellectuals were prepared to use extra-party forces to put pressure on the party leadership. They were prepared to discuss a multi-party system. But they did not recognize that the mass of the Czechoslovak population were exploited by a privileged bureaucratic class and that the Communist Party was this ruling class's own instrument. Many of them managed to believe that if only they had reformed the party a little more than the leadership wished then society would be transformed.

Some intellectuals took their criticism further. The shift in *Literarny Listy*'s position was in part the outcome of organization and agitation led by intellectuals who were not in the party. A few intellectuals and students made attempts to establish direct links with workers in the factories, their efforts enjoying some degree of success.

Those student leaders who had been fighting for the right to control their own student organizations long before Dubcek leapt into prominence naturally distrusted many of the pretentions of the new leadership.

> (They) found few people they could believe in since so many of even the reformers had Stalinist or opportunistic pasts . . . The resulting ambivalence even towards the reform regime was made clear by student leader Lubos Holacek who said at the 20 March 1968 Prague rally that the present support for the progressives should not be taken as something definitive. He warned that if the 'political monopoly of the Communist Party' failed to secure the activity of the masses the students would have to seek a model of socialism not identical with the vision of the reformers.[78]

The paper *Student* published articles which warned of the dangers to 'democratization' from the liberal Party leaders:

> Within the next year the paradoxical reality will show the representatives of this political renewal as ministers, ambassadors and secretaries of state, who will have an immediate interest in the preservation of the status quo, just as today they have an interest in breaking the bounds of the existing totalitarian dictatorship. We support the

young guard who want to take up positions in the party as against the old bureaucrats, but we must clearly understand that we support their programme, not as personalities, and that their maximum programme is our minimum one . . . The entente between the critical intellectuals and the top party representatives is the momentary expression of the unity of their interests which will vanish as soon as the young guard assumes full power in the state and as soon as they consider the democratization as finished and the stage arrived at at which they have to consolidate power.[79]

Ideological Confusion

However, even the most radical of the intellectuals were confused in various ways. The myth that the coup of 1948 had been some sort of socialist revolution carried through by the working class remained prevalent.[80]

But if the myth were true it followed that the existing Czechoslovak state was some sort of working-class state, and that it ought to be open to reform from within. Such was the view accepted by the reform wing of the party leadership itself and by the intellectuals who clustered around them. It was a view which could only serve to aid the party leadership's efforts to reconsolidate its power.

The more radical intellectuals rejected that particular view of current possibilities. But they shared the confusion over 1948, and paid the price in other ways. They tended to feel that, since 1948 had been a revolution carried through by a working class and led by a centralized party, then the outcome of any future workers' revolution – and certainly any revolution led by a party – could be equally disastrous.

Petr Pithart expressed the logic of the argument in *Literarny Listy*:

> To . . . suggest, for instance, that instead of being channelled through autonomous political parties, the people's will can be expressed in some direct way or that it can be expressed in a socialist syndicalism . . . all these suggestions are symptoms of an already incurable incapacity to learn from the tragic history of socialist ideas up to now.[81]

Such fears reflected a widespread feeling among many of the

best Czechoslovak intellectuals that party activity, or even individual 'fanaticism', lay at the root of Stalinism. Personal experience played a big part in creating this feeling. After 1945 large numbers of young, middle-class intellectuals had joined the Communist Party, where – in return for unquestioning loyalty – they seemed to be offered the chance to reshape society. Milan Kundera (in his novel *The Joke*) has described how many of them must have felt:

> The thing that attracted me, even infatuated me about the Communist movement was the feeling, however illusory, of being close to the helm of history. In those days we really made big decisions about the fate of men and things . . . in the initial years the Communist students ran the universities almost unaided . . . We were bewitched with history, intoxicated at having jumped on its back and being able to feel it beneath us . . . There was at the time, and with us youngsters in particular, an altogether idealistic illusion that we were inaugurating a human era, an era when every man – every man – would be neither outside history nor under the heel of history, but would direct and create it himself.[82]

But the dream had turned into a nightmare. The intellectuals blamed their own youthful enthusiasm and were adamant that they would not make the same mistakes again:

> Youth is a terrible thing: it is a stage peopled by supposedly innocent children, who stride about on stilts and in the most varied costumes, pronouncing speeches they have learnt by heart and only half understood, but which they regard with fanatical reverence. History too is a terrible thing, because it becomes the plaything of adolescence: the youthful Nero, the youthful Napoleon, the frenzied mobs of children whose simulated passions and primitive poses are suddenly transformed into catastrophic reality.[83]

But, in the conditions of 1968, organization and 'fanaticism' were essential if the opportunity to break once and for all from the Stalinist system was to be seized. Inhibitions about playing an activist role could only leave the stage vacant for those who had no such inhibitions – the proponents of a return to untrammelled bureaucratic rule.

The precondition for coming to terms with such fears was an absolutely clear analysis of the changes that had taken place after

1945. Only if it were clearly understood that the 1948 coup was in no sense a workers' revolution could there be any faith in the potentiality of working-class action in the future. What lay behind the Stalinization of society, it had to be understood, was not a single minded dedication to social progress, but the attempt to base social progress on accumulation and exploitation.

This understanding was all the more important because in Czechoslovakia, in 1968 as in 1948, there were those – among the 'progressive' as well as among the 'conservative' wing of the bureaucracy – who identified 'progress' with more efficient exploitation and accumulation. They and their devotees among the intellectuals, by spreading illusions in the possibilities of limited reforms, were laying the ground for a reconsolidation of bureaucratic power.

A real democratization of society demanded an ideological struggle against such viewpoints, both among intellectuals and in the factories. But such a struggle could only be successful if it were co-ordinated and made effective by some coherent, activist political organization, a revolutionary socialist party with members in every work place and every working-class district.

Without such an organization the debates of the intellectuals could well end up as no more than a verbal accompaniment to the re-establishment of bureaucratic rule – as had those of the October Left in Poland in 1957. Yet the most radical of the intellectuals feared the development of any such organization. Those who learn mistaken lessons from history increase the likelihood that history will repeat itself.

The Workers

In the early months of 1968 the movement for reform hardly touched the biggest single group in the population, the working class. In this respect, the situation was in marked contrast to East Germany in 1953 or Hungary and Poland in 1956. Although workers rejected the demagogy of Novotny, they did not seem inclined to throw themselves heart and soul into the movement against him. While the intellectuals and students hurled defiance at the old order, the factories remained quiet.

The workers were less impressed than the intellectuals by superficial changes in the personnel and policies of the bureaucracy. In the factories the old-time functionaries still hung on to their positions, biding their time for an opportunity to reassert authority. Workers were not yet prepared to take the risks entailed in challenging them. And the programme of the economic reformers, with its talk of 're-deployment' and increased differentials, was not likely to inspire them to do so.

Ivan Svitak has described the mood at this time:

The liberal intelligentsia took as its goal the implementation of democratic freedom, especially the freedom of the press and the freedom of association, and elections by secret ballot in which independent candidates could stand – in short, the democratization of political life. But this had no effect upon life in the factories, because the re-establishment of civil liberties did not give any real new opportunities for action to the labour organizations, and especially to the trade unions, while for the workers the economic reforms represented a real and tangible danger in that they called for the closing of uneconomic enterprises. The middle classes and their intellectual spokesmen had reason to be enthusiastic about the new dimensions which creative activity took on in hitherto forbidden spheres. But what reason did the workers have for such enthusiasm? None. The conservative groups in the party apparatus, in the unions and in the militia in the plants cleverly turned these facts to their own use and made it appear that there was no support for the democratization programme in the factories. That was not true, and it soon became apparent that the local gorillas of the militia did not even have the backing of those Communists who were militia members and that Novotny was as discredited in the eyes of the average worker as he was for every other section of the population . . .
(But) the leading Communist intellectuals were so dominated by their feeling of solidarity with the new leadership that they tried only to expand the freedom of the press and to popularize the programme of political rehabilitations. Though this programme was good in itself and opened up many political possibilities for the future, it meant nothing to the average worker because the slogans of the *Literarny Listy* did not express the basic interests and needs of the factories. The absence of enthusiasm and the distrust with which the workers awaited the outcome of the reforms then in preparation were just as well-founded and far-sighted as the reservations of the sceptical intellectuals who saw behind the scenes and realized that,

apart from a change of elite, almost nothing could be expected from the Communists. The class character of the state did not allow the state elite to do anything about its monopoly of power. The intellectuals' programme therefore cut itself off from the people, because the leading Communists insisted on the leading role of the party, made no attempt to formulate any goals and contented themselves with supporting the progressive faction. So political life went on in the form of mere backroom quarrels with no mass involvement and no support among the population.[84]

But beneath the superficial calm in the factories, changes were beginning to take place. The elements that later gave rise to a massive movement of opposition to the Russians and to bureaucratic 'normalization' were beginning to coalesce. There were growing numbers of meetings, strikes and resolutions from the shop floor. At first, these related in the main to the workers' immediate economic problems.

The editor of the trade-union daily, *Prace*, described the early period:

> Shortly after January 1968 a multitude of demands for settlement of wages and social problems arose ... Workers in the factories seemed far less disturbed over political questions. Only in the following weeks did enterprises and party and trade union organizations begin, with growing intensity, to express their opinions.[85]

By the beginning of April, demands for wage increases had been put forward amounting to a total value of 20,000 million crowns. These wage demands were often backed by the threat of strike action.

Prace also reported that 'there are countless economic, social and wage pressures' which 'thanks to the January plenary session (of the Central Committee) have been able to come out of their underground hiding'.[86]

An example of such 'pressure' was a seventy-minute strike at the Pisek Electropristoje plant against changes in production with detrimental effects on wages. The workers remained inside the plant, and formed a strike committee which kept order by appointing strike guards with red armbands.[87] At the Optimist rubber and plastics plant at Ordry a strike forced the manager and chief engineer to resign after production bonuses were introduced that overwhelmingly favoured technical and office staff rather than manual workers.[88] At the Ruzyne airport in Prague the threat of a six-hour strike by electricians forced the management to make concessions over conditions in the engineering workshops.[89]

When a strike broke out at the Lednicke Rovne glassworks both the management and the trade union committee were taken completely by surprise. Demands included improvement of conditions and the 'creation of independent workshop committees of the RTUM (the official unions) composed of people they (the workers) will suggest themselves'.[90]

In the West Slovak town of Zilina, thousands of railway workers struck for three hours to force the resignation of unpopular management officials.[91]

Democratization within the Unions

The first strikes broke out at a time when the whole apparatus of bureaucratic control was in turmoil. This was reflected in the attitude of local bureaucrats to the strikes. One automatic reaction was to condemn the strikes out of hand – as in June when the official leader of the unions, Polacek, warned local trade-union officials that 'they should not support wildcat strikes'.[92] But some sections of the bureaucracy saw possible benefit to themselves in the strikes. Junior managers often regarded them as a lever to remove more senior, Novotnyite officials or to gain a degree of autonomy for the plant they controlled.

Certain trade-union bureaucrats stood to gain even more. Traditionally they had played a fairly subordinate role, being chiefly concerned with attempting to prevent friction between management and workers. Any upsurge of workers' struggle, however, could rapidly transform their role. A strike movement threatened to undermine their position completely, by proving that they could not fulfil their mediating function. But it could also increase their power and prestige immensely, by making their support an indispensable condition for the success of any other bureaucratic group.

More ambitious and younger trade-union officials, less committed to the practices of the previous twenty years, saw immense opportunities in the situation, if only they adopted militant language and broke from the old structures. The trade-union machine began to splinter into various, opposed fragments.

The convulsions in the unions followed rapidly on the convulsions within the party. The defeat of the Novotnyites within the party made the removal of the Novotnyite union leader, Pastyrik, inevitable. But his replacement, Polacek, was far from secure: many workers were very dissatisfied at his appointment. Some unions threatened to withhold union dues unless a leader more responsive to the new mood was chosen. In Prague strike action by 70,000 workers was threatened.

Polacek managed to survive in office. However, lower down the union machines the dissidents were much more successful. Sometimes they succeeded in using the threat of strike action to force old bureaucrats to resign: it had been estimated that about fifty per cent were removed from their positions in the following twelve months. Sometimes the component unions of the RTUM gained a new measure of independence from the trade-union centre. Sometimes whole sections of workers succeeded in gaining the right to formal separation from the old centralized union federations. The 4 June meeting of the central committee of the trade unions was faced with no less than 37 different demands from different sections of the membership for organizational independence.[93] The massive metal workers' union demanded complete autonomy for itself and – an omen for the future – made political demands for its members, including the right of workers' councils to appoint factory managers, enterprise directors and the Economics Minister.[94]

Polacek and the other conservative union leaders could not completely ignore these movements developing from below. They were forced to concede increased autonomy to the various sub-sections of the RTUM – if only because, otherwise, there was the threat that workers at the rank-and-file level would seize such independence for themselves, as, for instance, when an attempt was made to set up an 'Independent Federation of Railway Crews'.[95] The official daily paper of the RTUM, *Prace*, became a mouthpiece for the more extreme reformists. And the unions began to offer at least verbal backing to their members' wage demands.

But once the working class began to take advantage of the political crisis to organize itself, it was bound to define its position in opposition to the new party leader as well as the old. On the question of wages the Dubcek government was at first quite adamant. Cernik warned that there was 'an absolute lack of resources to meet the legitimate demands for wages and investments'.[96] Under growing pressure from the factories, he was forced to promise that 'the government is determined to solve the most urgent wage problems within two years', adding however that only a few of them could be dealt with immediately.[97] Sik argued in public for measures to control 'excessive growth of wages and prices' by controlling the income at the disposal of firms,[98] and declared: 'As regards the raising of the standard of living, this is not the time to distribute more from the state budget which would only increase inflationary pressures.'[99]

Despite Sik's pronouncements, the government did finally agree to 'distribute more from the state budget' by increasing pensions, and maternity and children's allowances. Again, although in March Cernik had seen little chance of a reduction in the working week, by June the five-day week had been agreed.

But the biggest contradiction between the government's programme and the growing involvement of workers concerned the question of 'redeployment'. Cernik made this clear as early as March when he spoke of the biggest difficulty trade unionists had raised as the 'problems connected with the labour transfers'.[100] In a number of cases the local trade-union organizations used their new-found freedom to organize opposition to management plans that implied redundancy: for instance, miners in Ostrava objected to any transfer of workers from the mines unless other jobs were available in the area. [101]

Kabrna warned at a central committee meeting of the party in April that within the trade unions there was developing

> a spontaneous process which takes place without party influence . . . The slogan 'Trade Unions without Communists' begins to assert itself in some places. Four shop committees which have already emerged in the Aero plant are completely without Communists . . . Demands that the old democracy be restored are not lacking either. We already have demands from two plants that it be re-established.[102]

Certain sections of workers were drawing conclusions from their own experience that led them to align themselves with the more 'extreme' intellectuals. *Literarny Listy* reported in May that in a number of factories 'Workers' Committees for the Defence of Freedom of the Press' had been formed.[103] It has been claimed that 'this spontaneous workers' movement spread rapidly and, by the end of June, there were hundreds of such committees involving thousands of ordinary workers'.[104]

The Czechoslovak party leadership saw such trends as a threat not just to old-style Stalinism, but also to their own newly-won control over the country. In its reply to the Warsaw letter (written *before* the invasion) the Praesidium boasted that it had been able to overcome

> political demagogy . . . which attempted to utilize the justi-
> fied demands of the workers to disorganize our system
> and which fanned an impromptu movement in the name
> of 'workers' demands' in order to make the economic and
> political situation more difficult.[105]

Resistance to 'Normalization'

Before the Russian invasion the workers' movement had been an irritation to Dubcek: after the end of August it became an independent force completely beyond his control. As in Hungary in 1956, the national and democratic demands that were first formulated by sections of the bureaucracy and by the intellectuals were taken over and given a new depth and significance by the organized workers. As the editor of *Prace* later wrote:

> Suddenly a new social movement surged forth . . . neither
> the journalists nor the scientists started it – they could not
> because of the censorship. The new wave . . . was the clear
> and unequivocal voice of the factories and the over-
> whelming majority of the working class.[106]

Hundreds of thousands of workers expressed their hostility to the 'normalization' by taking part in the demonstrations of November, January and March. Through their trade-union committees and through factory meetings they expressed their growing resistance as a class to the abandonment of 'democratization' by the regime.

When, in November, the government was restructured to strengthen the conservative forces, the workers of the Tesla plant in Prague demanded 'No retreat from the post-January policy' and protested at the activities of the pro-Russian group in the party leadership.[107] Similar resolutions were passed by the trade union and Communist Party committees in the railway repair shop in Ceska Lipa, the CKD steel smelting plant in Vysocany and the CKD Tatra motor works in Prague.[108]

Students in the Czech lands staged a three day sit-in as a symbolic protest at the erosion of the reforms. To their amazement they found themselves receiving messages of support from workers in factories throughout the country. In Prague many workers went beyond mere verbal support. There were scattered sympathy strikes, and the railway workers threatened that if the government acted against the students 'not a single train will move out of any Prague station'. A few weeks later a formal agreement to keep pressing jointly for democratization was signed between the Czech student union and the metal workers' union.

At the beginning of December Dubcek accepted a Russian demand that Smrkovsky be excluded from a delegation to discuss the progress of 'normalization' with the Kremlin leaders. In anger Smrkovsky criticized Dubcek in public: 'I have always been in favour of open politics.'[109] Factories and union branches took up his protests against 'any change in the composition of our leadership with the help of policies conceived behind closed doors'.[110]

> The workers give full support to Mr. Smrkovsky and expect him to remain as chairman of the federal assembly.[111]
>
> Workers of Prague's Naradi Vrsovice factory . . . sent a resolution to the Central Committee of the Czechoslovak Communist Party . . . saying that they would only work under the socialist set-up begun in January.
> Workers at the Vojnske Stavby military construction works demand an end of the whittling away through constant concessions and compromises of the pre-invasion action programme and oppose the systematic curtailment of human and civil rights such as freedom of the press, freedom of assembly and of expression and freedom to travel abroad.[112]

At the Malice tool factory, workers threatened to use all means 'including a general strike' to oppose the removal of Smrkovsky.[113]

Not only were such resolutions passed, they also received nationwide publicity. The trade-union daily, *Prace*, gave particular prominence to them.

A movement was developing that could no longer be contained behind the compromising policies of the Dubcek group. Dubcek himself looked desperately for ways to handle it. Duplicity was one weapon: he apparently promised Smrkovsky in private that he would not be removed,[114] while preparing to eliminate him. Coercion was another: he threatened to take measures which 'will appear to be undemocratic. But they will be in the interests of democracy.'[115] By 'saving democracy' Dubcek seems to have understood saving himself.

Millions of workers were unimpressed. When the first conference of the 900,000 strong Czech metal workers' union (as opposed to the single union for the Czech and Slovak lands that had existed previously) met in December, it was addressed by Smrkovsky. The conference threatened a general strike if he or any of the other leading reformers was removed.[116] The builders' union and the miners' union backed this call, and several columns of *Prace* were taken up with resolutions backing Smrkovsky. Only when Smrkovsky dissociated himself from the campaign was the strike threat withdrawn.

Printworkers refused to print a new conservative party weekly, *Tribuna*, which contained articles opposing the reform movement. At the Printers' Conference

> many of the 450 union delegates whistled and jeered at Mr Vladimir Solecky, a magazine official, when he protested at their ban on publication . . . The union said that under a workers' censor the decision on whether or not to print an article would rest with their members in the printing works.[117]

At the Seventh Congress of the RTUM (the Czechoslovak TUC) which was held at the beginning of March, the delegates asserted their independence both from the government and from the occupying forces. Polacek who, as we have seen, was not the most radical of men, responded to the mood by asserting that the unions would continue to 'maintain an independent and critical approach on all questions, economic as well as political, affecting individuals and the nation alike'.[118]

Other trade-union leaders were more outspoken. Toman of the Metal Workers said that he was not ready to 'buy appeasement by sacrificing civil rights and the freedom of the press'.[119]

In the first months of 1969 there seemed to be two rival sources of power in Czechoslovakia – the Russian army and the unions. The other sections of the population, including the 'reforming' bureaucrats, had to choose between them. However, unanimity and strength of feeling are never enough by themselves if workers are to enforce their demands on any government. Action is also needed. But those to whom the workers still looked for leadership – Smrkovsky and the union leaders – refused to translate their words into deeds.

No doubt, in a country occupied by hundreds of thousands of foreign troops, any such initiative would have had to be carefully organized if it were not to be smashed in the first few hours. But a mass strike movement would have pushed the Russians on to the defensive for the first time since August. It would have again isolated the collaborators and put an immense obstacle in the path of bureaucratic consolidation. And even if it were defeated, the outcome could not have been worse than what followed from the path of gradual 'normalization'.

Smrkovsky and the national leaders of the trade unions were no more prepared to organize such a movement than they had been in August. They threatened action as a way of strengthening their own position in the various manoeuvres within the party leadership. But they even withdrew the threats when the crunch came.

The result was that the energy and anger of the workers was dissipated. It exploded once more on to the streets with the 'ice hockey riots' but then, section by section, factory by factory, the workers gave up the fight in the face of seemingly overwhelming odds.

The union leaders, having failed to utilize the strength of their members, now had little choice but to retreat before the re-organized forces of the bureaucracy. The leaders of the RTUM (whose members had probably constituted the majority of the participants in the ice hockey riots) 'unequivocally condemned anti-democratic and anti-socialist actions' committed by the demonstrators.[120] The Metal Workers' leaders, too, paid lip-service to the condemnation, although they continued 'to demand the positive principles of the post-January policy'.[121]

Organizations of the working class closer to the rank and file spoke with a completely different voice. Typical was the statement of the CKD Dukla Works Trade Union Committee which was 'extremely concerned and disgusted at the style, content and argumentation of the (party praesidium) statement, which is returning to the style of the 1950s'.[122]

The difficulty was that there were few links between workers in different factories outside the formal trade-union structure. They 'still had not overcome the isolation imposed by the Novotny regime when no horizontal communications existed even between two neighbouring factories, let alone between different industries'[123]

Student activists were of some assistance here. 'In many cases, the students helped to arrange meetings of workers' deputies from various factories. In these cases the students in due course retreated to the background, leaving the workers to intensify contacts themselves'.[124] 'On the grass roots level there was emerging an informal, spontaneous network of conscious workers, a network which could circumvent the official trade-union bureaucracy and exerted pressure on the latter.'[125]

The party leadership could not stop such factory discussions. But it could move to isolate the different centres of opposition from one another. Full preliminary censorship was reimposed and publication of all factory and union resolutions condemning the censorship was banned.[126] The main dissident periodicals were forced to cease publication, and editors of daily papers who had permitted free discussion were replaced.

In an attempt to save their own position, the trade-union leaders pressed further into the embrace of the party leaders. The praesidium of the RTUM, at its meeting on 21 April, approved the decision taken by the central committee to accept Dubcek's resignation. Polacek went on a visit to Moscow, and returned committed to bringing to an end trade-union opposition to the regime. (No doubt his determination to do so was heightened by the position he was given as a new member of the party praesidium). A fortnight later the leaders of the RTUM sacked the editor of *Prace*, in an attempt to end its identification with the dissident movement.[127] The Metal Workers' Union joined the other unions in forbidding its members to support student demonstrations, although it still refused to promise positive support to Husak.[128]

At the rank-and-file level protest and action continued into the summer. When the Union of University Students of Bohemia and

Moravia was dissolved on 15 June, there were reports of token fifteen-minute strikes at a number of industrial plants.

In July, *Rude Pravo* complained of 'rightist forces among trade unionists', and a meeting of senior party officials still objected to the contents of *Prace*. Not until the autumn, with the purging of Toman and others, was the control of the apparatus over the unions complete. And even then there were protest meetings in factories throughout the country.

The Workers' Councils

No class ever intervenes in history aware of its own interests in a pure sense, and the working class is no exception. Brought up within the confines of the old society, its members share many of the old society's ideas. At the very time when they are beginning to carve out a new future, they are weighed down by the inheritance of the past.

Only resolute action, involving conflict and further conflict with the old structure, confused battles which the workers often lose, leads to a shaking off of the burden. And even then, every worker does not learn all the lessons at once. The precondition for the working class coming to a full consciousness of its situation is a process of polarization within itself.

In Hungary in 1956, as we have seen, the very speed of events and the intensity of the conflicts hastened all these developments. Nevertheless they were far from completed when the Russians finally re-established their control.

The much slower tempo of events in Czechoslovakia meant a slower assimilation of the lessons by shop-floor workers. A further factor also contributed to this: the very chaotic and confused state of the ruling apparatus, while enabling workers to take action, also meant that there was no unified opposition against which workers could test their own demands.

Such tendencies can be seen in the progress of the workers' councils in Czechoslovakia. The demand for workers' councils arose with the first successes of the January reforms. But it had different meanings for different sections of the population.

For those at the top, as well as for many existing enterprise managers, workers' councils meant no more than mechanisms that would give workers the impression that they had some involvement in production, while effectively leaving the focus of control elsewhere. What was offered the workers was to be 'participation', not genuine control. The first government edict on the creation of councils (April 1968) was phrased in this sense. It spoke of 'equal representation of the state, specialists external to the enterprise and the workers' collective'.[129] Sik, one of the most outspoken reformers within the party hierarchy, asserted that workers' councils 'would not assume any managerial functions, these would rest with management'.[130]

However, the collapse of the centralized apparatus in the early months of 1968 created problems for the reformers. The functioning of the economy became increasingly chaotic. Those who now ran the key economic ministries did not wish to return to the old centralized system which they regarded as being the source of all the problems. But the vast majority of enterprise managers and party functionaries were incapable of working under any other system. They continued to react in the old ways within the new market structure. The result was an increase, not a diminution of the irrationalities in the economy.

Among a section of the leading economic reformers and among a layer of lower (and younger) managers in the factories the idea of a complete break-up of the old centralized mechanism began to gain influence. It was argued that what was needed was an elimination of all direct state controls from the enterprise and a thorough purge of old senior managers. The state was to be reduced to the role played by shareholders or creditors in the West, while the actual decision-making would rest within the factory itself. In effect, what was wanted was a system close to the Yugoslav one, in which independent nationalized enterprises compete with one another, make their own contracts abroad, and are responsible for their own financing.

Such a structure could not be brought into being, however, without a struggle against the bureaucrats who held power in each locality and enterprise. The workers' councils seemed able to offer a weapon in this struggle – providing the councils could be dominated by those in the enterprise who shared the ideals of the economic reformers, i.e. the lower managers and specialists.

So it was that some of the partisans of 'managerialism' (with Sik in the lead) rallied to the idea of 'self-management' in the spring of 1968. They saw it as the only means to liquidate those structures that treated the whole economy as a single enterprise.

Proponents of this position could and did use the most extreme forms of language, referring to 'workers' democracy', the 'struggle against bureaucracy' and the like. But it is important to note that their model was not one which would have given the workers (as opposed to a new set of managers) real power.

One of them wrote in *Rude Pravo*, for example, that 'the logical point of arrival of the new economic system of direction is self-management of the enterprises . . .'[131] He went on:

> The existing level of productive forces . . . demands the activity of many types of enterprises . . . These various enterprises must be judged by the results effectively obtained from their work, which will be indicated through the control of the market; it is necessary that this develop effectively a managerial activity that does not hide behind the state balance sheet.[132]

The logical outcome of such a system was that different groups of workers would compete with one another, attempt to win markets from each other, and, in the process, even force one another out of business.

As Bukharin pointed out fifty years ago such a situation would be far from the workers' real interests:

> If a state of affairs came about in which every factory belonged to the workers of only that particular factory, the result would be competition between factories: one cloth factory would strive to gain more than another, they would strive to win over each others' customers; the workers of one factory would be ruined, while those of the other would prosper; the latter would employ the former, and, in a word, we would have again the old familiar picture . . . capitalism would revive.[133]

Even short of this extreme situation, the market process would actually take decision-making from the workers' own hands. They would be compelled to work as hard as possible in order to provide the enterprise with the resources necessary to pay interest to the state bank, raise capital for reinvestment and oust other enterprises from the market. Their actual area of free decision-making over the use of the products of their labour would be extremely limited. Furthermore, in the drive for ever greater competitive efficiency, workers would lose faith in the value of voting in workers' council elections, and the power of managers and supervisors in the factories would increase.*

Supporting the notion of workers' councils with power to determine policy in individual enterprises, Vaclav Kraus pointed out in the reform-oriented Communist Journal, *Politika*:

> There are managers who are for self-management. They are for total self-management, or at least for equal participation of the councils in the running of the enterprises . . . They know that the enterprise council would have a primordial interest in labour discipline in the enterprise, in profitability and efficiency . . . In order to run the enterprise successfully, the councils would have to be able to choose to whom and when they sold their products at economic prices . . . they would have to modernize production as well as its management. In order to modernize, it is necessary to invest in machines and equipment for the workshops.[136]

In brief, to survive on the market, the self-managing enterprise would have every interest in accumulating in order to accumulate further.

Such a programme had obvious appeal to certain, although by no means all, 'technocratic' elements.

However, there was also a more radical current in the workers' councils movement, characterized above all by a tendency to see the councils as a political weapon for transforming society, rather than just as a means of improving the economy.

One of the first public formulations of such a position was made by K. Bartosek in an 'Open letter to the Czechoslovak workers'. This was refused publication in three major Czech papers in May

---

*Such is the reality of the situation in Yugoslavia. Although the country has the highest unemployment rate in Europe, the management structure works, as M.Todorovic has pointed out, so that 'workers find it in their interest . . . that the working collective . . . number as few as possible . . . because they must share the joint product with them'.[123] Svetozar Stojanovic has concluded that 'fragmented and disintegrated, the working class displays a potential egoism, particularism and competition. Only in an integrally self-governing society can it manifest its social character, solidarity and universalism. Far from negating statism, an exclusively group self-government only nourishes it. Only horizontally and vertically integrated self-government, i.e. a self-governing system, will enable the working class to become the dominant social force.'[135]

1968 as a 'provocation of the masses', and instead appeared in the dissident weekly, *Reporter*. Bartosek argued that so far

> All (that has happened)... is only a beginning. The system that impedes the liberation of man in our country can only be negated by actions, not words; a revolutionary disavowal – the only authentic sort – cannot be attained by a pure and simple substitution of persons. Otherwise the tottering thrones will remain thrones from which a new oligarchic bureaucracy will exercise control over us all ... The act which can begin to change your condition is the election and activity of organs of workers' self-management, in which together by yourselves you administer what belongs to you ... What is important is that you elect them immediately and choose for them the most honest and able members of your collectivity ... Without democracy in the factories one cannot speak of a democratic society.[137]

The radical concept of workers' intervention in public affairs could not be limited to the idea of self-management in the isolated factory. It raised the whole question of the nature of central control over society, even if a clear answer to the question was not always provided.

The point was later made by the same writer in a discussion shortly afterwards: 'When in our society we have five thousand workers' councils, they will not only be an economic but also a political force, in which the collective opinion of the factories is expressed.'[138]

Another contributor to the same discussion was explicitly critical of the Yugoslav model:

> We cannot hold that self-management is a step towards solving political problems. The Yugoslavs have tried to found the whole political system on the system of self-management, but the situation is that self-management pre-supposes a competition of political forces. To put the emphasis on the idea of self-management could therefore take on a conservative or retarding character ...
> More important than productive self-management is social self-management ... Self-management must be an expression of civil society, must be independent from state power.[139]

However, few people went so far as to counterpose a national structure of workers' councils instead of the bureaucratic state structure as a means of running society. To this extent they did not fully separate themselves from the 'technocrats'.

The distinctions we have drawn are important from the point of view of seeing what was necessary if Czech and Slovak workers were really to develop an independent class standpoint. They could not do so without breaking completely from the programmes of the 'technocratic' tendencies.

But the 'technocrats' also faced a problem. Their own conception could only be fulfilled if the old ruling stratum was fundamentally weakened without, however, the workers taking an independent class position. But the technocrats themselves did not have the necessary social base to put their scheme into effect. They could only do so by using the workers against the old bureaucrats. And doing that increased the likelihood of the workers developing independent ideas of their own.

The different views as to the role played by the councils were reflected in arguments over their structure and functions. According to government texts, the councils should have been elected from lists drawn up by the trade-union committees in the enterprise. If this had been rigorously enforced, it would have provided an easy mechanism for reversion to bureaucratic control. In practice, however, in many enterprises, nomination could also be moved by ten per cent of the work-force in any particular section.[140]

There was similar division over the role of the General Assembly of all the workers in the enterprise. Government texts did not define its role and prerogatives, whereas in many factories statutes (such as, for instance, the W. Pieck factory) the General Assembly was defined as the 'supreme organ of control', while the role of the council was reduced to carrying out its instructions.[141] The official texts left the initiative for calling meetings of the assembly to the Trade Union Committee ; but again, in practice, this right was often exercized by the council, on many occasions under pressure from the shop floor.[142]

However, one particular feature of the councils encouraged the separation of their members from those on the shop floor who elected them: members were voted into office for a long term of four years. The whole experience of the workers' movement internationally teaches that only by regular elections, combined with the right of recall by shop-floor meetings, can rank-and-file delegates be made really responsible to those who elect them. This has been true of experiences as diverse as the shop stewards' movement in Britain today or the Russian Soviets of 1917. Indeed, in a period of very rapid political change, as in Czechoslovakia in 1968-69, the elections would have needed to be more frequent than once a year to keep pace with the changing needs of the workers.

The four-year period between elections could accord with the interests of those wanting workers' 'participation' in the old bureaucratic structure or of those wanting the 'Yugoslav' pattern. But it could not accord with the needs of a programme for workers' democracy. There are, in fact, various indications that, as the councils developed through 1968 and 1969, they did remain to a large extent under the influence of the 'technocrats'. This is shown above all by their composition. Although 82.6 per cent of workers took part in the ballots for the councils, the delegates elected were by no means ordinary workers. A survey carried out by the Industrial Sociology Laboratory of Prague University Engineering Faculty revealed that 62.3 per cent were engineers or technicians and only 20 per cent were 'workers'.[143] A commentator in *Prace* pointed out that 'unqualified workers are not in practice represented on the councils'.[144]

Although *potentially* the workers' councils offered a means for the rank and file shop-floor workers to express their own direct power, in reality they do not seem to have developed beyond being a mechanism for the exercise of *indirect* pressure. Like the union bureaucrats, the 'technocrats' of the councils depended on shop-floor support for their attempt to assert their own independence as against the bureaucracy at large. To that extent, like the unions, the councils were an integral part of the process by which the workers began to intervene in politics. But a full intervention would have meant (as it did for the Russian workers of the summer of 1917) completely changing the personnel of the councils.

Conclusion

The mass of the Czechoslovak population put up one last display of resistance to the restoration of bureaucratic control in August 1969. On the anniversary of the Russian invasion there were demonstrations hundreds of thousands strong, in Prague and Brno, which ended in clashes with the police. The authorities used brutish strength to drive the demonstrators from the streets, with tear gas and baton charges and the threat of tanks.

From that point on, overt opposition to the occupation and 'normalization' of the country subsided: it was quite clear that the armed might of the Russians was now able to impose its will.

The repression directed against those who had played some role, however minor, in the events of 1968 increased in intensity in the months that followed. Those hit were not just the big names of the reform movement in 1968. Dubcek was down-graded – first to ambassador to Turkey, and then to a minor managerial post. Cernick, Smrkovsky and so on suffered similar fates. Svoboda himself remained as president.

But for many of the lesser figures of the reform movement, the punishment was much more severe. Teachers, lecturers, government officials were sacked from their jobs. The writers' union was closed down and authors deprived of the ability to get a livelihood, unless they agreed to become publicists for Husak. They were lucky to get manual work, and some were even denied this. And more than 50,000 Czech and 13,000 Slovak trade-union officers were removed from office for having given expression to the feelings of their members.[145]

Activists who continued to speak openly of opposition to the regime were faced with threats of imprisonment. For some, such as Kosik and Vaculik, it has remained at the level of threats ; for others the threat has become the reality. Individuals like Milan Huebl, Jaroslav Sabata, Jan Tesar, Jiri Mueller, Rudolph Battek, and a host of others have faced prison sentences varying from a few months to six or seven years.

Yet the repression does not seem to have forced any positive acceptance of the regime by the population at large. In this respect, Husak seems to have been rather less successful than Kadar was after 1956. By the early 1960s Kadar was beginning to gain a grudging acceptance for his rule. Husak still has not achieved even this minimal aim: the fact that his government takes punitive action against the radicals of 1968 today, six years later, shows that he fears they might have an audience. At another level also, repression alone has been unable to heal the wounds of 1968. The reform movement originated out of the economic failings of the Novotny regime:

these failings remain and no amount of repression can end them.

The government, of course, has attempted to paint a glowing picture of economic success. Although the economy is supposed to have been growing fairly rapidly and living standards have certainly been raised a little, the underlying deficiencies revealed in the mid-1960s have been untouched. This is admitted in the academic economics journals at least:

> The Czechoslovak economy is losing a significant portion of its labour force capacity in the non-effective growth of material costs, in the increasing amount of ineffective co-operation, and also in the growth of inventories and slow utilization of the results of technological progress . . . This loss is disguised by the fulfilment of volume indicators of output.[146]

The Husak regime has been unable to solve these economic problems – in part, at least, because of its fear of the political instability that might accompany any real attempt to come to terms with them. But without solving the economic problems there can be no satisfying the desires of any major section of the population. And that means that the anger of millions of people is merely bottled in by the threat of physical force, not in any way placated. At some point it is liable to burst out – and much more explosively than in 1968.

9.
1970: Poland

The invasion of Czechoslovakia proved beyond question that the rulers of Russia were not prepared to relax their control over Eastern Europe any further. The collapse of the overt resistance to the Husak regime in the summer of 1969 demonstrated their ability to impose their will by force.

But the spectre of revolution had not been vanquished. It raised its head in the industrial centres of Poland barely a year after the consolidation of bureaucratic power in Prague.

Gomulka's regime has been much praised by the liberal press in the West, particularly in the years immediately after 1956. Commentators spoke of 'the spring in October'. Even on the revolutionary left there were those who preferred the course events had taken in Poland to that taken in Hungary. The journal of the Fourth International claimed that in Poland

> the political revolution of the masses against the bureaucratic regime economizes on mistakes in the uncertainty and confusion and evades the dangers inherent in the situation . . . In Hungary the absence of all centralized political direction provoked, on the contrary, after a certain point, exactly these mistakes and dangers.[1]

But by the mid-1960s Poland presented a very different face to the world. Gomulka had made his peace with the old Stalinists and increasingly aligned himself with them against the intellectuals who had backed him in 1956. The closure of *Po Prostu* in October 1957 was followed by a purging of the editorial board of *Nowa Kultura* in 1958. When a new debate about 'freedom under socialism' began within the intellectuals' 'club of the crooked circle' in 1962, the club was closed and further restrictions were imposed on the press.

Przeglad Kultur and *Nowa Kultura* were shut down. Thirty-four intellectuals signed a letter of protest to the premier, Cyrankiewicz, in 1964: the party retaliated by denying them various privileges (such as taking part in official cultural delegations abroad) and by imposing a suspended three year prison sentence on one of them, the elderly writer Melchior Wankowicz.

Small groups of individuals began going beyond complaints about the restrictions on the rights of intellectuals and raised political and social questions. To this the party leadership responded far more sharply, no longer restricting itself to suspended sentences. Ludwick Hass (a pre-war Trotskyist who had already spent 17 years in Russian labour camps) and Kazimierz Badowski (a pre-war Communist Party member, who had also been imprisoned by the Russians after the war) were imprisoned for three years each. In a separate trial, Jacek Kuron and Karol Modzelewski went down for three and for three-and-a-half years respectively for writing an *Open Letter to the Party*, in which they analyzed Poland in a marxist sense as a bureaucratic, class society.[2]

Warsaw students who protested at these trials were themselves subjected to disciplinary proceedings. Other people were imprisoned for writing, privately, an account of the trials (Nina Karsow) and tape recording a satirical opera (Janusz Szpotanski).

By the tenth anniversary of Gomulka's return to power, the police were effectively suppressing any form of open dissent. That is not to say they enjoyed the power they had had in Stalin's time; they did not have thousands and thousands of people confined to labour camps. But they could pick on individuals at will, intimidate them, and hang over them the threat that they could lose their jobs and possibly be sent to prison. They tolerated private grumbling about the state of affairs, but clamped down the moment private grumbling looked like translating itself into political or social action.

At first, support for the out and out dissenters seemed very limited:

> After Jacek (Kuron) and Karol (Modzelewski) were arrested . . . even the faintest attempts at protesting were a failure. Those who sympathized with the heresy – and they suddenly turned out to be a very small group – found no support either among the students or the professors. The views of Kuron and Modzelewski were condemned on every hand.[3]

In March 1968, however, the situation changed rapidly. A student demonstration, four thousand strong, occurred in Warsaw after the university authorities expelled two leaders of the protest movement, Adam Michlick and Henryk Szaifeen. Lorryloads of steel-helmeted militia men arrived and began breaking the meeting up with their batons.

This overt brutality moved other sections of students into action. The next day there were ten thousand students on the streets. Again the militia attacked, this time with tear gas as well as truncheons. The students fought back, chanting 'liberty' and 'Czechoslovakia'.

Students continued to demonstrate for about a week, and not only in Warsaw. There were demonstrations in Lodz, in Poznan, in Wroclaw, in Katowice. Other sections of the population were beginning to join in. The Polish authorities complained that 'hooligans (i.e. young workers) had participated in the student demonstrations. There were reports that groups of young workers from the Nowa Huta steel works had expressed their solidarity with Cracow students.[4]

The party leadership lashed out in all directions in its attempts to restore control. Students were beaten up in the streets with rubber truncheons. There were 1200 arrests – the majority of them young workers. A campaign of hate was directed against the liberal intelligentsia, driving many of its most prominent members into exile. The extreme dissidents, like Kuron and Modzelewski, were thrown back into the jails from which they had only recently emerged.

In addition, the party leadership resorted to another weapon in its efforts to discredit its opponents: anti-semitism. Three days after the demonstrations began, the party daily, *Trybuna Ludu*, printed a long list of student 'trouble makers', most of them with Jewish names. Another paper openly blamed the troubles on 'Zionists'. This was the cue for a concerted campaign in the press. One party leaflet, for instance, claimed that all the important Polish Stalinists had been Jewish and that there had been 'an excessive concentration of Polish citizens of Jewish origin' in the security police.

There were only 25,000 Jews in Poland at this time (0.01 per cent of the population). But now party leaders gave the impression that they dominated the country. Such was the climate created by this playing on old-established prejudices that something like half the Jewish population was forced into exile in the summer of 1968.

By such methods, the ruling group rode the storm of March 1968. In the months that followed, Poland became the most repressive of all the East European states (except for the USSR itself). The power of the police increased considerably and the leeway for dissent was reduced to a minimum.

The Economy

The Polish party leaders' reversion to the crudest forms of repression was not merely the result of their own personal nastiness, nor simply of their personal determination to maintain power. It also reflected the growing economic difficulties they faced.

In 1956 and 1957 substantial wage increases had been granted. The regime bought itself time. But the underlying economic problems had not been solved. It grew more difficult to sustain a high rate of economic expansion as the following table shows:

Growth of national income per unit of investment[5]

1951-54	0.373
1955-58	0.335
1959-63	0.201

To compensate for this decline in the effectiveness of investment, there was a considerable increase in *total* investment (from 271 billion zloty in 1955-58 to 501 billion in 1959-63) and in the rate of growth of investment, from 6.3 per cent a year increase in the former period to 8.9 per cent in the latter period.[6]

But this increased level of investment could only be achieved by holding back or even cutting into workers' living standards. Official estimates show that real wages fell in 1960, rose very slowly (at about 2 per cent per year) in the early 1960s, and then fell again in 1964.[7] Kuron and Modzelewski suggest that 'taking into consideration the hidden price rise, not included in the official statistics, we conclude that over the last four years (1960-64) the average worker's standard of living not only failed to rise, but fell somewhat'.[8]

In the late 1960s the level of accumulation was further stepped up – from 23 per cent of the national income in 1965 to 27 per cent in 1967[9] – and wages again suffered.

Under these conditions the ruling group in the bureaucracy could not satisfy the most elementary aspirations of the mass of the population. Nor could it achieve its own aim of developing

Poland fully into a modern industrial power. It had to sacrifice workers' wages to accumulation, and even then faced repeated difficulties in balancing its foreign trade payments. Inevitably it began to lose faith in itself: the leaders no longer believed, as they had in the past, that their goals corresponded to the highest ideals of mankind. Instead, their only aim became survival. And survival meant using the police to atomize all other groups in society and using anti-semitism to deflect attention from their leadership's own faults. For individual members of the bureaucracy, the main concern became fighting to climb up the bureaucratic structure at the expense of other bureaucrats. Cultural life was stifled and political life became a continual bitter combat between rival factions within the party hierarchy, which were divided by personal ambition alone.

Bureaucratic society was in permanent crisis, but the ruling class still seemed able to frighten and atomize other social classes. After 1968 the intellectuals went into exile, the student movement disintegrated, and the workers maintained their sullen silence.

Gdansk

Then, when no one expected it, in December 1970, the silence was broken. Poland was shaken from below as it had been at the time of the Poznan events in 1956.

Gomulka's economic policy after 1968 had continued to be based upon shifting resources to investment and cutting real wages. The experience of the March 1968 disturbances should have hammered home to the party leadership their need to placate the population – particularly the young workers who joined in the fighting. But other pressures were at work, much more compelling for the ruling group than the desires of the population – the pressures of competitive accumulation.

The plan targets spoke of a five per cent increase in consumption;[10] Edward Gierek later told how:

> We voted (at party congresses) for a solid plan for the construction of dwellings. The plan was dropped into the void. We voted for a whole series of other things, for example, for increasing living standards, wages etc. These were ignored . . . because . . . it was not wished to annul certain decisions on investments which were very drawn out and which had to be completed.[11]

When investment plans started coming unstuck because of the cost of buying goods abroad, Gomulka resorted to pushing up food prices, deliberately aiming to cut home consumption so as to permit greater exports. On Saturday, 12 December 1970, average food prices were put up 20 per cent, while prices of certain luxury goods were cut. A new 'incentive wage system' was also announced for the factories.

The workers in the three adjoining coastal towns of Gdansk, Gdynia and Sopot were the first to react. On the Monday, instead of working, they held a mass meeting, drew up a list of demands and arranged a march to the local party headquarters. Fighting soon broke out as police attacked with batons. But they were driven back by the workers, who armed themselves with chains and Molotov cocktails. The party building was burnt down and fighting continued through the day. That evening the provincial party secretary, Kociolek, spoke on television in a conciliatory tone, promising concessions to the workers.

Many of the workers seemed to feel they had won some sort of victory. They prepared to return to work the next morning. But as they approached the factory gates they were fired on by riot police armed with machine guns. Many workers were killed or wounded. Others took refuge in the railway station, where bitter fighting with the police continued. Despite a massive concentration of police and soldiers in the cities, the strike continued and, with it, the street fighting.

In Szczecin, like Gdansk a major ship-building city on the Baltic, a strike broke out in the shipyards when news came through of what was happening further along the coast. A strike committee was elected and a demonstration organized to the Szczecin regional party building. As they marched the workers carried red banners and sang the Internationale. As in Gdansk, bitter fighting with the police broke out. The strike was joined by the majority of the other workers in the city and took on the aspect of an armed rising. Workers obtained guns to return the police fire and organized an armed guard to keep the police from approaching the shipyards.

According to official figures, 17 workers were shot dead in Szczecin, but one of the shipyard workers' delegates claimed that the real figure was at least 30.[12]

Once again, the repression did not succeed in suppressing the movement. By the weekend it was spreading to other industrial centres –to Koszalin, to Slupsk, to Nowa Huta, to Silesia. And by the weekend, too, workers in most of Warsaw's main factories had let it be known that they would be coming out on strike the following Monday.

The Polish bureaucracy was now faced with a popular movement as powerful as that which had ushered Gomulka into power 12 years before. Only this time it was directed *against* Gomulka. In desperation, the other leaders of the regime were forced to attempt a repeat of the manoeuvre carried through in 1956.

On the Sunday evening, Edward Gierek, previously regional boss in Silesia, told the Polish population that Gomulka had been removed from power and that he, Gierek, would henceforth be running the country. A two-year freeze on food prices and certain economic reforms were promised.

Action was taken just in time, from the point of view of the bureaucracy. The changes removed the immediate likelihood of a general strike in Warsaw, and persuaded the workers of Gdansk to return to work – temporarily.

However, the situation remained highly volatile. Workers were still bitter at the 20 per cent rise in prices, which remained in effect. The rise in the cost of living was hardly compensated for by increases in minimum wage rates and family allowances (which only increased the total government budget by about 4 per cent).

The first three weeks of January saw repeated strikes in both Gdansk and Szczecin, with workers demanding the release of all those arrested during the disturbances; the creation of free trade unions, based on the workers' committees elected in December; the abolition of the new production norms; freedom of the press. Gdansk shipyard workers struck on 5, 10, 16 and 18 January. On the nineteenth the Gdansk transport workers struck for four hours and elected a permanent strike committee.

Finally, on 22 January, 3000 Szczecin shipyard repair workers went on a sit-down strike and were joined by 12,000 workers in the A. Warksi shipyard, and by transport workers. The next day fighting broke out when a number of scabs tried to cross the picket line, but the workers remained in occupation of the yards.

Gierek faced the dangerous possibility that a movement would develop as powerful as that which had precipitated Gomulka's removal a month before. In a desperate attempt to avert it he went personally to Szczecin to plead with the workers to call off their strike.

A unique confrontation, lasting several hours, followed as Gierek argued with five hundred workers' delegates. He tried to give the workers the impression that he himself had opposed Gomulka's worst excesses, but had been helpless before the December events. He went on to argue that the demand for a return of prices to their pre-December level was impossible because 'we would be plunged once more into chaos'.[13]

> Whether you believe me or not is your affair, but we have not the least reserve which would enable us to carry through a more rapid increase in the standard of living than we have already. We are in an impasse . . . In the last five years we put 23 per cent of the national income into investments. Fifty per cent of the investments were fixed for a long period, for we are developing the base, production of energy and raw materials. A series of these investments have already begun and to stop them would be to cause a useless loss not of dozens but of hundreds of millions of zlotys. And I say that such a manoeuvre, holding back certain investments, is from this point of view impossible . . .
> You are demanding the lowering of prices for foodstuffs to the level of 12 December 1970 . . . But, dear comrades, it is all a complex system. If we were to go back on this measure, then the whole economy would once more be plunged into chaos . . . That is why I say to you: no return is possible to the price of foodstuffs before 12 December 1970.

The workers centred their demands on particular grievances. Issue after issue was raised – the dangerous working conditions in the shipyards, the remoteness of trade-union officials, the distorted stories about their actions published in the local press, the continued imprisonment of strikers.

Some of the delegates gave vivid accounts of what had been happening in 'socialist' Poland:

> We did not fight to burn down the party committee building . . . But the militia forces provoked it . . . when they began to use tear gas against us and to beat us with batons . . . The authorities have lied to us with impudence, have treated us like little kids, like babies. And because of that,

it is not surprising that when our militia flew into a rage
and the babies began to march we were called hooligans . . .

(Later) they used blackmail against us, although we had
received solemn assurances that no sanction would be
taken against us . . . They trapped the workers in the shipyards like rats. They pushed them quietly into a corner,
where several had already been very badly beaten . . .
There was a case here of a man who was beaten . . . he
was black and blue because of the beatings . . . And only
because he wanted to make a note of the number of a
militia man who inspected his papers . . .

It is said that the militia fired only against those who attacked the prison or the seat of the regional committee.
That is not true. They fired next to our buildings, in the
area of the shipyard, in order to frighten us . . . One burst
of gunfire was fired, then another, and two people had been
killed and two injured.

Another delegate underlined these points: 'Too many young
people have been killed, too many are dead, shot not from the front,
but from behind, through the head. There are proofs. The doctor told
me that about 30 people had been killed.'

Others raised the question of wage differentials.

At every meeting there is talk of the high wages of the
shipyard workers . . . without any mention of the long
hours of overtime . . . We ask the question: what are the
salaries of the directors and the ministers?

We must take the money of those who live too well from
(our) work. I'll put it to you bluntly, comrades. It is
spoken of within the working class. For our society is
divided into determined classes. There are men who . . .
have too much money and too many means for making
money. And we know perfectly well what goes on in our
shipbuilding yards. A director gave up his job as director-
general . . . At the end of twelve months he had made
170,000 (zlotys) . . . We must work to ensure that there is
no division into classes. Yet this division into classes is
being created at the top. Why?

Discontent is developing and will continue to develop . . .
But where is the evil? . . . These leaders are not trying to
improve the situation of the workers, but are turning into
simple bosses as in the time of the colonels . . .

But many of the delegates were clearly confused by Gierek's
arguments.

Everyone in (Department) W7 knows that every strike makes the economic situation of the country more difficult . . .

We were not informed of the situation in the country. Now we know it and the workers of the Department (W6) support . . . comrade Gierek. We are going to resume work . . . It is really necessary to do our best to produce as many ships as possible (to sell) abroad.

I want to say to all the workers of the shipyards that, in the present difficult situation, we must, comrades, resume work. We must give the government a chance.

The majority of the delegates still felt they had some sort of national interest in common with those who ordered them about, even if they did not trust the local representatives of the regime. Some of them felt they were maltreated not as workers in general, but as workers in Szczecin: 'Why is our region of Szczecin treated differently to the others . . .?'

Even the delegates who referred to the trust they had put in Gomulka twelve years before had the illusion that things could be different with Gierek:

I almost had tears in my eyes seeing that there really are men capable of speaking frankly with us about our affairs. It is difficult to imagine, is it not, what will happen in the future . . . For the experience of the previous years tells us that we gave Comrade Gomulka our confidence in the same way . . . and people expressed their enthusiasm even . . . they offered him their help. Nevertheless they were deceived. We want to be spared this deception now. We give our confidence in hoping that, despite everything, things will really be quite different now.

The workers understood their particular grievances only too well. But they were not so clear about the overall nature of Polish society. It was only too easy to blame the horrors of the past on Gomulka, and on local officials, while believing that the new man at the top would change things.

Gierek's trump card was, as Gomulka's had been in 1956, ideological. He was able to get them to call off the strike by presenting himself as an opponent of Gomulka and the representative of society as a whole. The vast majority of workers had only just begun to enjoy the opportunity to argue with one another openly about the nature of the society in which they lived. When it came to fitting their demands into a wider political framework, they were still groping in the dark. Their vision was obscured by local prejudices, nationalistic fears, and by the illusion that somehow or other the regime remained socialist.

Gierek was also aided by rumours of a split in the party leadership. It was said that a powerful minority wanted to launch an all-out military attack on the shipyards. Gierek, by seeming to oppose such a physical onslaught, appeared a friend to the workers. The fear of a 'hard cop' made the job of the 'soft cop' easier. If the workers rejected Gierek's requests, they felt bloodshed was the alternative.

But the support Gierek was able to obtain for a return to work was not unqualified. The attitude of the majority of workers was one of 'giving the new government a chance'. 'We will support Gierek if he will support us.'

This attitude meant that Gierek had only won a temporary respite. And his problems were further increased by the fact that a minority of the strikers were still intransigent. One delegate insisted that

> The situation in the department is that everyone answers unanimously, 'We wish to continue the strike' . . . I wish to draw attention to the fact that the workers of our department reproach all those who have spoken previously with having given in so easily on the concrete point of annulling the price increases . . . Comrade Gierek, Comrade Jaroszewicz, your intervention has not convinced the workers of our department . . . And I tell you that we are calling off our strike, not out of conviction, but because the other departments are ending it.

The vote to end the Szczecin strike did not enable Gierek to return to the situation of total bureaucratic control that had existed prior to December. The workers' committee remained in existence as an independent working-class force that could not be ignored.

A month later a massive strike by textile workers in Lodz forced Gierek to carry through the measures he had told the Szczecin workers were impossible – he rescinded the December price increases. Nor was that the end of the matter. Workers had been tricked into returning to work. They had not been defeated. Two years later, the workers of the Baltic port were continuing to take strike action when they wanted to express their grievances. Gierek's government still dare not turn openly against the workers. Even more than before, its chief hope is that the economic deficiencies of the system over which it rules will not drive it into further clashes with a working class that has proved its power.

Conclusion: Reform or Revolution

The history of the Eastern European regimes has been one of repeated crises. Those who thought that the explosions of 1956 were an accident were proven wrong in 1968 and 1970. The monolith, it is very clear, contains the seeds of its own destruction.

The significance of this fact extends far beyond the boundaries of the states concerned. It affects the very future of humanity, for well over a third of mankind now lives in societies structured along essentially the same lines as the countries of Eastern Europe.

For many years the majority of the left took it for granted that the sort of society pioneered in Stalin's Russia and copied in Eastern Europe was economically superior to that in the west. For Stalinism seemed to have found a way of guaranteeing sustained economic growth at breakneck speed without repeated economic crises.

In the mid-1950s it was possible for an avowed enemy of Stalinism like Ernest Mandel to write:

> The Soviet Union maintains a more or less even rhythm of economic growth, plan after plan, decade after decade, without the progress of the past weighing on the possibilities of the future . . . All the laws of development of the capitalist economy which provoke a slow down in the speed of economic growth are eliminated.[1]

However, these popular beliefs have proved to be weakly rooted in fact. We have seen in earlier chapters that the Eastern European states have experienced recurrent economic difficulties. It was precisely these that opened up cracks in the seemingly monolithic organization of bureaucratic control. The stagnation of the Czechoslovak economy in the 1960s laid the basis for the disintegration of police power in 1968 ; Gomulka's inability to provide for investment without cutting into living standards provoked the uprisings on the Baltic coast in 1970. The blood on the pavements began as red ink on the balance sheets.

The revolutionary movements in Eastern Europe have not been mere mechanical reflection of economic crisis. Those who participated were reacting against a total experience. Such factors as police repression and cultural impoverishment have played a key part in determining the platform and perspective of the various movements.

Nevertheless, without the economic crises the movements could never have gathered momentum as they did. In the years before 1956 and 1968 only the confusion over economic questions could break the police discipline of the ruling stratum. In 1953 and 1970, only the compulsion of acute economic deprivation could drive enough workers into action at the same time to throw the repressive apparatus of the regime into disarray.

To that extent, the future of all the state capitalist societies depends on their future economic development. If they can provide continual, harmonious growth in all sections of the economy, of consumption and accumulation simultaneously, then they can survive. The grumble at the work bench will not become the roar of revolution. But if economic crisis is endemic, then the threat of social revolution will not have been averted.

Economic Malaise

All the East European economies are subject to a long-term tendency for their rates of economic growth to decline, as shown in the following table:

Compound Annual Growth Rates of National Income[2]

	1950-55	1955-60	1960-65
	per cent		
E. Germany	11.4	7	3.5
Czechoslovakia	8.0	7.1	1.8
USSR	11.3	9.2	6.3
Hungary	6.3	6.5	4.7
Poland	8.6	6.6	5.9
Bulgaria	12.2	9.7	6.5
Rumania	13.9	7.0	8.7

The point has been reached where according to official figures their growth rates are more or less equal to those of the advanced western states (less than those of Japan, greater than those of Britain). Calculations by western economists would indicate that the situation is even worse than official Communist figures suggest. But, whichever calculations are used, it is clear that the aim of 'catching up and over-taking' the West is unrealizable.

Yet the rate of accumulation in the Communist states is as high as ever: today about 75 per cent of the industrial output of the USSR consists of producer goods, compared with only 70 per cent in 1950-55; in Czechoslovakia, 61 per cent as against 55 per cent; in Poland 65 per cent as against 55 per cent.[3]

Despite the relatively low growth rates, accumulation absorbs a much higher proportion of the national income than in the West (the only western state with a rate of accumulation comparable with those of Eastern Europe is Japan – and it has a very high growth rate).

Rates of Gross Economic Investment (1967)[4]

	per cent		per cent
Bulgaria	39	West Germany	16.7
Czechoslovakia	23.7	Italy	14.4
Poland	24.7	Japan	31.5
USSR	28.5	Britain	14.6
Yugoslavia	27.0	Belgium	16.3

The discrepancy between investment and growth has forced many East European and Russian economists to recognize that their economies are immensely wasteful. There are repeated complaints in the economic press, and occasionally in the speeches of major politicians, of particular failings of the economy: the difficulty of ensuring a sufficiently high quality of output; the excessively high level of unfinished investment; the tendency for inventories of goods to accumulate; the fact that shortages of spare parts and raw materials prevent capital equipment from running at full capacity; the excessively high production costs of many goods; the technological backwardness of much of the economy.[5]

The Russian statistics for 1971 noted that 600 million roubles worth of goods were of too low a quality to be used. The official account adds 'such losses were actually much higher'.[6]

Izvestia has complained that in the motor vehicle industry as many as 30 per cent of the components are too badly produced to be of any use and have to be sent back for resmelting.[7]

Baibakov's report of the Economic Plan for 1970 mentioned that 'large losses of raw materials continue to take place during extraction and processing. For example, there are still great losses of wood in sawing and extensive metal wastes in machine building . . .'[8]

In Czechoslovakia in 1964, only a third of the products of the mechanical engineering industry were of world standard and about 25 per cent 'had to be withdrawn from production' because their quality was so low.[9]

The Rumanian leader Ceausescu has admitted that

> in heavy industry, particularly in the machine building sector, there are disproportions which are getting more visible, creating difficulties in the development of the whole economy . . . This situation is reflected in the prices we get in the export of machine tools per ton . . . In 1964 we got £420 sterling per ton, while Bulgaria got £500, France £968, the German Federal Republic £946 and Switzerland £1,724.[10]

A few economists have attempted calculations as to the total extent of this waste.

The Yugoslav, Branko Horvat,[11] estimates that in the years 1960-67 ten per cent of the total output of the Yugoslav economy was lost due to side-tracking into piles of inventories and unfinished investments. This waste has a cumulative effect, in that it could have been used to further expand production. Horvat calculates that this cumulative loss of output amounted to a figure equal to 25.6 per cent of the total social product for the years 1952-57, and 50.2 per cent for 1960-67. Such figures ignore other forms of waste, through low quality output and so on.

Figures for Hungary, Czechoslovakia and Poland indicate that the average yearly loss due to accumulated inventories and unfinished investments accounted for from 5 to 7 per cent of industrial production in the early 1960s. In Czechoslovakia in 1967, three quarters of increased production went into increased inventories;[12] in Hungary in 1961 to 1964 'about eight per cent of the national income went into the increase of inventories and reserves'.[13]

From these figures it would seem that the cumulative loss of production in these countries must approximate the Yugoslav figure:

that is, without the tendency for unfinished investments and inventories to pile up, the national income in each case would be somewhere around 50 per cent higher than at present.

The Russian economist, Kantorovich, has suggested a similar figure of a 30-55 per cent increase in production were that country's resources more rationally utilized.[14]

The Czechoslovak, Ivan Strupp, has used a different method to attempt to calculate the effect of all forms of waste in the economy. He has contrasted the level of output per head in Czechoslovakia, which is 15-17 per cent above the corresponding figure for France, with average living standards, which are considerably lower in Czechoslovakia, and draws the conclusion that the difference can only be explained if it is accepted that at least half of the output of Czechoslovak industry goes to waste.[15]

Waste and Competition

Such levels of waste are not marginal features of the Eastern bloc states, susceptible to removal by a few reforms. They are the in-built price which Eastern Europe's rulers have to pay for participating in a world system based upon competitive accumulation.

They participate in this world system in two ways. Firstly, through their involvement in the arms race – either as part of the Russian bloc, or, as in the case of Yugoslavia and Rumania, as independents trying to balance between rival great powers – they are compelled to match any expansion of the level of military spending in the West (or China) with an expansion of military spending of their own. So, for instance, when US arms spending rose by about 30 per cent in the late 1960s, a rise of 53 per cent in the military outlay of Russia's Eastern European allies followed.[16]

They are also involved in economic competition, both with the West and with one another. As small states, with relatively few native resources, they are heavily dependent on foreign trade. This dependency increases the more they develop. 'The higher the new level of development, the higher the import factor.'[17]

To pay for imports they have to export, and they export in competition with one another, since they are at similar levels of development. Until recently, few attempts were made to plan their economies jointly. 'Up to now, no supranational integration has been achieved at the enterprise level.'[18]

Survival in these conditions imposes harsh demands. Each national ruling class has to match the levels of accumulation achieved by its rivals, and individual industrial investments have to be comparable in terms of both size and level of technology to the most advanced anywhere in the world.

The level of development in the shipyards of Poland, the engineering industry of Czechoslovakia or the chemical industry of Hungary does not depend on the internal resources available to sustain development, but on the pace of industrial advance internationally.

The most technologically advanced industries now demand a scale of operation that exceeds the resources of most countries. None of the West European countries is able to stand up to IBM in computers; in oil, chemicals and synthetic fibres, the trend is towards domination by cartels made up of the giant international firms; even in the less technologically sophisticated motor vehicle industry, US firms dominate much of the European market, with General Motors having an annual turnover greater than the GNPs of all but twelve countries in the world. In other industries, such as aero-space, only a deliberate state-sponsored concentration on a few projects allows national industries to survive. But that concentration leads to massive investment in very expensive individual projects, such as Concorde or the RB211. If the cost of these projects escalates (and that is likely, given the unpredictable nature of innovation in technologically advanced industries) or their viability is put into question, whole industries and the life of whole industrial areas can be ruined.

These problems are not peculiar to western states. They confront their Eastern rivals too – in a magnified form. Because of the smaller size of their economies –and even the USSR's economy is much smaller than that of its main competitor in the arms race – the proportion of national resources tied up in accumulation has to be greater.

Those who control the economies of the various countries know that unless they achieve a certain level of investment, they will not be competitive in foreign markets. Similarly, those who run the Russian military machine want a level of arms spending in the countries under their control which will match that achieved by the US and its allies. These external pressures mean that the targets set for accumulation inside each country are as high as possible. 'The tendency is to make highly optimistic evaluations of the capacity of the economy to sustain a piling up of investments.'[19]

If such evaluations involve miscalculations – either of the cost of completing investments or of the resources really available for accumulation – then the inevitable effect is to distort the whole development of the economy and to produce precisely the levels of waste that have been noted above. And miscalculations do occur, inevitably, as the attempt is made to match the scale of investment of larger and more advanced competitors. 'The overspending on projects – and not by trifling amounts but by 50 to 100 per cent – of appropriations for construction, has become widespread.'[20]

A Vicious Circle

The real condition of the state capitalist economy is very different from that suggested by talk of 'planning'. Competitive accumulation means that large chunks of the national income are devoted to a number of massive investment projects. After a time it is found that the resources to complete all these projects at once do not exist. Bottlenecks begin to appear in the supply of components and raw materials which delay their completion. According to Brezhnev in 1972: 'The time taken to complete projects was far too long and the proportion of "near complete" projects grew larger last year than the year before.'[21]

Instead of the economy expanding at breakneck speed, it stagnates. Resources are tied down in unproductive idleness.

The central authorities cannot just ignore such problems. They have to clear the bottlenecks and complete projects which they regard as essential either for building up their arms potential or for exports. If necessary other investments must be frozen so as to release the resources needed. So some projects are left in a half-finished state and the factories which previously supplied them with raw materials and components are ordered at short notice to switch to supplying the priority projects.

The effects reverberate throughout the economy. The production schedules laid down for particular factories change at short notice. There is a continual chopping and changing in the demands made by the planners on the manager. 'Enterprises still do not have stable long-term plans ; in the course of a year they receive additional obligations and assignments.'[22]

Some plants are forced to stand idle because needed components and materials have been diverted from them to priority projects. When finally the necessary supplies arrive, they are then expected to work overtime. Typically, *Izvestia* could report in 1972 that '20 per cent more work was done in June than in May (in the light and food processing industries)'.[23]

Some factories continue to turn out components for other factories where they are no longer needed, so that stocks of unfinished goods accumulate throughout the economy. Chaos creates further chaos. Because managers are continually being instructed to fulfil new and unexpected tasks, 'the temptation arises to keep something in reserve' and they hoard labour and materials.

The planners end up having no real idea of the resources that actually exist. 'We have been unsuccessful in impelling enterprises to disclose fully their reserves.'[24]

Those who manage particular enterprises know that what matters to the authorities immediately above them is that they should turn out large quantities of the components needed by the key sections of the economy. The urgent need to overcome bottlenecks means that cost and quality of production become quite secondary considerations. In their haste to fulfil the physical norms they have been set, enterprises often do things that are to the detriment of the economy as a whole.

> Fulfilment of planning indices appears more important to the factories than adhering to contracts entered into by them . . . Factories sometimes produce a product of a certain quality merely in order to reach a high . . . index figure, although it would be quite possible to replace that use value by another, cheaper use value.[25]

The authorities find themselves trapped in a vicious circle. The scale of waste and hoarding makes rational calculation of the resources available for investment impossible. Everyone knows that the statistics provided by the factories underestimate the resources that actually exist. The planners attempt to compensate for this by setting excessively high production targets. Their attitude is that the necessary resources have to be squeezed out of the factories.

This, however, has the opposite effect to that intended. Some resources are of course squeezed out. But fears of further pressure from above increases the desire of managers and workers to protect themselves by further hoarding as the opportunity arises. It also creates on the factory floor a contempt and resentment against those at the top, a refusal to do more than the absolute minimum necessary to keep the foreman off the workers' backs.

The planners have only two ways out of the vicious circle, but both add to the other problems they confront.

One way out is to redress the internal imbalances of the economy via foreign trade. Components and raw materials that are needed can be obtained as imports – but only by cutting consumption of other imports or by increasing exports.

The easier alternative for the planners – and the one they usually resort to – is to hold back or even cut workers' living standards. Funds intended for consumer goods industries and agriculture are diverted towards heavy industry and arms. The level of investment 'acts to diminish . . . the growth of real wages . . . (This) is not an accidental phenomenon, but a logical consequence of other premises in the field of development policy.'[26]

The effect is to increase workers' resentment and contempt for the system. Even if this does not erupt into rebellion on the streets, it makes more difficult the long-term goal of raising labour productivity and it increases the proportion of low quality goods that are produced.

When the bureaucratically centralized economies were at a fairly low level of industrialization, this difficulty could be ignored to a large extent. Providing the workers could be prevented from open rebellion, they could be compelled to build up industry. Under Stalin, millions of slave labourers were ruled by fear of the bullet alone. But with sophisticated modern industry and with certain sorts of agriculture – particularly animal husbandry – the initiative and involvement of the worker is vital. This commitment by workers cannot be obtained without a minimal satisfaction of their physical requirements. Failure to meet consumption demands is inevitably reflected in low productivity. By opting for a raid on workers' consumption in order to provide for excessive accumulation, the bureaucracy merely stores up problems for itself in the future.

The Crisis

Crisis is endemic in such a situation although it is not always overt. As a number of East European economists have noted, the pattern of economic development is cyclical, so that the elements of crisis are concealed for much of the time.[27]

For a period the economy expands rapidly, the bureaucracy becomes optimistic and plans its massive investment projects. Then these come unstuck. More resources are used up than had been planned, more workers than expected are taken on and more wages paid out, yet fewer new goods than expected result. Stagnation, inflation, balance of payment deficits, all develop at once, producing uncertainty, awareness of the underlying economic chaos – in short, all the elements which can erupt into a political and social crisis.

But the crisis does not last indefinitely. Eventually the investments which were frozen do come to fruition, producing more goods and boosting growth rates. There is a new optimism among the bureaucracy as to the potentialities of the economy. This in itself prompts them to be over-optimistic in their future investment plans, a trend which is accentuated by the pressures of international competition and the need to expand in certain sectors (particularly raw materials) where bottlenecks have been encountered. But this new optimism merely makes the next round of crisis inevitable. Not only do crisis conditions arise again, but they tend to do so in an ever more serious form.

In the early stages of development of the state capitalist societies, it was possible to compensate for failings in industry by using resources from the agricultural sector. Foodstuffs seized from the peasants could be used to buy essential raw materials and industrial components abroad, as well as to feed the urban population. Massive amounts of man power could be siphoned from the countryside to plug gaps in industry: in Russia an average of two million people a year migrated to the towns between 1945 and 1954, and even in relatively advanced Czechoslovakia, half the rural labour force left the countryside between 1948 and 1968.

But a point is eventually reached at which this is no longer possible. There is little surplus population left in the villages. In the USSR today there is hardly enough rural labour left to ensure that essential agricultural tasks are performed. 'Nearly all agricultural areas now suffer from a shortage of labour, especially young and skilled labour, in periods of intense activity.'[28] At the same time, increased food production is needed if the towns are to be adequately fed and workers' discontent kept in check. Rather than grain being exported to cover industrial shortfalls, industrial goods have to be exported to buy food. The countryside no longer alleviates industrial crisis. Quite the reverse: if bad weather leads to a poor harvest, it can push the crisis in the towns to breaking point.

The Failure of Reform

The faults in the bureaucratically centralized economies have prompted certain sections of the ruling class to press for economic reform.

They have argued that a few men at the top of the planning apparatus can never know what resources are really available, nor, as a result, can they organize production rationally. The central apparatus' attempts to plan necessarily produce over-investment, bottlenecks, shortages of supplies, output of unwanted goods, stockpiling and so on. The only way to overcome all these problems is, according to the economic reformers, by reorganizing the structure of economic decision-making, so that managers at the plant or enterprise level themselves decide what they are to produce, without undue outside interference. The free play of the market will then force them to produce what other enterprises, consumers or the state are willing to buy. Enterprises producing goods which are not wanted or are of low quality will be forced out of business unless they change their ways. Further, if enterprises have to compete with each other to borrow investment funds from state banks then only the more efficient will make sufficient profits from their sales to get resources for new investments. 'Over-investment' will be ended and the more efficient sections of the economy will expand. Managers will have a positive incentive to work out means to dispose of hidden reserves of labour, and so raise productivity. And, as prices begin to reflect production costs, some overall assessment of the resources in the economy will at last be possible.

At the same time, there should be a gradual removal of the restrictions preventing individual enterprises from entering directly into economic relations with trading partners outside the country.

This, it is argued, will force them to measure their own performance against the level of efficiency prevailing internationally. 'The cold blast of competition' will ensure that only the fittest survive and that the component parts of the national economy are efficient by international standards.

> Computations of value, return, expenditure and other methods employed to indicate whether or not certain transactions or products are profitable, must become an organic part of planning . . . These computations call for objective criteria, i.e. comparison with the gain from other transactions, comparison with world technical and cost levels . . . Individual value categories – prices, profits, wages, credits etc – must be effectively used to make enterprises expand the production of products in high demand, introduce new products and cut down unnecessary production.[29]

The form of the economy depicted in the reformers' proposals is very similar to that in the West, with the difference that the enterprises, the banks and so on are not owned by private capital, but by the state. Nevertheless, in their competition with one another managers of enterprises would behave just like western managers, and the managers of banks would behave like western bankers. Finally, the state's intervention in the economy would no longer involve the issuing of detailed orders to particular enterprises, but would take the form of creating an overall framework for economic decision-making and speeding up or slowing down the tempo at which the market forces operate.

Economic reforms along these lines were proposed in Hungary and Poland in the mid-fifties, and throughout most of Eastern Europe in the second half of the 1960s. However, in each case their full implementation was prevented by essentially non-economic forces.

The political difficulty, as we have shown above in our analysis of the political crisis in particular countries, is that any economic reform involves a reorganization of the power structure of the ruling bureaucracy itself. In a regime where the state bureaucracy controls all industry, any rearrangement of the economy involves a re-shuffling of the bureaucratic hierarchy. Sections of the bureaucracy that previously held enormous power—in particular those whose control of the party machine at national and local level enabled them to intervene in economic decision-making – lose out. They do their utmost to maintain their power to intervene in the economy, regardless of the changes in the formal structure of control. They tend to be backed in this by managers of inefficient enterprises, who turn to them for assistance in resisting pressures to curtail their own activities. There is a 'continual tendency towards an obvious or disguised use of directives . . .'[30]

After a period of initial enthusiasm, these political pressures halt the drive for reforms. Such was the fate of the Polish reforms of the mid-1950s, the reforms in Russia in the mid-1960s, the Czechoslovak reforms of the late 1960s and, it seems, the more recent Hungarian reforms.

It is not only political pressures which lead to the abandoning of reform. The economic benefits of the reforms have never turned out to be as great as their enthusiastic supporters promised. Over-investment, growth of inventories and inflation have all continued after the reforms. They seem more fundamentally rooted in the system than even the most radical reformers suggested.

In Czechoslovakia in 1968-69, 'the negative tendency to an unbalanced development was intensified and reproduced at a higher level'.[31] There remained 'a distressing chain of insufficient output, capacity, services, labour power etc., disturbing both the continuing process of production and the standard of living . . .'[32] The inflationary pressures grew rather than diminished. Over-investment was as great as ever. Planned investment in 1967 was 14 billion crowns, actual investment 20 billion ; in 1968 planned investment was again 14 billion, actual investment more than 18 billion.[33]

In Yugoslavia, reforms carried through in the mid-1960s were likewise ineffectual in overcoming imbalances in the economy. Massive fluctuations in the rate of industrial growth continued. Stagnation in 1967 was followed by years in which output grew much faster than planned – nearly fifty per cent faster in 1969 and a hundred per cent faster in 1971. Yet the overall growth rate for 1966-70 was only 6.7 per cent, as opposed to a planned rate of 9 per cent.

Investment projects continued to be started without regard to the availability of resources to sustain them. Raw materials had to be imported to make up the gap, while exports lagged : by 1972 exports covered the cost of only 55 per cent of imports. The effect of the increased pressure on resources was to push up prices, unleashing an endless inflationary spiral, which in 1971 reached an annual rate of

17 per cent. Meanwhile, unemployment remained at around the 300,000 mark – with a million more workers forced to seek employment abroad. Part of the remedy to these faults put forward by the Yugoslav government at the beginning of 1973 was a wage freeze, despite rising prices, and wage cuts of up to 10 per cent for many workers.

In the late 1960s the favourite country for many western economists was Hungary. The New Economic Mechanism seemed to them to offer a solution to all the problems of the bureaucratic economies. The adoption, albeit in a limited form, of the market mechanism seemed to justify their faith as apologists for private capitalism. In western writings on the Hungarian economic reform hardly a hint of doubt was to be found.

Yet in the summer of 1971 statements from Hungarian leaders revealed that the reform was running into all the old difficulties. Rezso Nyers, head of the Hungarian Communist Party's economic department admitted that 'current investment expenditure . . . appears to have broken all bounds and is running 23 per cent higher than during the first half of last year'.[34]

The President of the national bank reported that capital tied up amounted to 65 thousand million forints – more than the total investment expenditure for the year.[35] Investment was rising twice as fast as the national budget, complained the prime minister, Fock. 'Too frequently investments were being embarked upon which were not feasible either technically or financially.'[36] Imports were growing twice as fast as exports, and only 11 out of 19 planned investment projects were completed.[37] Once again, those who suffered from the excessive investment were the workers. Although the main targets of the 1966-70 plan were overfulfilled, 'the most generally known and most perceptible problem is the slow, hardly perceptible rise in real wages'.[38]

The failure of reform to produce the promised benefits brings new support to the conservative elements in the bureaucracy who opposed change all along. The need for immediate action to prevent further over-investment and inflation strengthens the hand of those who hanker after full administrative control of the economy. Central intervention is necessary to ensure that some investment projects rather than others are given top priority, regardless of market and profitability considerations. The state is stepping in to compensate other enterprises for losses. And in no time at all the limited market mechanism is replaced by a return to central bureaucratic control.

The path to reform is blocked, not just by political obstacles, but even more by the fact that reform cannot deal with the basic faults of the system. Ending central state direction of enterprises and permitting them to compete individually on a world market does cope with certain forms of waste and inefficiency. It certainly produces pressures on less efficient enterprises to force them out of business. But it also gives rise, inevitably, to new sources of waste and distortion. In particular it results in the national economy being dominated even more than before by particular industries and their investment projects. The efficiency of these investments is as dependent as ever upon uncontrollable factors – the success of applying technological innovation to production processes, fluctuations in the world economy which create or destroy markets for particular products.

Certainly, the omens from Yugoslavia – the East European state that has gone farthest in this direction – have not been very hopeful. The country has a massive deficit on its trade transactions, only counter-balanced by massive revenues from tourism and the remittances of emigrant workers, revenues not available to the other states. And its economy has been subject to massive fluctuations in its growth rate. 'The Yugoslav economy is significantly more unstable than that of the ten (major) economies . . . including the US.'[39]

Such a state of affairs is not surprising. The market mechanisms of the western economies *do not* guarantee stability and balanced economic development. For a relatively short historical period (since 1940) the advanced western countries have experienced a prolonged bout of economic growth and stability, on the basis of a massive waste on armaments.[40] But whole sections of world capitalism have not benefited from this growth. While the already advanced economies have made progress, the less developed economies have suffered stagnation and increasing poverty. They simply have not been able to compete with the industry of Western Europe, Japan and the US.

There is no indication that the economies of Eastern Europe will be much more fortunate. Without state protection, many of their factories would rapidly be forced out of business, their development would be stunted in certain directions and exaggerated in others, in accordance with the demands of the world system, but not the needs of the local population.

No ruling class in the world could afford the social risks involved in such a devastating reorganization of industry under the impact of the world market. In the West there has been a steady advance of state control aimed at mitigating the immediate impact of market conditions. The nationalization by a Tory government of Rolls Royce and the Upper Clyde shipyards provides graphic examples. For the same reason the rulers of the East cannot abandon state centralization. To be sure, it is grossly inefficient to try to organize production which is international in scale within the confines of small nation states. But there is no alternative for ruling classes working within the present world system.

Nor is there any alternative within the framework of bureaucratic class rule to the continued subordination of consumption to accumulation. The Yugoslav plan for the early 1970s proposes a rise in net economic investment from its 1970 figure of 18.4 per cent of national income to an average figure of 21.0 per cent[41] a figure between 40 and 100 per cent higher than that for most western countries (except Japan). For relatively less advanced countries, like those of Eastern Europe, there is no other way to survive in international competition.

Such levels of accumulation inevitably involve holding down living standards and denying workers the right to organize to fight for higher wages. Under these conditions, the rights of intermediate sections of the population, such as intellectuals and students, are also necessarily restricted within tight limits. The moment intellectuals threaten to unite with other sections of the population against the party leadership, censorship and police repression are brought to bear.

In the cold light of these realities, the official schemes for economic and political reform amount to little more than utopian attempts to wish away the dominant features of capitalism as an international system.

Revolution

Yet if reform does not work, the future for the Communist states is grim. Their efforts to 'catch up and overtake' the West have produced a vicious circle of waste and inefficiency from which there seems no way out. Their high levels of accumulation adversely affect living standards, building up resentments among the mass of the population so that labour productivity fails to rise as planned. Ever greater levels of investment are needed to secure the same increase in output.

If growth rates are not to fall even more, still higher levels of accumulation are needed than in the past. But that means further investments in excess of resources to sustain them, further attacks on workers' living standards, further growth of resentment against the system.

Yet there is an alternative to the inefficient bureaucratically centralized economy, with its slowing growth rate, its low level of living standards and its massive waste. The alternative is an economy no longer dominated by the drive to accumulate and no longer relating to neighbouring economies through competition, but through co-operation.

The rival ruling classes that dominate the world are driven to competitive accumulation because the productive forces of mankind can no longer be contained within the boundaries of national states. Neither the closed bureaucratic economy nor the 'open' reformed economy can avoid this fact.

However, there is no need to accept that the development of an international productive system requires the existence of an international competitive system. It could mean instead, the development of a planned international division of labour expanding at a tempo determined by human need.

The precondition for such a development is the destruction of the present ruling classes and a reorganization of society. The replacement of an anarchic international system depends upon the displacement of the rival national ruling classes that sustain it.

The bureaucrats of Eastern Europe cannot even begin such a task. They measure their own power in relation to the amount of accumulated labour under their control. They accept and glorify the drive to accumulate as much as the private capitalists of the West. They cannot co-operate even with one another, except on the basis of calculation of individual competitive advantage. They reject any revolutionary movement internationally as a threat to their national privileges and power bases.

The importance of the events of 1953, 1956, 1968-69, and 1970 is because they show the bureaucratic regimes, as much as the private capitalist regimes of the West, to have created their own grave digger, a force that can carry through the necessary historical transformation of society: namely, an industrial working class, growing in size, self-confidence and hostility to the present system.

The system resorts to ever greater levels of accumulation in a futile effort to counter falling growth rates. But this ensures attacks on living standards which drive workers to rebellion. The bureaucrats testify to their own fears on this score by the scale of repression. A stable, secure ruling class does not need to machine-gun strikers and imprison poets.

But to say that working-class revolution is inevitable is not to say that it will necessarily be successful. The example of Poland in 1956 shows that bureaucracy can survive a virtual collapse of the centralized state machine. As with any other social class, the power of the bureaucracy is not only vested in the central government ministries or the party headquarters. Its representatives control the enterprises, set the goals and organize the co-ordination of the economy, sit in the local civil service and police centres, man the courts. From these bases the bureaucracy can reassert its hold over the central political mechanisms of society if political revolution does not become social revolution.

While reorganizing its forces the bureaucracy will make all sorts of promises. Some of its leaders may even believe their own words. But once bureaucratic power is consolidated again, the compulsion to accumulate will make it forget its fine phrases. It will inevitably return to the only structure that can guarantee the necessary rate of accumulation – a structure based on exploitation and repression.

The bureaucracy can only be prevented from successfully staging such a come-back if the most radical sections of the workers and intellectuals grasp what it is up to and struggle politically to lead the rest of the working class in opposition to it. They have to reject the notion that a political revolution will suffice and insist that the whole structure of political and economic control has to be transformed. A co-operative society based upon the satisfaction of human needs can only be built if the working class smashes the old, hierarchic state and takes over the whole of society from the bottom up, through a system of genuinely democratic and accountable workers' councils, linked together into a centralized national structure.

Those who really want to transform Eastern European societies also have to insist that the revolution cannot be merely national in its goals. So long as it is confined to one country only, it cannot indefinitely escape pressures to compete and accumulate. Under such conditions, those who are best at laying the basis for accumulation by exploitation will again raise their heads. The revolution can only survive by becoming permanent: basing itself internally upon the most far-reaching workers' democracy, linking itself externally to the struggles of other workers, East and West, and to the national liberation struggles in the third world.

It has been their isolation that has stopped the revolutions of Eastern Europe in their tracks so far. The presence of the Russian army on the streets or on the frontier has loomed as a major factor in people's calculations. Fear of the firepower that hit Budapest in 1956 helped to secure the acquiescence of the Czechoslovak workers in 1969 and the Polish workers in 1971.

But this constraint on the revolutionary movement will not exist for ever. The Russian economy is increasingly plagued by the same imbalances, the same faltering growth rates, that have produced the upheavals in Eastern Europe. At some point the monolith in the Kremlin itself will crack. When that happens the Russian soldiers will be as much affected by the general discontent as were the members of the Hungarian army in 1956 or of the Czechoslovak army in 1969. Sixty million Russian workers will then have the opportunity to make their mark on history.

Notes

Introduction

[1] V.I.Lenin, *Collected Works*, Vol. 33, Moscow 1965, p. 430

[2] J.V.Stalin, *Problems of Leninism*, p. 356, cited in Isaac Deutscher, *Stalin*, London 1961, p. 328

[3] Quoted in E.H.Carr and R.W.Davies, *Foundations of the Planned Economy*, Vol. 1, London 1969, p. 327

[4] Joseph Berger, *Shipwreck of a Generation*, London 1971, p. 90

[5] Karl Marx, *Capital*, Vol. 1, Moscow 1961, p. 592

[6] *ibid*, p. 595

[7] N.Bukharin, 'Address to the Fourth Congress of Comintern' in *Bulletin of Fourth Congress*, Moscow, 24 November 1922, p. 7

[8] *Pravda*, 24 April 1970

[9] Quoted in T. Cliff, *Russia, A Marxist Analysis*, London n.d. (1963), p. 42. See also L. D. Trotsky, *The Third International after Lenin*, New York 1937, p. 279

[10] Tony Cliff, *Stalinist Russia*, London 1955, reprinted as Book I of the 1963 edition. Jacek Kuron and Karol Modzelewski, *An Open Letter to the Party*, translated in English as *A Revolutionary Socialist Manifesto*, London 1968

Chapter 1

Eastern Europe after World War II

[1] Winston Churchill, *The Second World War*, Vol. VI, London 1954, p. 198

[2] For a full discussion of the various interests of the great powers see Gabriel Kolko, *The Politics of War*, London 1969. Kolko argues that the interview between Churchill and Stalin was much less important than Churchill thought. The spheres of influence that were eventually decided upon 'were less a creation of new relations than a formulation of the status quo'. Even so, the spheres of influence which eventually emerged were very much as laid down in the Stalin-Churchill discussion.

[3] Kolko, *op cit*, p. 174

[4] US Department of State, *Foreign Relations of US, the Conferences at Malta & Yalta 1945*, p. 783, quoted in Kolko, *op cit*, p. 359

[5] *ibid*

[6] Kolko, *op cit*, p. 50

[7] Economist Intelligence Unit, *Quarterly Economic Review, East Europe North*, 1968, No. 3.

[8] F.Zweig, *Poland Between Two Wars*, London 1944, p. 121 cf also L.Wellisz, *Foreign Capital in Poland*, London 1938, p. 145

[9] Royal Institute of International Affairs, *Agrarian Problems from the Baltic to the Aegean*, London 1944, p. 81, quoted in Y.Gluckstein, *Stalin's Satellites in Europe*, London 1952, p. 26

[10] B. Kidric, *On the Construction of Social Economy in* FPRY, quoted in Gluckstein, *op cit*

[11] Royal Institute of International Affairs, *South Eastern Europe, A Political and Economic Survey*, London 1939, p. 173, quoted in Gluckstein, *op cit*

[12] A.Zauberman, *Industrial Progress in Poland, Czechoslovakia and East Germany, 1937–62*, London 1964, p. 1

[13] *ibid*

[14] Zauberman, *op cit*, p. 106

[15] Estimate given in N. Bethell, *Gomulka*, London 1972, p. 118

[16] Article by Benes in *Manchester Guardian*, 15 December 1945

[17] For more details on the development outlined in this paragraph, see Gluckstein, *op cit*, pp. 26–29

[18] For accounts of the development of the Polish Communist Party, see Bethell, *op cit*, pp. 15-72, and A. Korbonski, *The Politics of Socialist Agriculture in Poland, 1945–60*, New York 1965, pp. 50–66

[19] For one account of the Rumanian Communists in the pre-war period, see Introduction to G. Ionescu, *Communism in Rumania, 1944–62*, London 1964

[20] Figures given by P.L.Zinner, *Communist Strategy and Tactics in Czechoslovakia*, London 1963, p. 30

[21] *ibid*, p. 63

[22] *ibid*, p. 75

[23] V.I.Lenin, *Collected Works*, Vol. 24, Moscow 1964, p. 69

[24] *Economist*, 7 October 1944, quoted in Gluckstein, *op cit*, pp. 132-33

[25] *New York Times*, 16 January 1954, quoted in *ibid*

[26] *New York Times*, 21 September 1944, quoted in *ibid*

[27] *New York Times*, 21 September 1944, quoted in *ibid*

[28] *Economist*, 7 October 1944, quoted in *ibid*, p. 133

[29] *New York Times*, 22 September 1944, quoted in *ibid*, p. 134

[30] Quoted in *ibid*, p. 134

[31] Account given in *ibid*, pp. 134–35

[32] *Observer*, 10 September 1944, quoted in *ibid*, p. 135

[33] 19 November 1938. For a long description of his actions in organizing repression against workers and peasants, see *Inprecor*, 8 December 1933, quoted in *ibid*, pp. 136-37

[34] *ibid*, p. 137

[35] Statement by Patrascanu in *Christian Science Monitor*, 12 December 1945, quoted in *ibid*, p. 140

[36] *New York Herald Tribune*, 7 November 1947, quoted in *ibid*, p. 140; cf also Ionescu, *op cit*, p. 131

[37] Speeches of Gheorgiu Dej and others at the November–December 1961 Plenum of the Central Committee of the Rumanian Workers' Party

[38] *New York Times*, 17 March 1945, quoted in Gluckstein, *op cit*, p. 138

[39] *Era Noua*, 8 November 1946. Quoted in *East Europe*, London, 20 November 1946, quoted in Gluckstein, *op cit*, p. 141

[40] *Era Noua*, 3 December 1946. Quoted in *East Europe*, London, 18 December 1946, quoted in Gluckstein, *op cit*, p. 141

[41] P.E.Zinner, *Revolution in Hungary*, New York 1962, p. 52

[42] Appeal of the Union of Polish Patriots broadcast by Moscow Radio, 29 July 1944. Quoted in Gluckstein, *op cit*, p. 144, cf also appeal of the UPP radio, Radio Kosciuszko, the day before the rising began: 'Peoples of Warsaw to arms. Attack the Germans . . . Assist the Red Army in crossing the Vistula', quoted in *Manchester Guardian*, 22 August 1944

[43] *Armia Ludowa*, 15 August 1944, quoted in Gluckstein, *op cit*, p. 148

[44] Quoted in Zaremba, *La Commune de Varsovie*, Paris 1947, pp. 39–40

[45] Speech of 29 February 1952. Extracts in *Problems of Communism*, 1952, No. 4, p. 35

[46] Facts given in H.Ripka, *Czechoslovakia Enslaved*, London 1950, p. 195. Ripka was Minister of Foreign Trade in the coalition government prior to the coup of February 1948

[47] Korbonski, *op cit*, p. 106. cf also Gluckstein, *op cit*, p. 168

[48] P.E.Zinner, *op cit*, pp. 43-44

[49] Gluckstein, *op cit*, p. 175

[50] A.Ciolkosz, *The Expropriation of the Socialist Party*, New York 1946, p. 3, quoted in Gluckstein, *op cit*, p. 176

[51] Gluckstein, *op cit*, describes the repression, pp. 177–81

[52] *Robotnik*, 5 May 1947, quoted in Gluckstein, *op cit*, p. 179

[53] P. Nettl, *The Eastern Zone & Soviet Policy in Germany*, London 1950, pp. 56, 58; cf also W.Leonhard, *Child of the Revolution*, London 1957. Robert Havemann tells that when he was sacked from his university job for criticisms of Stalinist practices in the mid-sixties 'the rector of the university and the state secretary for universities who sacked me were former members of the Nazi party'. *An Alienated Man*, London 1973, pp. 60–61

[54] Nettl, *op cit*, p. 88

[55] *ibid*, p. 70

[56] *ibid*, p. 71

[57] Taborski, *Communism in Czechoslovakia 1948–60*, New Jersey 1961, p. 18; see also Zinner, *Communist Strategy and Tactics in Czechoslovakia*, p. 123

[58] Bethell, *op cit*, p. 93

[59] Zinner, *op cit*, p. 124

[60] Ionescu, *op cit*, p. 114

[61] Gluckstein, *op cit*, p. 186

[62] Zinner, *op cit*, p. 62

[63] Gluckstein, *op cit*, p. 187

[64] *Inprecor*, 1 June 1935

[65] Huebl in the Czechoslovak Writers' Union monthly, *Host do Domu*, 1968 translated in *Studies in Contemporary Communism*, April 1969, p. 189. For descriptions of the expulsions as seen in one village, cf L.Vaculik, *The Axe*, London 1973

[66] Declaration of Gottwald, 12 May 1945

[67] Statement of Zdenek Nejedly, 29 May 1945

[68] R.Luza, *The Transfer of the Sudeten Germans*, London 1964

[69] G.Beuer, *The New Czechoslovakia*, London 1947, p. 193

[70] R.Luza, *op cit*

[71] Zinner, *op cit*, p. 79

[72] G.Beuer, *op cit*, p. 194

[73] *ibid*, p. 214

[74] *ibid*, p. 214

[75] I.Deutscher, *Stalin*, London 1966, p. 576

[76] For descriptions of the events of the Prague coup, see Zinner, *op cit*, pp. 202–206; Korbel, *Communist Subversion in Czechoslovakia;* H.Ripka, *Le Coup de Prague*, Paris 1949, pp. 53ff

[77] Gluckstein, *op cit*, p. 84

[78] *Pravo Lidu*, 9 January 1948

Chapter 2

The Russian Interest

[1] G.Ionescu, *Communism in Rumania 1944–62*, London 1964, p. 137

[2] S.Newens (ed.), *Nicolae Ceausescu*, Nottingham 1972, and R.R.Betts (ed.) *Central & South East Europe*, London 1950, pp. 20-21

[3] UNRRA quoted in Y.Gluckstein, *Stalin's Satellites in Europe*, London 1952, p. 60

[4] Gero quoted in Gluckstein, *op cit*, p. 61

[5] *ibid*, p. 62

[6] *ibid*, p. 139

[7] The Yugoslav UN delegate, Vilfan, quoted in Gluckstein, *op cit*, p. 32

[8] M.Kaser, *Comecon*, London 1967, p. 78

[9] *ibid*, p. 78

[10] *Borba*, 31 March 1949

[11] *Pravda*, 31 October, 1956

[12] Figures quoted in Gluckstein, *op cit*, p. 64

[13] Kaser, *op cit*, p. 144

[14] Economist Intelligence Unit *Quarterly Economic Review, East Europe North*, London 1970, No. 3

[15] Economist Intelligence Unit, *Motor Business*, London, July 1972

Chapter 3

From Control to Subjection

[1] For an account of these, see the report produced by Piller and others;

for the Czechoslovak CP in 1968, published as Jiri Pelikan (ed.), *The Czechoslovak Political Trials 1950–54*, London 1971

2 Figures quoted in Taborsky, *Communism in Czechoslovakia 1948–60*, New Jersey 1961, p. 27

3 *Rude Pravo*, 9 November 1951, quoted in Taborsky, *op cit*, p. 71

4 Quoted *ibid*, p. 27

5 Quoted in *News from Behind the Iron Curtain*, 1956, No. 5, p. 21

6 Kural Kaplan in *Nova Mysl*, No. 6–7, 1968

7 Figures quoted by Zoltan Sztarany in *The Review*, Brussels, Vol. III, No. 2, p. 16

8 From A. Zauberman, *Industrial Progress in Poland, Czechoslovakia and East Germany 1937–62*, London, 1964, p. 107. For a comparison with western estimates see Zauberman, pp. 119-120

9 Imre Nagy, *On Communism*, New York 1957, p. 185

10 Zauberman, *op cit*, p. 40. Peter Kende, *The Review*, Brussels 1960, No. 4, p. 102, gives a figure of 33.4 per cent for accumulation in Hungary in 1952

11 Zauberman, *op cit*, p. 95

12 P.Kende, *The Review*, Brussels 1960, No. 5, p. 34

13 *Eastern European Quarterly*, Vol. 2, No. 1

14 According to P.Zinner, *Revolution in Hungary*, New York 1962, p. 116, by as much as 50–60 per cent in 3–4 years

15 Zapotocky in *Hospador* 15 October 1949, quoted in V.Chlupa, *The Rise and Development of a Totalitarian State*, London 1959, p. 202

16 *Neue Züricher Zeitung*, 6 September 1949, quoted in Y.Gluckstein, *Stalin's Satellites in Europe*, London 1952, p. 106

17 *ibid*. Note this figure compares with a 30 per cent wastage rate in sectors of the Russian metal industry recently noted in a recent edition of *Izvestia* (18 December 1969)

18 For details see Gluckstein, *op cit*, pp. 107-109

19 P.Kende, *The Review*, No. 4, Brussels 1960, pp. 58–61

20 'Basic Principles of International Socialist Division of Labour', *New Times*, Moscow, No. 27, 1962, reported in M.Kaser, *Comecon*, London 1967, p. 40

21 This 'autarchic' development in many ways paralleled the similar well-known autarchic development in the different units of the Russian economy.

22 Karl Marx & Friedrich Engels, 'Manifesto of the Communist Party', *Selected Works* Vol. 1, Moscow 1962, p. 37

Chapter 4

1953: The German Workers' Revolt

1 *Pravda*, 6 March 1953, quoted in L. Pastrak, *The Grand Tactician*, London 1961, p. 243

2 *Labour Monthly*, April 1953

3 Arnulf Baring, *Der 7 Juni 1953*, Cologne 1965, p. 55, and Heinz Brandt in *The Review*, Brussels, No. 2, October 1959, pp. 95, 102

4 Baring, *op cit*, p. 51

5 Document printed in *ibid*, p. 143

6 *ibid*, p. 59

7 *ibid*, p. 59

8 Robert Havemann, *An Alienated Man*, London 1973, pp. 93–94

9 Brandt, *op cit*, pp. 105–106

10 Havemann, *op cit*, pp. 95–96

11 *ibid*, p. 98

12 Baring, *op cit*, p. 168

13 Speech at the Fifteenth Plenum of the Central Committee of the SED, quoted in Baring, *op cit*, p. 67, and in M.Jaenicker, *Der Dritte Weg: Die Anti-Stalinistische Opposition gegen Ulbrichtseit 1953*, Cologne 1964, p. 43

14 Baring, *op cit*, p. 69

15 Jaenicker, *op cit*, p. 43

16 Baring, *op cit*, p. 68

17 Brandt, *op cit*, p. 108

18 *ibid*, p. 87; Jaenicker, *op cit*, p. 45

19 Stefan Brant, *The East German Rising*, New York 1957, pp. 79–97

20 Baring, *op cit*, p. 113

21 Statement on dismissal and arrest of Justice Minister, Max Fechner, by his successor, Hilda Benjamin, quoted in Baring, *op cit*, p. 113

22 Quoted in Brandt, *op cit*, pp. 105–106

23 Baring, *op cit*, p. 99

24 *ibid*, p. 100; cf also Brant, *op cit*, p. 70

25 Brant, *op cit*, p. 79

26 *ibid*, p. 68

27 Statement of 24 June 1953, quoted in *ibid*, pp. 68–79

28 For the situation in the giant Leuna works, see Jaenicker, *op cit*, p. 49

29 *ibid*, p. 51

30 Estimates given in A.Zauberman, *Industrial Progress in Poland, Czechoslovakia and East Germany 1937–62*, London 1964, p. 95

31 For German rulers' economic problems, see Baring, *op cit*, pp. 23ff

32 B.Garland, a Berlin journalist who spent eight years in Russian labour camps, in *The Observer*, 3 June 1956. Quoted in Cliff, *Russia: A Marxist Analysis*, London n.d. (1963), p. 286

33 Jaenicker, *op cit*, pp. 28ff; Baring, *op cit*, p. 40; Brandt, *op cit*, p. 96

34 Decisions of the SED Politburo meeting of 9 June 1953, quoted in both Jaenicker and Baring

35 Speech of March 1953, quoted by W.H.Kraus in K.London (ed.) *East Europe in Transition*, Baltimore 1966, pp. 50–51

36 Quoted in Brant, *op cit*, p. 57

Chapter 5

1953–56: Prelude to Revolution

1 Figures given in Imre Nagy, *On Communism*, London 1967, p. 185

2 *ibid*, p. 66

3 *ibid*, p 66

4 Miklos Molnor and Lazlo Nagy, *Imre Nagy, Reformateur ou Révolutionnaire,* Geneva 1959, pp. 24–37

5 T.Aczel and T.Meray, *The Revolt of the Mind,* London 1960, pp. 151–154 and P.Kecskemeti, *The Unexpected Revolution,* Stanford 1961, p. 39

6 For a description of the ensuing crisis of conscience among Communist writers see Aczel and Meray, *op cit*

7 According to Aczel and Meray, *op cit*, p. 382. However, according to Kecskemeti, *op cit*, p. 69, no police measures were taken against the writers, although attempts were made to close down their journals

Chapter 6

1956: Poland – Aborted Revolution

1 cf A.Korbonski, *Politics of Socialist Agriculture in Poland,* New York 1965, pp. 208–9

2 See various estimates in A.Zauberman, *Industrial Progress in Poland, Czechoslovakia and East Germany,* London 1964, pp. 95–97

3 *ibid,* p. 40

4 Address of Gomulka to central committee of PUWP, 20 October 1956, reproduced in P.Zinner (ed.), *National Communism and Popular Revolt,* New York 1956, p. 199

5 *ibid,* p. 200

6 *Economic Commission of Polish Council of Ministers,* quoted in Zauberman, *op cit,* pp. 102-104

7 Gomulka in Zinner, *op cit,* p. 199

8 *ibid,* p. 202

9 Figures based on Polish sources, given in Korbonski, *op cit,* p. 194

10 F. Lewis, *The Polish Volcano,* London 1969, p. 31

11 *Po Prostu,* quoted in *World Today,* July 1956, p. 300

12 Sections here quoted are from translation in Zinner, *op cit,* p. 40

13 *Po Prostu,* 26 January 1956

14 *ibid,* 1 April 1956

15 Quoted in Zinner, *op cit,* p. 128

16 *Pravda,* 1 July 1956, quoted in *ibid,* p. 136

17 Cyrankiewicz, *Trybuna Ludu,* 30 June 1956, quoted in *ibid,* p. 136

18 Quoted in K.Syrop, *Spring in October,* London 1957, p. 53

19 Lewis, *op cit,* p. 200

20 *Evening Standard,* 20 October 1956

21 *Tribune,* 26 October 1956

22 *ibid,* 9 November 1956

23 Isaac Deutscher in *Universities and Left Review,* London, Vol. I, No. 1, 1957

24 Ernest Mandel in *Quatrième Internationale,* December 1956

25 Tony Cliff in *Socialist Review,* London December 1956

26 *The Times,* 25 October 1956

27 Quoted in Syrop, *op cit,* p. 164

28 Quoted in Zinner, *op cit,* p. 215

[29] L. D. Trotsky, *History of the Russian Revolution*, London 1945, Vol. I, p. 186

[30] Wyszynski, speech of November 1956, quoted in N. Bethel, *Gomulka*, London 1969, p. 227

[31] *World Today*, 1957, p. 347

[32] Korbunski, *op cit*, p. 207

[33] N. Bethel, *op cit*, p. 232

[34] Jacek Kuron and Karol Modzelewski, *An Open Letter to the Party*, translated as *A Revolutionary Socialist Manifesto*, London 1968, p. 45

[35] *ibid*

[36] Speech to Provincial Party Secretaries, 23 November 1956

[37] *The Times*, 25 October 1956

[38] *ibid*

[39] *Glos Pracy*, 18 December 1956

[40] Printed in *Po Prostu*, 9 December 1956. Texts of this and the following material are collected in J–J Marie and Balazs Nagy (eds.), *Pologne–Hongrie*, Paris 1966

[41] *ibid*, pp. 90–95

[42] *Nowe Drogi*, February 1958, in *ibid*, pp. 139–42

[43] in *ibid*, p. 95

[44] Report to Ninth Plenum of the central committee in *ibid*, pp. 139–42

[45] M.Borowska, J.Balcerek and L.Gilejko, 'Workers' Councils or a System of Councils', *Po Prostu*, 6 January 1957, in *ibid*, p. 118

[46] S.Chelstowski and W.Godek, 'Workers' Self-Management in Danger', *Po Prostu*, 30 January 1957, in *ibid*, p. 128

[47] W. Skulska in *Po Prostu,* 30 June 1957, in *ibid*, p. 144

[48] *Trybuna Ludu*, 17 May 1957, in *ibid,* p. 149

Chapter 7

1956: The Hungarian Revolution

[1] Economist Intelligence Unit, *Quarterly Economic Review, Eastern Europe South*, February 1956

[2] *ibid*, May 1956

[3] Resolution of the central committee of the Hungarian party of 30 June 1956. Quoted in J.–J.Marie and B.Nagy (eds.) *Pologne-Hongrie 1956*, Paris 1966

[4] Gero in *Szabad Nep*, 19 July 1956

[5] *ibid*

[6] Quoted in Melvin J.Laski (ed.), *Hungarian Revolution*, London 1957, p.29

[7] Kadar's words, according to a report quoted in Kecskemeti, *The Unexpected Revolution*, Stanford 1961, p. 76

[8] Quoted in Laski (ed.), *op cit*, p. 40

[9] F.Toke, 'What were the Hungarian Workers' Councils?' in Marie and Nagy (eds.) *op cit*, p. 242. The English translation, in *The Review*, Brussels, January 1960, does not contain this passage

[10] B.Nagy in Marie and Nagy (eds.), *op cit*, p. 183

11 ibid, p. 183

12 Quoted in Laski (ed.), *op cit*, p. 48

13 Radio speech reprinted in Laski (ed.), *op cit*, p. 51

14 Zolyan Zele, quoted in Tibor Meray, *13 Days that Shook the Kremlin*, London 1959, p. 87

15 Kadar government's 'White Book', quoted in Meray, *op cit*, p. 87

16 Peter Gosztonyi, 'Diary – Revolutionary Days at the Killian Barracks', *The Review*, Brussels, No. 6, October 1960

17 According to the account given by Charlie Coutts to Peter Fryer, *Hungarian Tragedy*, London 1956, p. 46

18 Nagy's speech is printed in Laski (ed.), *op cit*, p. 74

19 *New York Times*, 27 October 1956

20 *Politika*, Belgrade, 26 October 1956

21 Gosztonyi, *op cit*, p. 73

22 Radio Gyor, 27 October 1956, in Marie & Nagy (eds.), *op cit*, p. 187

23 Radio Kossuth, in *ibid*, p. 188

24 *ibid*, p. 192

25 Radio Miskolc, quoted in Laski (ed.), *op cit*, p. 98

26 Peter Fryer, *op cit*, p. 51

27 Toke, *The Review*, Brussels January 1960, p. 75

28 Radio Miskolc, 27 October, quoted in Laski (ed.), *op cit*, p. 98

29 Radio Gyor, 28 October, quoted in Laski, *op cit*, p. 120

30 Speech printed in Laski (ed.), *op cit*, p. 139

31 Zoltan Tildy, quoted in Laski (ed.), *op cit*, p. 140

32 Quoted in Laski (ed.), *op cit*, p. 134

33 Quoted in Laski (ed.), *op cit*, p. 152

34 *Po Prostu*, 25 November 1956

35 Kadar on Radio Kossuth, 1 November, quoted in Marie and Nagy (eds.), *op cit*, p. 210

36 Interview in *Der Spiegel*, 12 December 1956

37 The President of Borsod National Council on Radio Miskolc, 2 November 1956, printed in Marie and Nagy (eds.), *op cit*, p. 205

38 For an elaboration of this approach see Jacek Kuron and Karol Modzelewski, *An Open Letter to the Party* printed in English as *A Revolutionary Socialist Manifesto*, London 1968

39 L.G. in *The Review*, Brussels, Vol. v, No. 2, p. 37

40 Reprinted as *Imre Nagy on Communism*, London 1957

41 M.Molnar and L.Nagy, *Imre Nagy, Réformateur ou Révolutionnaire*, Geneva 1959, p. 133

42 Balazs Nagy in Marie and Nagy (eds.), *op cit*, pp. 183–84

43 Both instances related in *ibid*, p. 182

44 'Hungaricus Pamphlet' produced in Budapest, November 1956; translated into English, Brussels, 1959

45 *ibid*

46 Szigeti had been a fellow travelling peasant M P who was later 'exiled' to Gyor, where he took charge of a collective farm and was, during Nagy's

first premiership, vice-president of Gyor department. He was later to die in Kadar's prisons. Marie and Nagy (eds.), *op cit*, p. 81

47 F.Fejto, *Budapest 1956*, Paris 1966, p. 205

48 P.Zinner, *Revolution in Hungary*, New York 1962, p. 291

49 *Borba* (Belgrade), 1 November 1956

50 Radio Kossuth, quoted in Laski (ed.), *op cit*, p. 172

51 Quoted in Laski (ed.), *op cit*, p. 127

52 Hungarian News Agency, quoted in Laski (ed.), *op cit*, p. 148

53 Toke, *op cit*, p. 77

54 For accounts see Felix Morrow, *Revolution and Counter-Revolution in Spain*, London 1963, and George Orwell, *Homage to Catalonia*, London 1962

55 Radio Miskolc, 2 November 1956

56 Statement of the 'Revolutionary Worker-Peasant Government', 4 November 1956. Quoted in Laski (ed.), *op cit*, p. 236

57 G. Urban, *Nineteen Days*, London 1957, p. 158

58 Speech of 14 November 1956

59 Toke, *op cit*, p. 77

60 *ibid*, p. 78

61 *ibid*, p. 79

62 Miklos Sebestyen in *The Review*, Brussels 1961, No. 2, p. 43

63 Quoted in *ibid*, p. 47

64 See the record of these negotiations in the second duplicated bulletin of the Central Workers' Council, 30 November 1956, translated in *The Review*, Brussels, 1960, No. 2, p. 112

65 Toke, *op cit*, p. 81

66 Sebestyen, *op cit*, p. 50

67 Translated in *The Review*, Brussels 1960, No. 4, pp. 108ff

68 Apro on Radio Kossuth, 25 November 1956

69 *Observer*, 25 November 1956

70 Economist Intelligence Unit, *op cit*, January 1957

71 Quoted by B. Nagy, 'Budapest 1956: The Central Workers' Council', *International Socialism* 18, p. 19

72 Quoted in Laski (ed.), *op cit*, pp. 295–96

73 *ibid*, pp. 295-96

74 cf two of the bulletins translated (in French) in Marie and Nagy (eds.), *op cit*, pp. 292 and 307. One of the bulletins appears in *The Review*, Brussels, 1960, No. 4

75 Reproduced in Marie and Nagy (eds.), *op cit*, pp. 314ff

76 Quoted in *ibid*, p. xlvi

77 In *Neparakat*, 13 December 1956

78 *Borba*, 12 December 1956, quoted in Laski (ed.), *op cit*, p. 296

79 Bulletin reproduced in Marie and Nagy (eds.), *op cit*, pp. 307ff

80 All the above quotes on the changing government attitude to the workers' councils are contained in T.Schreiber, 'The Fate of the Hungarian Workers' Councils', *The Review*, Brussels, October 1959

Chapter 8

1968: Czechoslovakia – Arrested Reform

1 Russia, China and the other East European regimes gave the Hungarian government loans which had to be paid back in the mid-1960s. M.Kaser, *Comecon*, London 1967, p. 78

2 Perry Anderson, 'The Left in the Fifties', *New Left Review*, 29, London 1965, p. 14

3 Speech of 21 April 1968. Translated in A.Oxley, A.Pravda and A.Ritchie, *Czechoslovakia, The Party and The People*, London 1973, pp. 78–82

4 A.Oxley et al, *op cit*, p. 123

5 Figures given in P.Windsor and A.Roberts, *Czechoslovakia 1968*, London 1969, p. 106

6 Text of Communiqué on Moscow Agreement of 27 August 1968. Translated in R.Rhodes James (ed.), *The Czechoslovak Crisis 1968*, London 1969, p. 183

7 Dubcek's radio address of 27 August 1968. Translated as an appendix to W.Shawcross, *Dubcek*, London 1970, pp. 267-74

8 *Statistika rocenka CSSR 1968*, Prague 1968, p. 289. Quoted in C.Boffito and L. Foa, *La Crisi del Modello Sovietico in Cecoslovacchia*, Turin 1970, pp. 34ff

9 A.Zauberman, *Industrial Progress in Poland, Czechoslovakia and E. Germany 1937–62*, London 1964, p. 95

10 K.Cerny (of the Institute of Politics and Economics in Prague), 'Historical Background to the Czechoslovak Economic Reform', *East European Quarterly*, Vol. III, No. 3, p. 346

11 *Facts of Czechoslovak Foreign Trade*, Prague 1966, p. 30

12 See report in the *Economist*, 29 June 1968, p. 33; cf also Economist Intelligence Unit, *Quarterly Economic Review, East Europe North*, January 1967, p. 5

13 For accounts of these problems, see the various articles collected in Boffito and Foa, *op cit*, pp. 125-211

14 'Analysis of the Party's Record and of the Development of Society since the Thirteenth Congress; The Party's Main Tasks for the Immediate Future (a rough outline).' Translated in Jiri Pelikan (ed.), *The Secret Vysocany Congress*, London 1971, pp. 193-94

15 For a detailed account of meetings of the central committee, October 1967–January 1968, see P.Tigrid, 'Czechoslovakia, A Post-Mortem', *Survey*, Autumn 1969, pp. 133–48

16 *ibid*, p. 146

17 *ibid*, pp. 151ff

18 *Smer*, 12 June 1954, quoted in Shawcross, *op cit*, p. 55

19 According to Shawcross, *op cit*, p. 142

20 *ibid*, p. 138

21 Speech of 8 April 1968, quoted in *ibid*, p. 157

22 On 11 April 1968, quoted in *ibid*, p. 247

23 Statement of 30 June 1968, quoted in *ibid*, p. 248; cf also pp. 161–62

[24] V. V. Kusin, *Political Groupings in the Czechoslovak Reform Movement*, London 1972, p. 172. For other reports of attempted censorship see, for example, Shawcross, *op cit*, pp. 157ff

[25] Speech of 31 August 1969. Translated in Shawcross, *op cit*, p. 230

[26] A translation of the appropriate section of the Action Programme appears in Oxley et al, *op cit*, pp. 125–26

[27] Dubcek, speech to the central committee of the Communist Party, 29 May 1968. Translated in *ibid*, p. 147

[28] Quoted by J. Spacek in *Rude Pravo*, 16 March 1968, according to Kusin, *op cit*, p. 165

[29] Kusin, *op cit*, p. 174

[30] Quoted in P.Tigrid, 'Czechoslovakia, A Post-Mortem, II', *Survey*, Winter-Spring 1970, p. 122

[31] Dubcek, speech to the central committee, 26 September 1969. Translated as an appendix to Shawcross, *op cit*, p. 275

[32] Speech to Party Congress in Brno, 16 March 1968, in *ibid*, p. 150

[33] Speech to central committee, 26 September 1969, in *ibid*, p. 279

[34] 'Reply of the Presidium of the Central Committee of the Czechoslovak Communist Party to the "Warsaw Letter" from the Central Committee of the Communist Parties of the USSR, East Germany, Hungary, Poland and Bulgaria.' Translated in R. R. James (ed.), *op cit*, p. 177

[35] Dubcek, speech to the central committee, 29 May 1968, translated in Oxley et al, *op cit*, p. 146

[36] *ibid*

[37] Prague Radio, 10 July 1968

[38] Figures given in Pelikan, *op cit*, p. 292

[39] Translated in *ibid*, p. 231

[40] *ibid*, p. 231

[41] *ibid*, p. 232

[42] Shawcross, *op cit*, p. 154

[43] According to Shawcross, *op cit*, p. 179

[44] Dubcek, speech to central committee, 26 September 1969, in *ibid*, p. 291

[45] *ibid*, p. 291

[46] Speech by Martin Vaculik to the Congress, in Pelikan, *op cit*, p. 19

[47] Communiqué of central committee of the Czechoslovak Communist Party, quoted in *ibid*, p. 22

[48] *ibid*, p. 53

[49] *ibid*, p. 49

[50] Speech to central committee on 26 September 1969, in Shawcross, *op cit*, p. 292

[51] Communiqué of central committee etc., in Pelikan, *op cit*, p. 22

[52] Speech to Vysocany Congress, in *ibid*, p. 37

[53] Radio address of 27 August 1968, translated in Shawcross, *op cit*, p. 268

[54] P. Tigrid, *op cit*, p. 124

[55] Speech to central committee, 26 September 1969, in Shawcross, *op cit*, p. 294

[56] *ibid*, p. 294

57 *ibid.*, p. 296

58 *The Times*, 6 January 1969

59 P.Tigrid, *op cit*, p. 140

60 Their speeches are translated in *Studies in Contemporary Communism*, January 1970

61 The economist, Radoslav Selucky, could note, for instance, that consumption of meat per capita in Slovakia was 14.8 kilos a year less than in the Czech lands; consumption of fats and oils 7.2 kilos less; consumption of eggs 63 less. *Czechoslovak Economic Papers*, 1964, No. 3

62 M. Pecho in *Pravda*, Bratislava, 13 May 1967, quoted in Shawcross, *op cit*, p. 101

63 Speech on Prague Radio, 31 May 1969. Translated in *Studies in Contemporary Communism*, January 1970

64 Neal Ascherson in the *Observer*, 18 March 1968

65 Quoted in A.Shub, *An Empire Loses Hope*, London 1971, p. 350

66 *ibid.*, p. 351

67 Analysis of the Party's Record etc., in Pelikan, *op cit*, p. 229

68 *ibid.*, p. 220

69 *ibid*, p. 218. For Stalin, see quotes in T. Cliff, *Russia: A Marxist Anaylsis*, London n.d. (1963), pp. 55–56

70 Figures for various categories of workers and the middle class given in A. Kudrna, *Planovane Hospdarstvi*, 1968, No. 9, translated in *East European Economics*, Vol. VII, No. 4. He shows that a third of men got more than 2000 crowns in 1966, while the average labourer's pay was 1600 crowns. Two per cent of the population got more than twice the Labourer's wage. Ivan Svitak, in *The Czechoslovak Experiment, 1968–69*, New York 1971, suggests that the really privileged 'power elite' was 100,000 strong (less than one per cent of the population). The 'intelligentsia' of white collar and professional workers was much larger, about 18 per cent of the population.

71 Speech translated in Oxley et al, *op cit*, pp. 30-40

72 According to Ivan Svitak, 'The Gordian Knot: Intellectuals and Workers in the Czechoslovak Democratisation', *New Politics*, New York, January 1969

73 *ibid*

74 For one translation of *2000 Words*, see Oxley et al, *op cit*, pp. 261–68

75 Prague Radio, 2 July 1965

76 Vaclav Harvel in *Literarny Listy*, 4 April 1968

77 *ibid*

78 G.Golan, *Reform Rule in Czechoslovakia*, London 1973, p. 71, quoted in J. Kavan, 'Czechoslovakia 1968: Workers and Students', *Critique* No. 2, Glasgow 1973

79 Ivan Svitak, 'Heads Against the Wall', in I.Svitak, *The Czechoslovak Experiment 1968–69*, New York 1971

80 *ibid*, p. 187

81 Petr Pithart, 'Political Parties and Freedom of Speech', *Literarny*

Listy, 20 June 1968. Translated in Oxley et al, *op cit*, pp. 141-45
82 Milan Kundera, *The Joke*, London 1970, p. 69
83 *ibid*, p. 86
84 I. Svitak, article in *New Politics, op cit*
85 *Prace*, 4 January 1969
86 R. Selucky in *Prace*, 23 April 1968
87 Report in *Prace*, 27 March 1968
88 Report by Ceteka, 14 April 1968
89 Report in *Prace*, 24 April 1968
90 *Pravda*, Bratislava, 14 May 1968
91 Report of Ceteka, 7–8 June 1968
92 Speech at a meeting of local trade-union leaders, 18 June 1968
93 Prague Radio report of 4 June 1968 on the meeting of the central committee of the RTUM
94 Report on Bratislava Radio, 27 March 1968
95 Referred to by K.Pasek, in *Literarny Listy,* 18 April 1968
96 Prague Radio, 24 April 1968
97 Ceteka, 20 June 1968
98 *Prace*, 31 May 1968
99 Ceteka, 21 May 1968
100 Prague Radio, 3 March 1968
101 Ceteka, 13 June 1968
102 *Rude Pravo*, 7 April 1968
103 J.Skvoracky (ed.), *Nachrichten aus der CSSR*, Frankfurt/Main 1968, p. 346
104 J.Kavan, *op cit*, p. 65
105 Translated in James, *op cit*, pp. 177–78
106 *Prace*, 4 January 1969
107 Quoted by Sam Russell, in the *Morning Star*, 15 November 1968
108 Quoted *ibid*
109 Prague Radio, 10 December 1968
110 Lorry Works resolution published in *Prace*, quoted in *The Times*, 13 December 1968
111 From a pipeline factory near Prague, *ibid*
112 *Morning Star*, 14 December 1968
113 *The Times*, 14 December 1968
114 According to Shawcross, *op cit*, p. 194
115 Speech of 21 December 1968, quoted in *ibid*, p. 195
116 cf Kusin, *op cit*, p. 39
117 *The Times*, 13 January 1969
118 *The Times*, 4 March 1969
119 *Financial Times*, 6 March 1969
120 Resolution quoted in *East Europe*, New York, May 1969
121 *ibid*
122 *ibid*
123 Kavan, *op cit*, p. 68
124 *ibid*

125 Tomalek, *Czechoslovakia 1968–69, The Worker-Student Alliance,* quoted in *ibid,* p. 68

126 Quoted in *East Europe,* New York, May 1969

127 *ibid,* June 1969

128 *ibid*

129 Referred to in J. and U.Fisera, in *Revue de l'Est,* Paris, Vol. 2, No. 1, 1971, p. 46

130 Quoted in Economist Intelligence Unit, *Quarterly Economic Review, East Europe North,* 1968 No. 3. Sik shifted his position to one which gave more influence to elected delegates soon after this, although 'they still lacked decisive political power and had only a limited workers' representation' (Kavan, *op cit,* p. 63)

131 Pavel Ernst in *Rude Pravo,* May 1968. Translated (into Italian) in Carlo Boffito and Lisa Foa, *op cit,* pp. 232-37

132 *ibid*

133 N. Bukharin, *The Programme of World Revolution,* Glasgow 1920.

134 Quoted in D.D.Milenkovitch, *Plan and Market in Yugoslav Economic Thought,* p. 192

135 *Praxis* (Zagreb), 1968, p. 104

136 *Politika,* 27 February 1969

137 *Reporter,* 8 May 1968. There is a translation in Oxley et al, *op cit,* pp. 193–96

138 In the discussion 'Self-management, yes or no', *Reporter,* 5–12 June 1968

139 Samalick, in *Reporter,* 5–12 June 1968

140 Fisera, *op cit,* p. 49

141 *ibid,* p. 48

142 *ibid,* p. 50

143 *ibid,* pp. 53ff for a statistical break-down of the successful candidates

144 *Prace,* 19 February 1969

145 According to the *Czechoslovak Trade Unions, 1870–1970,* Brussels, International Confederation of Free Trade Unions, 1970, p. 34

146 J.Dvorak and T. Jezek in *Politica Economica* (Czechoslovakia), 1972 No. 6. Translated in *East European Economics.* Vol. XI, No. 4, Summer 1973

Chapter 9

1970 : Poland

1 Both extracts from *Quatrième International,* December 1956

2 Published in English as *A Revolutionary Socialist Manifesto,* London 1968

3 N.Karsow and S.Schechter, *Monuments are not Loved,* London 1970, p. 285

4 A.Shrub, *An Empire Loses Hope,* London 1971, p. 356

5 J. Pajetska, *Ekonomista* (Warsaw) 1965, No. 2, translated in *East European Economics,* Vol. V, No. 2

6 *ibid*

[7] Figures given in Kuron and Modzelewski, *op cit*, and in L.Beskid, *Ekonomista*, 1968, No. 6, translated in *East European Economics*, Vol. VII, No. 3

[8] Kuron and Modzelewski, *op cit*

[9] Figures on accumulation from GUS, *Roswoj gospodarczy krajow RWPG*, 1950-68, Warsaw 1969, quoted in Z.M.Fellenbuchi, *Comecon Integration: Problems of Communism*, May–June 1973

[10] Economist Intelligence Unit, *Quarterly Economic Review, East Europe North*, January 1968

[11] Gierek's speech to the Szczecin shipyard workers, 24 January 1971 printed in E.Gierek, *Face aux Grévistes de Szczecin*, Paris 1972, p. 37

[12] *ibid*, p. 85

[13] The precis of Gierek's speech is based, as are the various quotes from the discussions which follow, on the texts printed in *ibid*

Chapter 10
Conclusion: Reform or Revolution

[1] *Quatrième International*, année 14 (1956), Nos. 1–3

[2] The figures, from the official statistics of the different countries were collated in this form in *Lloyds Bank Review*, October 1968, p. 9. For a different presentation of similar figures, cf W. D. Connor, in *Problems of Communism*, March/April 1973

[3] Figures given in J. Klewt, *Warost intensywny w krajacch socjalistyycznych*, Warsaw 1972, pp 104–105, quoted in W.D. Connor, *op cit*

[4] Figures from K.Bogaev, *Ekonomist* (Yugoslavia) 1970, Nos. 2–3. Translated in *East European Economics*, Summer 1972

[5] For a few outlines of the failings of the East European Economies, cf: Karel Cerny, 'Background to the Czechoslovak Economic Reforms', *East European Quarterly*, Vol. III, No. 3. T.Berend, 'Background to the Recent Economic Reforms in Hungary', *ibid*, Vol. II, No. 3. J.Goldman and K.Korba, *Economical Growth in Czechoslovakia*, Prague 1969. *Rude Pravo*, 17 October 1964, translated in *East European Economics*, Vol. III, No. 4. M.Bottcher, *Die Wirtschaft*, East Germany 1965, No. 48. Translated in *East European Economics*, Vol VI, No. 3. Essays by Brjeski, Fekete, Holosovsky and Pisek, in G.Grossman (ed.), *Money and Plan*, Berkeley 1968. O.Sik in K.Coates (ed.), *Czechoslovakia and Socialism*, Nottingham 1969. T.Cliff, *Russia: A Marxist Analysis*, London n.d. (1963), Book 2

[6] *Financy SSSR*, May 1972, pp. 7–12

[7] *Izvestia*, 18 December 1970

[8] *Pravda*, 17 December 1970

[9] Ota Sik, *op cit*, p. 162

[10] S.Newens (ed.), *Nicolae Ceausescu*, Nottingham 1972, pp. 121–22.

[11] Branko Horvat, 'Business Cycles in Yugoslavia', translated in *East European Economics*, Vol. XI, Nos. 3–4

[12] Pisek, in Grossman (ed.), *op cit*, p. 126

13 J. Fekete, in Grossman (ed.) *op cit*, p. 14

14 *The Best Use of Resources*, London 1965, quoted by H. Ticktin in *Critique* No. 1, Glasgow 1973, p. 27

15 *Politika Economica* (Czechoslovakia), 1968, No. 2, translated in *East European Economics*, Vol. VI, No. 4. Strupp assumes that the level of investment is the same in France as in Czechoslovakia. In fact it is probably rather lower – although exact comparisons are difficult. However, the error would not seem to affect Strupp's overall conclusion a great deal

16 *SIPRI Yearbook*, Stockholm 1969-70, p. 9

17 Ferenc Janossy in *Kozgadasagi Szemle*, 1969, No. 2, translated in *East European Economics*, Summer 1970

18 Jaroslav Sokol, *Planovane Hospodarstvi*, 1969, No. 1, translated in *East European Economics*, Vol. VII, No. 4, p. 19

19 Joseph Pajetska in *Economistika* (Poland) 1965, No. 2, translated in *East European Economics*, Vol. V, No. 2, p. 19

20 Brezhnev in *Pravda*, 24 April 1970

21 Quoted in the *Financial Times*, 20 July 1972

22 A.Birman in *Literatura Gazeta*, 11 February 1970

23 *Izvestia*, 11 August 1972

24 A. Birman, *op cit*

25 M.Bottcher, *Die Wirtschaft*, East Germany 1965, No. 8, translated in *East European Economics*, Vol VI, No. 3

26 Pajetska, *op cit*

27 See, for instance, Goldman and Korba, *op cit*; Horvat, *op cit*; Pajetska, *op cit*; N.Cobeljik and R.Stojanovic 'A Contribution to the Study of Investment Cycles in the Socialist Economy', *East European Economics*, Fall/Winter 1963/4

28 Mervyn Matthews, *Class and Society in Soviet Russia*, London, 1972, p. 208; See also K.Wadekin, *Soviet Studies*, Glasgow, Vol. XX, No. 3

29 *Rude Pravo*, *op cit*

30 Sokol, *op cit*

31 A.Balek et al, 'Linee fondamentale di sviluppo della riforma economica', translated from Czech in C.Boffito and L.Foa (eds.), *La Crisi del Modello Sovietico in Cecoslovacchia*, Turin 1970, pp. 170ff

32 Sokol, *op cit*

33 A.Balek et al., *op cit*

34 *Financial Times*, 9 August 1971

35 *ibid*

36 *ibid*, 26 October 1971

37 *ibid*, 4 February 1972. See also Economist Intelligence Unit, *Czechoslovakia and Hungary*, 1972, No. 2

38 Jozsef Batiut in *Kozgazdazagi Szemle*, 1969, No. 6, translated in *East European Economics*, Fall 1970

39 Horvat, *op cit*

40 See, e.g. Michael Kidron, *Western Capitalism since the War*, rev. ed. London 1970

41 Bogaev, *op cit*

Index

Absenteeism; punishments for, 62

Accumulation; in Russia, 15,16,17, 18; and Stalin era, 16; and competition, 17,259; and planning, 260; in West and East, 17,256; and revolution, 186; and attacks on workers' rights, 269

Action Programme (of the Czechoslovak Communist Party), 189-90, 200

Anderson, P., 188

Apro, 177; begs Petofi circle to lead demonstration, 150; denounces workers' councils, 185

Armia Ludowa on Warsaw Uprising, 34

Arms spending in Eastern Europe, 55

AVH, 125; fires on demonstration 132-3

Badowski, K., 243

Baibakov, N.K., 257

Bali, Sandor, 177,178

Barak, R., 189

Bartosek, K., 236-7

Battek, R., 240

Behind the Yellow Curtains, 100-1

Berend, I.T., 61

Beria, L., 81,83

Berman, J., 97

Bierut, 58,97,100

Bolsheviks; view of possibilities for Russian revolution in 1917, 11; number driven out of CPSU by Stalin, 14

Borba, 52; on Hungarian revolution, 143, 183

Brandt, H., 71-3,76-7

Brezhnev, L., 260; on economic competition between Russia and West, 18

Budapest telephone factory, 127

Budapest Workers' Council: *see* Greater Budapest Central Workers' Council, 235

Bulganin, N., 105

Bulgaria; Communist Party opposes 'Sovietization' 31; ministers and members of Politburo arrested, 57; expulsions 1949-50, 58; foreign capital in, 26,28; postwar revolutionary wave in, 31; order restored, 31; tobacco sold to Russia, 52

Bureaucracy; growth in Russia, 13; abandons principles of October, 14; as a class, 19,147-8

Ceausescu, N.; on extent of Rumanian reparations, 50; on failings of Rumanian economy, 257

Cernik, O., 190,191,201,226-7,240

Chelstowski, S., 115,120

Chudynski, J., 100

Churchill, W., 23

Cliff, T., 20; on Poland 1956, 108

Clementis, V., 211

'Club of the Crooked Circle', 242

Collectivization; aim of, 63; in Poland, 94; in Hungary, 63; efficiency compared with private farms, 95

Cominform conference of November 1949, 60

Counter-revolution under Stalin Russia, 14

Communist Party of the Soviet Union (CPSU); members forced to use special shops, 16; Twentieth Party Congress, 125; effects of Twentieth Party Congress in Hungary, 125; politburo fly to Warsaw (1956), 106

Csepel; workers denounce Russian propaganda, 163; fighting in January 1957, 183; workers' council dissolves itself, 184

Cyrankiewicz, J., 38,104,243

Czechoslovakia:
  Communist Party; attitude to German speakers, 42; strength in 1930s, 29; membership, 40,59; role of workers in, 202, 203; lack of democracy in, 59; purges 58, 188; execution of leaders, 58; control over Ministry of Interior, 35-6; control over media, 214; attempt to integrate intellectuals, 216; Presidium, 199,200,227; Vysocany Congress, 206
  Economy; role of state in industrial production in 1930s, 26; German ownership, 27; looting by Russian troops, 50; nationalization before and after Prague coup, 47; Russian control, 55; dependence on foreign trade, 194-5; migration of labour, 263; in 1950s, 193; crisis in 1960s, 194, 195,241,257-8,266
  Generals try to back Novotny, 197
  Impact of destalinization, 189
  Intellectuals, 214-22,223,240; confusion over 1948, 220
  Prague Coup, 46-7
  Students, 189, 215-16, 219, 229, 232 agreement with Metal Workers' Union, 229; union dissolved, 232-3
  Trade unions; in late 1940s, 44,48; in 1968, 225-6; Czech Metal Workers' Union, 229,230,232; Printworkers Union Conference, 230; leaders after April 1969, 231-3: *see also* RTUM

Workers; promoted to bureaucratic posts, 41; living standards, 193; absenteeism, 62

Writers Congress of 1967, 217

1968; initial reaction of workers, 223; wage demands, 224; strikes, 225; union reactions, 225; pension increases, 227; reactions of workers after invasion, 228-33; journalists, 216; reaction of party leadership to new political organizations, 199-200; role of workers' militia, 223

1969; lack of leadership for workers, 231; role of radical students, 232; censorship of union resolutions, 232; purge, 191

Dahlem, F., 83

Deutscher, I., view of Prague coup, 46; on 1956, 108

Differentials; in Czechoslovakia in 1968, 217

Dimitrov, G., 32

DISZ, 125

Donath, F., 90

Dual power, 156-61

Dubcek, A., 189,191,200,201,204, 209,230,240; prior to 1968, 198-9; denounces 'anarchy', 199; denounces *2000 Words*, 199; gives jobs to Novotnyites, 204-5; removes Prchlik, 205; flown to Moscow, 190; during invasion, 205-6; and 'normalization', 208, 210; similar aims to Gomulka, 202

Dudas, J., 153, 159, 183

Eastern Europe:
  Arms spending, 258
  Bankruptcy of pre-war rulers, 25;
  Economy: capital formation, 61, 256; crisis, 263; international competition and, 268-9; foreign trade, growth of, 258; growth rates, 255; investment overspending, 260; international planning, lack of, 64,258; production 1948-55,61; proposals for reform, 264
  Living standards 1945-55, 60-1

East Germany:
  Economic difficulties in 1952,
    80-1
  Real wages 1935-50, 80
  Rising of 1953; attitudes of West
    German government and of
    Western occupation forces, 79;
    casualties, 78; extent and organi-
    zation of the general strike, 75-7
  Russian occupation forces build
    new bureaucracy, 38-9
  SED; formed in 1946, 39; leader-
    ship call for increased accumu-
    lation, 70; leadership admit to
    mistakes, 83; membership
    purged, 80
Egyetemi Ifjusag, 158
Eisenhower; deprecates armed
    resistance in E. Europe, 164
ELAS, 24

Farkas, General Mihaly, 128
Fechner, 79
Fourth International; on 1956, 242
Fryer, P., 138
Fucik Park, 215

Gero, G., 126,128,131,134
Gierek, E., 246,248,252; argues
  with Szczecin workers, 249-51
Gimes, Miklos, 149; executed, 163
Godek, W., 115,120
Goldstucker, E., 200
Gomulka, W., 45,96; purged and
  arrested, 57-8; reintegrated into
  leadership, 105-6, 187; criticizes
  chaos in economy, 95; policy after
  October 1956, 108; on workers'
  councils, 109,118; on right to
  strike, 122; puts up prices (1970),
  247; ousted, 248
*Greater Budapest Central
  Workers' Council;* formation, 167;
  tries to organize national meeting,
  168; broadcast discussion, 176-7;
  see also Workers' Councils, Hungarian revolution
Greece, Stalin accepts British
  sphere of influence in, 23-4
Grotewohl, 39
Gyor National Committee, 138

Haraszti, 90
Hass, L., 243
Havemann, Professor, R., 71-4
Herrnstadt, 83
Holacek, L., 219
Horvat, B., 257
Huebl, M., 240
Hungarian Revolution:
  Arms, how the workers got them,
    132-4,135
  Armed resistance to Russian
    troops, 163-4
  Casualties, 163
  Class composition of fighters, 151
  Confused ideas of fighters, 153-5
  Final defeat, 184-5
  General strikes in, 135,163,167,
    170,175-6,182
  Lessons of, 185-6
  Parliament Square demonstration,
    135
  Political parties, in the govern-
    ment, 138; role of, 155-6
  Student activities early in October
    1956, 128
  Workers; oppose any return of
    factories to private capitalists,
    146; concessions made to after
    revolution, 176, 183-4
  Workers councils; first formed,
    137-42; background of members,
    152; in first month of Kadar
    government, 164-85
  Writers Union demands of 23
    October 1956, 129-30
Hungaricus Pamphlet, 150-52
'Hungarian workers and university
  students', 135
Hungary 28, 51:
  Classes in, 147-8
  Communist Party; in 1920s and
    1930s, 28; supports private
    ownership, 33; purges in, 57;
    condemns Petofi circle, 125-6;
    inner party opposition, 143,150
  Economy: reparations, 50; first
    five year plan, 60,86,88; effects of
    land reform and collectivization,
    63; condition early in 1956, 124;
    excessive investments, 88, 267;
    failure of 'New Economic

Model', 267; level of waste in early 1960s, 257

New Course, 86-91; prisoners released under, 88; reaction of intellectuals to, 89

Real Wages, 1950-55, 61

Small Holders Party, 37,155

Husak, G., 211,216,240; on Novotny period, 189; on activities of intellectuals, 214

Industrialization, aim of, 15, 63

'Independent Federation of Railway Crews', 226

Intellectuals in Czechoslovakia, 214-22,223,240; in Hungary, 89,91, 128; in Poland, 98-101,106,114-15, 242-3

Internal Security Corps (Poland), 103,105-6

Irodalmi Ujsag, 91

Izvestia, 256,261

The Joke, 221

Juspad, 51

Justa, 51

Kabrna, 227

Kadar, J., 90,135,164; imprisoned, 57-8; praises Hungarian uprising, 143-4,161; denounces uprising, 161; negotiates with workers' council, 167-8; praises workers' self-management, 176; arrests leaders of Budapest workers' council, 178

Kantorovich, 258

Karsow, N., 243

Kende, P., 61

Kethly, A., 144

Khruschev, N., 69; on Beria and Malenkov policy on Germany, 83; on mistakes of Rakosi, 86; rapprochement with Tito, 91; at Twentieth Party Congress, 91,92; second attack on Stalin cult, 188; ousted, 188

Killian Barracks, 134,136

Klima, 189

Kliszko, Z., 57

Klosiewicz, 117

Kociolek, S., 247

Komar, General, 105-6

Kosik, K., 240

Kostov, T., 57, 58

Kraus, Vaclav, 236

Kriegel, F., 190, 200, 210

Kun, B., 28

Kundera, M., 221

Kuron, J. and Modzelewski, K., 20; on 'October Left', 112-13, 114; imprisoned, 243, 244

Left Opposition, the, 19

Lenin, V.I., 11,12,13,29-30

Liehm, A., 189

Literarny Listy, 200,218,219,220, 223, 227; circulation of, 217

Literarny Noviny, 189

Lithuania, industry under German Occupation, 145

Losonczy, 90

Luxemburg, Rosa, 11

Malenkov, G., 89,94

Maleter, P., 134,136,153,158,162; executed, 163

Mandel, E.; on Poland 1956, 108; on superiority of Russian economy, 254

Marx, K., on dynamics of capitalism and socialism, 16; definition of class, 18; on socialist revolution, 29

Marx, K. and Engels, F., on instability of bourgeois society, 64-5

Matyas Rakosi Works, 127

Michlik, A., 243

Mixed Companies, 51-2; *see also* SAGs

Mlada Fronta, 216

Modzelewski, K.: *see* Kuron, J.

Molotov, V.; on Bulgaria, 31

'Moscow Agreement' (1968), 191, 208

Mueller, J., 240

Nagy, Imre, 86, 87, 88, 141; history prior to 1953, 87; his ideas, 148-9; premier (1953); criticizes mistakes of previous government, 87;

removed from office, 90; re-admitted to party, 128; addresses demonstrators, 131; made premier (1956), 134; calls for 'order', 131; promises withdrawal of Russian troops, 141; proclaims Hungarian neutrality, 159; denounces Russian attack, 162; flees to Yugoslav embassy, 163; executed, 163

Natolin group, 105

Naumann, R., 73

Neues Deutschland, 84

New Left Review, 188

Newspapers; in Czechoslovakia, 214-15,216,218-19,230,232-3; in East Germany, 84; in Hungary, 91, 126,127,128,137; in Poland, 100

Nova Mysl, 60

Novotny, A.; takes repressive measures, 189; isolated, 196; ousted, 196-7, 201

Nowa Kultura, 99,242

Ochab, 101,104

An Open Letter to the Party, 243

Orwell, G., 64

Paducha, Major, 47

Palach, J., 192

Palme Dutt; on Stalin, 69

Pastyrik, 226

Patrascanu, 33,58

Pauker, A., 29,33

Pavel, J., 47

Peasant Parties, 36

Pelikan, J., 206

Petofi Circle; formed, 125; not a revolutionary organization, 149-50

Pilsen (1953), 70

Pithart, Petr, 220

Poem for Adults, 99

Polacek, K., 230, 226, 232

Political revolution, inadequacy of, 271

Poland:
Anti-semitism (in 1968), 244-5
capital accumulation, 94,245
Catholic church, reactions to 1956, 111 (*see also* Wyszynski)
Collectivization, 94

Communist Party (inc PUWP); in 1930s, 28; reconstituted, 29; membership in 1945, 40; expulsions in 1948, 58; worker membership 1945-55, 96; Polish Council of National Unity, pro-gramme during Warsaw Upris-ing, 34

December 1970, 246-8

Demonstrations of 1968, 27

Economy; pre-war foreign invest-ment, 26; pre-war role of state, 26; devastation caused by war, 27; coal sales to Russia, 52; in 1950s and 1960s, 95, 245

Intellectuals, 98-100,106,114-15, 242-3

Peasant Party, 34,37

Police, purged, 97

Poznan Rising, 102-3; reaction of party leaders, 104; trials follow-ing, 105-6

Socialist Party (PPS); pre-war, 37; in Warsaw Uprising, 34; con-ferences 1946-7, 38; merged with CP, 37

Special Shops, 101

Technocracy; reaction to October 1956, 110-11

Unemployment, 100

Unions; in November 1945, 37; in 1956, 110-17

Workers; conditions during in-dustrialization, 100; living standards, 94,245; reactions in early 1956, 98; strikes of 1971, 248, 252; support for Hungarian revolution, 116

Po Prostu, 117,142; circulation, 100; attitude after October 1956, 114-16; on workers' councils, 119-21; on Hungarian revolution, 143; banned, 122

Prague; coup of 1948, 46-48; demonstrations of 1968-9, 192

Prace, 216,224,227,228,223; on *2000 Words*, 218; support for Smrk-ovsky, 229

Pravda; on Poznan rising, 104

Prchlik, General, 197,205

Przeglad Kulturalny, 243

Model', 267; level of waste in early 1960s, 257
New Course, 86-91; prisoners released under, 88; reaction of intellectuals to, 89
Real Wages, 1950-55, 61
Small Holders Party, 37,155
Husak, G., 211,216,240; on Novotny period, 189; on activities of intellectuals, 214

Industrialization, aim of, 15, 63
'Independent Federation of Railway Crews', 226
Intellectuals in Czechoslovakia, 214-22,223,240; in Hungary, 89,91, 128; in Poland, 98-101,106,114-15, 242-3
Internal Security Corps (Poland), 103,105-6
Irodalmi Ujsag, 91
Izvestia, 256,261

The Joke, 221
Juspad, 51
Justa, 51

Kabrna, 227
Kadar, J., 90,135,164; imprisoned, 57-8; praises Hungarian uprising, 143-4,161; denounces uprising, 161; negotiates with workers' council, 167-8; praises workers' self-management, 176; arrests leaders of Budapest workers' council, 178
Kantorovich, 258
Karsow, N., 243
Kende, P., 61
Kethly, A., 144
Khruschev, N., 69; on Beria and Malenkov policy on Germany, 83; on mistakes of Rakosi, 86; rapprochement with Tito, 91; at Twentieth Party Congress, 91,92; second attack on Stalin cult, 188; ousted, 188
Killian Barracks, 134,136
Klima, 189
Kliszko, Z., 57
Klosiewicz, 117

Kociolek, S., 247
Komar, General, 105-6
Kosik, K., 240
Kostov, T., 57, 58
Kraus, Vaclav, 236
Kriegel, F., 190, 200, 210
Kun, B., 28
Kundera, M., 221
Kuron, J. and Modzelewski, K., 20; on 'October Left', 112-13, 114; imprisoned, 243, 244

Left Opposition, the, 19
Lenin, V.I., 11,12,13,29-30
Liehm, A., 189
Literarny Listy, 200,218,219,220, 223, 227; circulation of, 217
Literarny Noviny, 189
Lithuania, industry under German Occupation, 145
Losonczy, 90
Luxemburg, Rosa, 11

Malenkov, G., 89,94
Maleter, P., 134,136,153,158,162; executed, 163
Mandel, E.; on Poland 1956, 108; on superiority of Russian economy, 254
Marx, K., on dynamics of capitalism and socialism, 16; definition of class, 18; on socialist revolution, 29
Marx, K. and Engels, F., on instability of bourgeois society, 64-5
Matyas Rakosi Works, 127
Michlik, A., 243
Mixed Companies, 51-2; *see also* SAGs
Mlada Fronta, 216
Modzelewski, K.: *see* Kuron, J.
Molotov, V.; on Bulgaria, 31
'Moscow Agreement' (1968), 191, 208
Mueller, J., 240

Nagy, Imre, 86, 87, 88, 141; history prior to 1953, 87; his ideas, 148-9; premier (1953); criticizes mistakes of previous government, 87;

removed from office, 90; re-
admitted to party, 128; addresses
demonstrators, 131; made premier
(1956), 134; calls for 'order', 131;
promises withdrawal of Russian
troops, 141; proclaims Hungarian
neutrality, 159; denounces Russian
attack, 162; flees to Yugoslav
embassy, 163; executed, 163
Natolin group, 105
Naumann, R., 73
Neues Deutschland, 84
New Left Review, 188
Newspapers; in Czechoslovakia,
214-15,216,218-19,230,232-3; in
East Germany, 84; in Hungary, 91,
126,127,128,137; in Poland, 100
Nova Mysl, 60
Novotny, A.; takes repressive
measures, 189; isolated, 196;
ousted, 196-7, 201
Nowa Kultura, 99,242

Ochab, 101,104
An Open Letter to the Party, 243
Orwell, G., 64

Paducha, Major, 47
Palach, J., 192
Palme Dutt; on Stalin, 69
Pastyrik, 226
Patrascanu, 33,58
Pauker, A., 29,33
Pavel, J., 47
Peasant Parties, 36
Pelikan, J., 206
Petofi Circle; formed, 125; not a
revolutionary organization, 149-50
Pilsen (1953), 70
Pithart, Petr, 220
Poem for Adults, 99
Polacek, K., 230, 226, 232
Political revolution, inadequacy of,
271
Poland:
Anti-semitism (in 1968), 244-5
capital accumulation, 94,245
Catholic church, reactions to 1956,
111 (*see also* Wyszynski)
Collectivization, 94

Communist Party (inc PUWP); in
1930s, 28; reconstituted, 29;
membership in 1945, 40;
expulsions in 1948, 58; worker
membership 1945-55, 96; Polish
Council of National Unity, programme during Warsaw Uprising, 34
December 1970, 246-8
Demonstrations of 1968, 27
Economy; pre-war foreign investment, 26; pre-war role of state,
26; devastation caused by war,
27; coal sales to Russia, 52; in
1950s and 1960s, 95, 245
Intellectuals, 98-100,106,114-15,
242-3
Peasant Party, 34,37
Police, purged, 97
Poznan Rising, 102-3; reaction of
party leaders, 104; trials following, 105-6
Socialist Party (PPS); pre-war, 37;
in Warsaw Uprising, 34; conferences 1946-7, 38; merged with
CP, 37
Special Shops, 101
Technocracy; reaction to October
1956, 110-11
Unemployment, 100
Unions; in November 1945, 37; in
1956, 110-17
Workers; conditions during industrialization, 100; living
standards, 94,245; reactions in
early 1956, 98; strikes of 1971,
248, 252; support for Hungarian
revolution, 116
Po Prostu, 117,142; circulation,
100; attitude after October 1956,
114-16; on workers' councils,
119-21; on Hungarian revolution,
143; banned, 122
Prague; coup of 1948, 46-48;
demonstrations of 1968-9, 192
Prace, 216,224,227,228,223; on *2000
Words*, 218; support for Smrkovsky, 229
Pravda; on Poznan rising, 104
Prchlik, General, 197,205
Przeglad Kulturalny, 243

Racz, S., 178
Radek, K., 19
Radio Free Gyor, 137
Radio Free Europe, 112
Radkiewicz, 97
Rajk, Julia, 125-6
Rajk, Laszlo, 57,58; reburied, 128
Rakosi, M., 87,89,91,125,126; on tactics for Stalinist takeover, 35; complains about absenteeism, 62
Reparations, 49-51
Reporter, 237
'Revolution from Above', 35
RIAS, attitude to E. German strike and rising, 80
Rokossovsky, General, 105,109
RTUM, 226,231,232; congress of March 1969, 230
Rumania; reparations, 50; suffering of population, 50-1
  Communist Party: membership, 29,40; in coalition, 37; supports monarchy, 33; joined by sections of Iron Guards, 33; government of March 1945, 32
Russia:
  Army moves towards Warsaw (1956), 106; re-enters Budapest, 162; prevents meeting of Hungarian workers' councils, 168; threatens and then enters Czechoslovakia, 190
  Economic interest in E. Europe, 49-55
  Economy: industrialization, 15; migration of labour to towns, 263; agricultural crisis, 264; growth rate, 255; investment, 256; waste, 256-7, 258; failure of 'planning', 260-2
  Government; demands reparation from E. Europe, 50; divisions within after Stalin's death, 81-2
  Invasion of Czechoslovakia; Czech casualties in, 50; reaction of Czechoslovak state machine to, 207
  Reforms after Stalin's death, 81-2
  Revolution of 1917; role of working class, 11; devastation caused by civil war, 12

Revolution; prospects for, 272

Sabata, J., 240
SAGs, 50
Salgovic, 205
Selbmann, F., 74
Semyanov, General, 83
Sik, O., draws up economic reform, 227; supports wage restraint, 227; on workers' councils, 234
Skoda workers; denounce Moscow Agreement, 208
Slansky, R., 58, 188
Slovak nationalism, 211, 212, 213
Slavonic House, 215
Smrkovsky, J., 190,192,200,215,231, 240; criticizes Dubcek, 229; speaks to Metal Workers' Conference, 230; dissociates himself from his supporters, 210
'Socialism in One Country', 14; and interests of bureaucracy, 15
Solecky, V., 230
Soltesz, J., 183
Soviets, 1905, 182; 1917, 110,156, 178
Spacek, J., 200
Spychaliski, 57
Stalin, J.; organizes bureaucracy against Trotsky, 14; on industrialization and arms, 15; agrees to division of Europe, 23-4; motives, 15; executes leaders of Polish CP, 28; dies, 69; criticized by Khrushchev, 9,92
Stalinism; the historical alternative to, 19
Staszewski, S., 106
Stojanovic, S., 236
Strupp, I., 258
Students; in Czechoslovakia, 189, 215-16,219,229,232; in Hungary, 127-8, 129, 151; in Poland, 107, 244
Student, 200, 208, 219
Strahov incident, 189, 196, 214
Sudeten Germans, 41-5
Svestka, O., 204-5
Svitak, I., 223
Svoboda, L., 191, 240
Svobodne Slovo, 200

Swialto, 97
Szabad Nep, 126
Szabo, J., 153
Szaifeen, H., 244
Szilagyi, J., 243
Szpotanski, J., 243

Tanczos, G., 129
Tatarescu, G., 32, 37
Tesar, J., 240
Tito, J.B.; plan for Bulgarian-
  Yugoslav-Albanian Union, 54;
  breaks with Stalin, 57; rapproche-
  ment with Khruschev, 91
Todorovich, M., 236
Togliatti, P.; supports Badoglio
  government, 25
Toman, V., 230
Tomsky, M., 14
Trade; between E. Europe and
  Russia, 52-4
Tribune (E. Germany), 84
Tribune (London); on 1956, 108
Tribuna (Czechoslovakia), 230
Trybuna Ludu; on Poznan rising,
  104; on Hungarian revolution,
  143; criticizes *Po Prostu*, 122
Trotsky, L., 14,19,110
2000 Words, 218; reactions to, 218;
  denounced by Dubcek, 199

UB, purged 1954-5, 97
Ulbricht, W., reaction after Stalin's
  death, 83; on causes of 1953
  rising, 79
Ujhelyi, S., 90
Union of Polish Patriots, 34
Union of Revolutionary Youth
  (Poland), 117
United States; arms spending as
  proportion of investment, 17;
  reassures Kremlin in 1956, 164;
  refuses loan to Czechoslovakia in
  1968, 25

Vaculik, L., 189, 217, 240

Vodslon, F., 210
Vorkuta, 83

Wankowitz, M., 243
Warsaw Uprising, 34-5
Wazyk, A., 99
Wittfogel, K., 64
'Workers' Committees for the
  defence of Freedom of the Press',
  227-8
Workers' Councils:
  Czechoslovakia; 233-9; function-
  ing and limitations, 238-9
  Hungary; 137-142, 164-85; effect-
  ively run Budapest, 165; political
  functions, 177; denounced as
  'counter-revolutionary', 185, after
  crushing of revolution, 184-5
  Poland, 118-21
  Revolutionary Party and, 178,
  186-7
'Workers' Militia' (Czechoslo-
  vakia); in 1948, 47; in 1968, 223
Writers' Congress (Czechoslovakia,
  1967), 189, 196
Wyszynski, Cardinal; supports
  Gomulka, 111-12; calls for calm,
  122

Xoxe, Kochi, 58

Yalta Conference, 24
Yugoslavia; role of state and
  foreign capital pre-war, 26;
  denunciation of Russian trade
  terms and 'mixed companies', 52;
  economy, 257, 266, 269; unemployment 267; 'workers' control',
  reality of, 236
Yugov, 31-2

Zaisser, W., 83
Zauberman, 61
Zinoviev, G., 14
ZISPO factory, 102
ZMP, 116